BEER, MAN FOOD, MAN COOKING, AND BEER

**Recipes with Beer
And Beer Trivia for All Occasions**

By

ROSS FIGGINS

**Glenross Publishing
Claremont, California**

Beer, Man Food, Man Cooking, and Beer:
Recipes with Beer and Beer Trivia for All Occasions

Glenross Publishing Company
775 W. 10 Street
Claremont, CA 91711

ISBN 978-0-615-27434-8

Printed in the United States of America

Holy Saint Gambrinus,
Protect and preserve us forever!

INTRODUCTION

Let There Be Beer!

From the beginning of recorded time and before, humankind has had a continuing and unflagging love affair with beer. From the shaggy-browed primordial lost in the dreamy dawn of time to the sophisticated jet-setter who spans continents in hours, the hallmark of respite, the token of friendship, and the elixir of renewal has been the ever welcome thought of a tall, cold beer.

No one knows who discovered brewing, whether it was a man or a woman, where they lived, or, for that matter, how long beer has been around. Ancient records tell us two things: That beer was important in everyday life and that it was not even then a new discovery. Here in these pages we will explore its numerous dimensions, moving through time and place, legend and record, to bring stories, trivia, speculation, and fact to further the enjoyment of our most basic companions – good food, a mug of your favorite beer and a story to tell.

Typecasting Beer

Very likely old Noah provisioned the Ark with a goodly supply of beer. Yet even this intrepid mariner might have hesitated to embark on the modern flood we face – a deluge of beer itself. I've yet to find an Ararat label among the hundreds of imports and domestics available, but it wouldn't be a shock if I did. Common sense tells me that when faced with such a confusion of alternatives, it's wise to begin by dividing them into convenient groups.

When you think about it, brewing is a relatively simple process even in this modern world of technology and robotics. First barley is malted. This means the grain is allowed to germinate and sprout, and then it is roasted. The resulting malt is crushed and cooked slowly in vats of hot water. Next hops are added for flavor and preservation. Finally yeast is mixed in to start the whole thing fermenting. After that it's a matter of patience, bottling, and gluing on appropriate labels. But these first steps can and do lead to an infinite variety of tastes and pleasures.

Beer, from the Latin *bibere*, meaning "to drink," was most likely discovered some eight or nine thousand years ago in the Middle East, during the great agrarian revolution. This was when the nomadic tribes of the region first started to settle down in one place, plant crops, and begin the long journey toward modern civilization. This hypothesis makes beer, which requires the domestication of grain, younger in the pantheon of human delights than wine, which is an almost natural by-product of crushed wild fruit and berries.

Recipes on Tap

In most kitchens, restaurants, and cooking places of the world, from posh dining salons to campfires, men and women add to the enjoyment of dining with their favorite beer or wine. These are frequently more than an accompanying beverage, becoming in fact a subtle additive to the dishes themselves.

Wine cookbooks abound. Their numbers cause booksellers' shelves to sag, totter and collapse. Yet few volumes, and thin ones at that, have been devoted to the magic of beer cookery. The realm of epicurean dining contains many well-known and not a few secret beer recipes. The purpose of this collection is not to praise the virtues of beer over wine – the grain and the grape are equally enjoyable amenities of life – but to praise the real pleasures of cooking with beer and ale.

Beer is a subtle component in most of these recipes. Basically, beer is a liquid that can be substituted in most dishes that call for water, broth, milk, or wine. It does not strongly impart much of its own character to the food, as does cooking with hearty wines, but interacts as a flavor catalyst to enhance and intensify the character of other ingredients. It will not make dishes taste "beery" – as long as you don't drown them – but too much beer makes food bitter. Beer, like wine, can enhance inexpensive ingredients but, as in the case of wine, the better quality used, the better the table results.

But before you run off and up-end a half pint into Uncle Charley's famous bouillabaise or Nanny's Strawberry Chiffon Pie, try it out on a couple of proven beer recipes to get the feel of what works and what should be left alone. Then when you have a couple under your belt, so to speak, strike out on your own and explore other applications. Look over that favorite recipe. Does it call for a liquid? Do you feel beer will compliment the other ingredients? If they don't like each other, you won't like the results. If the answer is "yes" to initial questions, give it a go. You'll be surprised how well beer goes with most dishes.

Here are a few more guidelines for adventurous cooks:

- Use your favorite beer to start. Later, with more experience, you can branch out into dark beers, ales, stouts and porters.

- Be a bit on the stingy side. Don't assume that if some is good, more is better!

- Give the beer time to work. Don't pull it out of the fridge at the last minute, slop it in cold, and expect a miracle.

- Since beer will intensify flavors, you can afford to be frugal with other spices and seasonings.

- Let the beer warm up and go flat before using – an hour or so open and outside the refrigerator should do it. There are two good reasons, besides superstition, for doing this: It increases the beer's flavor and it makes it easier to measure. To bring beer to room temperature quickly, run some warm water into a large pan. Slip the can or bottle into the water for a few minutes, until it feels right.

- Don't worry about the strength of the brew you choose. Alcohol doesn't add flavor and besides, the heat in cooking will drive it all off anyway. Aside from what you serve with them, almost no recipe in this book contains any alcohol by the time it's ready to eat.

- The same reasoning holds true for calories, too. Cooking with beer is unlikely to add to your avoirdupois. More than half the calories in a cold beer are in the alcohol. In beer cookery this boils away, leaving a liquid that is less caloric than milk or stock.

- Finally, should you change a recipe? Certainly. Half the fun of cooking is making what you like. Look at every recipe as something that should be prepared twice – once as it's written and again with your own variations. So be brave! Be imaginative!

TABLE OF CONTENTS

CHAPTER ONE: OPENERS 1
    Amsterdam Fried Cheese 3
    Bowery Crock Cheese 4
    Baja Bean Dip 5
    Shrimps Daphne 7
    Huevos Diablos 8
    Bavarian Pickled Eggs 9
    Gold Rush Chicken Livers 10
    Beef and Cheese Nosh 12
    Liverwurst Pâté 13
    Colorado Mushrooms 14
    Old Time Beef Jerky 15
    Saratoga Chips 17
    Toad in the Hole.. 18

CHAPTER TWO: SOUPS AND SALADS 19
    Yankee Tavern Soup.. 21
    Sausage and Bean Soup 22
    Cheddar Bisque 23
    Stone Soup 24
    Danish Beer Soup 26
    Baked Onion Soup 28
    Red Cabbage Salad 29
    Sesame Seed Dressing 30
    Old World Potato Salad 31
    Hot German Potato Salad.. 32
    Caesar Salad 33
    Pennsylvania Slaw 34
    California Salad 35
    Four-Bean Salad.. 36

CHAPTER THREE: MEAT 37
    Beer-Braised Pot Roast of Beef 39
    Seaman's Beef 40
    Texas Flank Steak 41
    Vampire Steak 42
    Mushroom Steak.. 43
    Steak Iberia 44
    Corned Beef Brisket 45

Shish Kebabs 46
Humbles and Onions 47
Chops and Kraut 48
Carnitas Jalisco 49
Gypsy Steak 50
Smuggler's Ribs 51
Baked Polish Sausage 52
Bratwurst and Sauerkraut 53
Beef Rolls de Paris 54
Beef Stroganoff 56
German Meat Balls 58
Danish Meat Balls 59
International Meat Loaf 60
Baked Ham 61
Latin Pochero.. 62

CHAPTER FOUR: ENTREES AND ONE-DISH MEALS 63
Flemish Carbonnes 65
Hungarian Goulash 67
Uncle Sam's Barley Stew 68
Doughboy Stew 69
Steak and Kidney Pie 71
Hearty Steak and Guinness Pie 73
Polish Delight 75
Mexican Lamb Stew.. 76
Pork Chile Verde 78
Pecos Chili 80
Bartender's Chili 81
Chili Azteca 83
Spaghetti with Meat Sauce 84
Stuffed Green Peppers 86
New England Baked Beans 88
Beef Canton 90
Pork and Apple Ragout 91

CHAPTER FIVE: CHICKEN AND FISH 93
Barbecued Chicken 95
Irish Chicken Cretloe 96
Flemish Chicken 97
Hoosier Game Hens 99
Chicken Ecuador 100

Baked Curried Chicken 102

Chicken Stuffed with Rice 104

Spanish Paella 105

Fish and Chips 106

Canadian Salmon Steaks 108

Rolled Sole with Peanuts 109

Dixie Fish Turbans 110

Texas Gulf Shrimp 112

Asparagus and Shrimp 113

CHAPTER SIX: SIDE DISHES 115

Spanish Rice 117

French Fried Onion Rings 118

Succotash 120

Cabbage and Noodles 121

Braised Cabbage 122

Fried Green Tomatoes 123

Corn on the Cob 124

Frijoles Borrachos (Drunken Beans) 125

Potato Casserole 127

Spuds Au Gratin 129

Oriental Fried Rice 130

Stuffed Tomatoes 132

Brussels Sprouts 133

Candied Sweet Potatoes 134

Mandarin Carrots 135

Baked Red Onions 136

Breaded Eggplant 137

Red Cabbage 138

CHAPTER SEVEN: SANDWICHES 139

Broiled Hamburgers 141

Great Hamburgers 142

Salisbury Steak 143

Smithfield Special 144

Coney Island Franks 145

Prairie Dog Sandwiches 146

Red Hots and Kraut 147

Bratwurst in Ale 148

Barbecue Pork Sandwiches 149

Barbecue Beef Sandwiches 150

Reuben Sandwiches 151
The Queen of Denver 153
Grilled Cheese on Rye 154
Saucy Steak Sandwich 155

CHAPTER EIGHT: EGGS AND CHEESE 157
Spanish Omelet 159
Egg Foo Young 161
Heuvos Rancheros 163
Eggs Parmesan 164
Gascony Fried Eggs 165
Creole Soufflé.. 166
Eggs Provençal 168
Baked Eggs Español 169
Welsh Rabbit 170
Heathen Welsh Hare 172
Alpine Fondue 173

CHAPTER NINE: BREADS AND SWEETS 175
Radio Beer Bread... 177
Cheese Bread.. 178
Soft Rye Bread 179
Raisin Cheese Nut Bread... 180
Beer, Olive, and Sun-Dried Tomato Bread... 181
Sesame Beer Bread Sticks... 182
Superlight Beer Pancakes 183
Quick Beer-Batter Crêpes 184
Hot Spice Cake 185
Chocolate Cake... 186
Universal Chocolate Frosting... 187
Date Cake From the Desert.. 188
Alice's Unbirthday Fruit Cake 189
Brit Lemon Cake 191
Cherry Cake.. 192
Old English Plum Pudding.. 194
Butterscotch Tarts.. 195
New York Cheesecake... 196

BEER FACTS WE ALL REALLY NEED TO KNOW

Beer Turns Up Down Under 3
The Mighty Aztec Brew 6
Tricking the Trickster 6
Whistle for It! 8
Drink Responsibly 9
California Steam Beer 11
A Boat We All Miss 12
Curb Your Enthusiasm and Hitch Your Pony 12
Olde Frothingslosh 13
Mugs and Muggling 16
Hail to the Queen! 17
Hate to Pick a Favorite Beer, But 18
Take It to the Judge 23
Tipping a Yard 25
The Skinny on Low-Cal Beer 27
So Can Beer Help Me Lose Weight? 27
The Conversion of Hathor 29
Three Cheers for Uncle Sam! And Some of His Beery Relatives 30
Indoor Beer Gardens 32
A Friend Indeed 34
Record of Hops' Value Comes from Dark Ages Abbess 35
Whistle-Belly Vengeance 36
But Mr. Tax Man, It's Almost the Same as Bread 40
Happy Birthday, Granddad 41
A Noble Compliment 44
Hot Beer 45
Mind Your P's and Q's 48
A New Nation's First Brewery 52
The Ubiquitous Church Key 53
Naval Secrets Revealed 55
Old German Proverbs 55
Russians Take Beer Seriously 57
Spring Cleaning Myth 57
Beer in Politics 57
Kaiser Bill 60
Eric the Red and Greenland Ale 61
Only the Yeast Knows 66
Why We Drink – It's the Longevity 66
A Noggin of Old Rattle Skull 70
In Vassar Halls 72
Gin Lane 74

Tepache 75
I Think He Liked the Beer 77
Tavernkeeper's Verse 79
Bartender 'Bot 79
New Heights for Beer 80
And Speaking of Heat 82
Blue Ribbon Tweak 83
Stone Street 85
The Agony of Prohibition, From a Cockroach's Point of View 87
Go to Bed, Tom, Drunk or Sober 89
Indestructible Guinness 91
Sign of Prohibition 95
India Pale Ale 98
Cone Mouth Beer Cans 100
Old World Connection 101
Beer Comes to Japan 101
Rushing the Growler 103
Porter: A Strong Man's Drink 107
Tip a Black and Tan 107
Drawing Straws 108
King Gambrinus 111
What's Behind the Clink? 111
Beer Dreams Foretell Future 119
Wet Your Whistle 119
London Beer Flood – Free Beer by Force of Nature 124
A Pint and a Gill 125
Rally Round the Flagon 126
The First Bottle of Beer 126
A Mouthful of Beer Proverbs 128
When There WAS a Free Lunch 128
Old Ben's Elbow 129
Scholars' Theory Gauls Germans 131
Three Sheates to the Wind 131
Heather Ale 133
From the Wood 134
Charlemagne the Great on Beer Policy 135
A Bumper of Ale, Sir? 136
Penalty Horns 137
Middle Ages Staple 138
Ale in Song and Verse 144
High Society 148
Bottles, Barrels, Cans, and Box-o'-Beer 149
The First Brewers' Trademark 150

xii

Special Delivery 151
Once Upon a Riddle 152
Beere in Shakespeare's Time 154
Being at Loggerheads 160
The Little Mermaid, Gift of Beer 160
Wager Cups 162
Flip-Top Coup 165
What Prohibition? 167
Mencken on Sobriety 167
And Speaking of Ale 171
Hob Nobbing 171
When Taxes Were Really Sticky 180
Travelers Take Care! 181
Not Toasting With Beer 182
For Whom the Beer Bell Tolls 183
What's More Serious Than a Double Cross? 187
Toby Mugs 190
Beer Money 191
Pilsner Urquell 193
The Holy Hour 193

CHAPTER ONE

FOR OPENERS: SMALL THINGS TO SPREAD, NIBBLE & NOSH

Amsterdam Fried Cheese

Bowery Cheese Crock

Baja Bean Dip

Shrimps Daphne

Huevos Diablos

Bavarian Pickled Eggs

Gold Rush Chicken Livers

Beef and Cheese Nosh

Liverwurst Pâté

Colorado Mushrooms

Old-Time Beef Jerky

Saratoga Chips

Toad in the Hole

2

Amsterdam Fried Cheese

Try this for a tasty and unusual treat. Originally a Dutch snack, *kas mit bier*, it has obviously traveled widely.

1 ½	pounds Gouda cheese
1	egg, well beaten
3	tablespoons all-purpose flour
½	cup warm beer or ale
3-4	tablespoons cooking oil
1	dash ground nutmeg
	salt to taste

Begin by cutting the cheese into slices at least ½ inch thick. Then chill briefly in the refrigerator. Mix the egg, flour, beer, salt, and nutmeg to form a smooth batter.

Dip the cheese slices into the batter and fry quickly in hot oil until evenly brown on both sides. You may have to practice this part a bit: Keep the oil hot and be quick, otherwise the cheese will melt into globs. But those are good too, so you can even enjoy your mistakes. Alternate the nibbles with sips of a good Dutch beer.

Makes 6 to 8 servings.

Beer Turns Up Down Under

The first brewer in Australia arrived aboard the *H.M.S. Surprise* on October 25, 1794. Governor Hunter, representing the King's interests, reported of John Boston that he "will continue to be one of those whom the colony will derive no advantage from." After some altercations with the law, which he seems to have won with annoying regularity, according to the Governor, Boston began his fortune in home-made soap and beer — both essentials in the rough and ready territory. His concoction for brewing was composed of "Indian corn, properly malted and bittered with leaves and stalks of the love apple" (i.e., the Cape gooseberry).

Whatever his recipe, John Boston's beer must have had sufficient kick to become popular. His profits multiplied quickly. He soon acquired title to not only a brewery but also prime land, a mill, and a number of ships. Yet his adventurous spirit was not satisfied.

Mr. Boston, as he was then called, continued searching for new enterprises. In 1804, while on a trading expedition to Tonga, he and the captain of his ship met their demise in a cannibal village. There is no record in the ship's log if beer was served with the entree.

(John Boston did NOT write the famous bartender's guide called "Old Mr. Boston's," in case you're wondering.)

Bowery Cheese Crock

"Go jump off a bridge!" A young man accepted that invitation when he leapt from the greatest suspension bridge in the world and into American folklore on July 23, 1889. The scene was the Brooklyn Bridge and the man Steve Brody, a carnival barker in a dime museum. From the notoriety gained by this feat of derring-do he was able to talk a local brewery into giving him the money to open a lavish Bowery saloon.

Some scoffers say the event is apocryphal. Many claim that only a straw dummy and some of Steve's old clothes got wet. Regardless of detractors, his saloon and free lunches became famous. To "take a brody" came to be associated with any dangerous or risky activity.

Rest assured, there is no gamble in this crock cheese, reputed to have been a crowd pleaser at Brody's Saloon during the halcyon days of free lunches and nickel beers.

½	pound sharp grated Cheddar cheese
3	ounces cream cheese
4	ounces warm beer or ale
2	eggs yolks, hard boiled and mashed
1	teaspoon capers, mashed
4	ounces soft butter
1	dash of Angostura bitters

Chill Cheddar slightly before grating, to make it easier. Allow beer, grated cheese and butter to come to room temperature. Mix together with a fork. Add egg yolk and capers. Continue blending, moistening with a little beer if necessary. Do not add too much beer or the mixture will be thin. It should be firm, but still easy to spread – it will stiffen up in the refrigerator.

Pack the cheese mixture into a cheese crock or a favorite beer stein. Chill thoroughly.

Serve with crisp crackers and cold beer. Keep this recipe close at hand when you're planning a beer tasting party; it goes well with all sorts of brews.

A wonderful feature of this spread is its versatility; it smiles on imaginative variations. Try other spices, for instance, dry mustard, garlic, Worcestershire sauce, Tabasco, or crunchy additives such as chopped chilis, sunflower seeds, minced onion, bacon bits or mashed anchovies. You can even alter the cheese base successfully; a mild Gorgonzola makes a fine replacement for the Cheddar or a Bleu for the cream cheese. And, naturally, the beer can range from a mild lager, like Coors or Budweiser, to a hearty ale, like Watney's, for instance.

Makes enough for 10 to 12 people. Bottoms up!

Baja Bean Dip

When ad people dream, they envision their product indivisibly joined with people's everyday activities. Tecate, brewed in a quiet town on the border between Baja California and California, has become one of the best selling imported canned beers in the West because of a curious serving custom. The "three companions," *los tres amigos*, as they're called, are salt, lemon and Tecate beer.

Aficionados sprinkle a few grains of salt – a heavy rock salt works best – around the top of the can, squeeze some lemon (normally lime in Mexico) into the *cerveza*, and sip contentedly. This makes a lot of sense in climates where excessive perspiration and loss of body salts and liquids can play havoc with one's constitution. Let's not take risks. Better sip a cold one and make some dip to munch with salty chips.

1	cup dried pinto beans
1	12-ounce can warm beer or ale
1	14 ½ - ounce can beef broth
1	medium onion, chopped
1	4-ounce can diced green chilis
1	bay leaf
1	small tomato, seeded and diced
¼	teaspoon hot pepper sauce
½	teaspoon *each* ground cumin and oregano leaves
½	cup sharp Cheddar cheese, grated
	garlic salt and pepper
	chopped fresh coriander (also known as cilantro)
	lots of fresh tortilla chips

Wash dried beans in cold water. Rinse them well, pour off water. Place beans in a 3- or 4-quart pan. Add beer or ale, beef broth, onion, pepper sauce and bay leaf. Bring to a boil. Reduce heat, cover, and let simmer for 2 to 3 hours, or until beans are soft and mashable.

Abuse beans unconscionably in food processor to create a smooth paste. Pour into a serving bowl. Mix in chilis, cumin, oregano, garlic salt and pepper to taste. If you're a fire-eater, add more chilis and hot sauce. Cover bowl and chill in refrigerator for a couple of hours. Overnight is even better. Sprinkle grated cheese and chopped tomato over top just before serving. Garnish with fresh, chopped coriander. Arm guests with plenty of tortilla chips, a couple of bottles of Bohemia or Tecate, and stand back.

Makes about 2 ½ cups of dip. *Arriba!*

The Mighty Aztec Brew

Oc ye necha, "once upon a time" – as the Aztecs would have said, the great and kindly god of the sun, Tontiu, appeared before his chosen people in a sterner role, as Huitzilpochtli, the war god, and demanded nourishment. Only the living, beating hearts of human beings would appease his hunger and thirst, and so the Aztecs embarked on their own series of conquests throughout the area that surrounds the valley of Mexico to gather the divine fodder to propitiate their gods – and there were quite a few of those gods. The most important were the combination sun/war god, Huitzilpochtli, and the mighty Tlaloc, the rain god.

Those chosen to be sacrificed on the great sun stones at the Heart of the World, Tenochtitlan – now buried beneath the foundations of modern Mexico City – were often as not given large quantities of well-drugged pulque or octli to prepare them. Without going into the grisly details of the Flowery Death, so well described in Gary Jennings' epic novel Aztec, let it suffice to say that the pulque helped some get through a day they didn't have their hearts in.

It's an ironic touch of fate too that excessive pulque drinkers of the time, the equivalent of our skid row winos, very often found themselves standing numbly in line as offerings to ensure the glory of Montezuma's empire.

Tricking the Trickster

Numerous stories about the wiliness of early Yankee traders abound in folklore and song. One such incident began after a traveler had had a hefty meal and several beers in a colonial tavern. When the innkeeper presented the bill, the stranger discovered it had been padded outrageously. But when he noticed the room was filled with the innkeeper's cronies, he didn't complain; rather he spoke softly and offered to show the greedy man how to draw both beer and ale from the same barrel – a profitable trick since there was a substantial difference in their price.

When the tavern owner agreed, the trader asked to be shown to the cellar where the liquor was stored. Such important secrets, he explained, could only be disclosed in private. The two men retired to the cool confines beneath the inn. There the trader drew a brace and bit from his sack and drilled a hole in one end of a small cask of ale. He asked the innkeeper to plug it with his finger so none of the precious liquid would be wasted. Next he turned the cask over and drilled a hole in the other end and, again, had the owner insert another finger there.

Then, whistling to himself, the trader left the cellar, a fuming innkeeper and his bill. The gullible publican remained behind, neatly trapped, torn between losing a butt of fine ale, calling for help and having to admit his foolishness, and collecting his money.

Shrimps Daphne

Among the more poignant stories told by the Roman poet Ovid in *Metamorphoses* is the tale of Daphne and Apollo. This legend of dual transformations begins with the beautiful maiden Daphne pursued by the randy god Apollo, with less than good intentions. During her flight, she prayed to be concealed from him. Just as he reached out to seize her, she was changed, suddenly, into a graceful laurel tree, and his lust turned into a veneration for the ever green and stately laurel.

Later, the priestess who was Apollo's oracle at Delphi chewed laurel leaves before making her famous predictions about the future, which tells us something about the dedication of the priestess, if not her benumbed taste buds.

In this classic shrimp dish, after the laurel (which is called bay leaf on your spice rack) has enhanced the taste during cooking, be kind to your guests and remove it before serving. That way no one will chew it by accident.

2	pounds raw shrimp
3	tablespoons minced onion
4	tablespoons butter
2	teaspoons chopped parsley
2	tablespoons flour
1	cup warm beer
3	tablespoons lemon juice
¼	teaspoon hot pepper sauce
½	teaspoon thyme
1	bay or laurel leaf
	salt to taste

Peel, de-vein, and dry shrimp. Sauté quickly in onion and butter – about 1 minute to a side. Add salt, pepper sauce, flour, beer and lemon juice, stirring continuously.

Bring mixture to a boil. Reduce heat. Add bay leaf and thyme. Cook over low heat for 5 minutes. Discard bay leaf. Sprinkle shrimp with parsley flakes.

Serve either hot or chilled with a cocktail sauce. Supply participants with toothpicks, napkins and dark Belhaven beer, "the Burgundy of Scotland."

Makes 8 to 10 servings.

Huevos Diablos

Among the ancient Maya, at the ceremony they called *hetzmek*, an egg was fed to babies to endow them with understanding. Today eggs are still considered in many cultures to be a food with special mystique, as in our own custom of decorated Easter eggs. In Mexico, eggs also figure strongly in folklore, religious offerings and magic. The following, although not a traditional Latin delicacy, will bedevil the eggs and enchant your guests.

1	dozen hard boiled eggs
½	cup mayonnaise
1	teaspoon dry mustard
1	teaspoon Dijon mustard
¼	cup shelled sunflower seeds
1	teaspoon chopped fresh coriander (also known as cilantro)
¼	teaspoon Angostura bitters
2	tablespoons warm ale or porter
1	dash *each* of garlic powder and coarse ground pepper
	seasoned salt to taste
	ground nutmeg

Slice hard boiled eggs in half lengthwise. Remove yolks and set whites aside to fill later.

In a medium-sized bowl, mash the egg yolks with a fork and mix in mayonnaise, dry and Dijon mustards, sunflower seeds, coriander, bitters, garlic powder, ground pepper, and salt to taste. Add enough ale or porter to make the filling smooth but not sloppy. Mound mixture evenly into egg whites and sprinkle with nutmeg, as Grandma would say, "for pretty." Cover loosely and chill in refrigerator for a few hours before serving.

Makes 24 bedeviled egg halves.

Whistle for It!

The saying "if you want anything, just whistle for it!" was not an original Lauren Bacall line. It dates back to an ingenious, though nerve-rattling invention, the whistle tankard. This device boasted a small, shrill device built into the handle of an ornate mug. The whistle was used to attract the attention of the landlord whenever the mug was depleted.

Bavarian Pickled Eggs

Pickled hard-boiled eggs, called *soleier* in German, resting temptingly in large glass jars, have long been a popular backbar accompaniment for beer drinkers.

This version is brightened with the addition of pineapple juice, which symbolizes hospitality. Some say this is because pineapple was expensive when it first appeared in Europe and was saved for favored guests. Others trace it to the custom of West Indian natives of placing a pineapple outside their huts to let visitors know they are welcome.

6	ounces unsweetened pineapple juice
6	hard boiled eggs
1	medium onion, sliced thin
2	tablespoons sugar
½	teaspoon salt
½	teaspoon whole pickling spices
¾	cup white vinegar
¼	cup warm beer or ale

Boil eggs, soak in cold water and peel.

Combine onion, sugar, salt, pickling spices, vinegar, beer or ale and pineapple juice in a sauce pan. Bring mixture to a boil and allow to cool. NOTE: If you use sweetened pineapple juice, leave the sugar out.

Place eggs in a resealable container and pour liquid over them. Store in refrigerator overnight. Turn eggs once in a while so they will pickle evenly.

To serve, remove from jar and slice lengthwise. Serve with any Bavarian style beer, the kind that's made in almost every beer-loving country in the world, or some Swiss Löwenbräu Zurich.

Makes 12 servings for a picnic or for snack time. *Prosit!*

Drink Responsibly

Never leave beer in your glass. Finish it. Remember, there are sober children in India and China.

Gold Rush Chicken Livers

In the gold camps in California and Nevada, fortunes were made in many ways besides digging and panning. Two of the strangest involved fellows whose cleverness kept them from having to get their hands dirty. One was a bartender who always wore muddy boots and the other was a traveling cook who loved to cook chicken.

The first entrepreneur's job mixing drinks required him to collect gold dust from patrons for each beer or shot, a pinch at a time. In the process he usually managed to spill a little bit on the floor. He'd cover his "accident" by stepping on the spot. When his shift was over, he would walk back to his shack, careful not to step in any puddles, and wash the mud from his boots to retrieve the embedded pay dirt.

The second miner, known throughout the camps for his fried chicken, made it a rule to work alone and to search carefully the gizzards of every bird he dressed. He knew that chickens are curious and will peck shiny things like small bits of gold.

Whether or not he kept the livers for the pot we don't know. But here's a great snack or, if you have a gold tooth, a main course.

1	pound chicken livers
1	medium onion, finely chopped
1	teaspoon paprika
2	tablespoons butter
1	tablespoon flour
1	cup warm beer or ale
2	tablespoons heavy cream
½	lemon, juice only
1	dash orange bitters

Cut chicken livers in half. Sauté gently for two or three minutes – they taste best if still slightly pink inside. Remove from pan. Sauté onion until transparent. Return livers to pan. Stir in paprika and flour. Pour in beer gradually. Finally, add lemon juice and bitters. Salt and pepper to taste. Just before serving, stir in cream.

Serve as hors d'oeuvres on toothpicks, or over rice as a main dish.

Makes enough for 4.

California Steam Beer

This brewing oddity, referred to by some as a slightly eccentric ale, grew out of the necessity of frontier life. In the 1850's, shipping beer around the Cape to San Francisco was too costly and only small amounts could be made locally. This was because brewing requires ice and early California brewers found it virtually impossible to obtain ice in large enough quantities to reach temperatures at which normal lager beers would ferment. Brewers elsewhere (before modern refrigeration was introduced) simply waited for the best weather, usually spring and fall. But in the roaring camps of the West, there was an urgent demand for more beer, now!

Since no one wanted to wait, and ice couldn't be brought in by wagons in large enough amounts from the High Sierras to satisfy the brewers' needs, the problem seemed insoluble until someone remembered an old German technique called krausening.

Krausening is a beer finishing process in which a little "young" beer is poured into kegs of aging beer during the resting stage. The kegs are then resealed and a second or after-fermentation begins. The trick, for those who are familiar with brewing procedures, is to use a beer- or bottom-fermenting yeast at a higher, ale-fermenting temperature. The procedure not only worked, but it worked faster than normal brewing. The difference was that the final product, because of increased amounts of carbon dioxide, was notably different from regular lagers.

Steam beer builds up to a pressure of fifty or sixty pounds in the keg. When a new barrel was tapped, to the cheers of clamoring miners, the pressure released was accompanied by a loud popping noise and fine white spray, resembling steam, whence its unique name.

Even though dozens of brewers adopted the process by the 1880s, steam beer is best remembered as a quick, rather than a connoisseur's, beverage. According to an 1879 issue of the _Phoenix Herald_, "Steam beer is allowed from ten to twelve days from mash tub to glass." By way of comparison, some modern brewers, like Henry Weinhard, insist on two months to brew and age properly.

Today, one can still sit by the bay in San Francisco and enjoy a steam beer because of the efforts of one tiny company that continues this almost forgotten tradition. The Anchor Steam Beer Company's major product, which also includes a stout and porter, is rich in color and highly hopped with a lively head. The "new" steam beer is also gentler on the palate. Anchor has won many tasters' awards and much praise among knowledgeable beer drinkers.

Beef and Cheese Nosh

In pagan days, games, festivals and other celebrations were of indeterminate length. In Europe, for example, the guests brought their own beer and, when it was gone, went home. In the middle of the 10th century, one King Haakon the Good of Norway mandated that "Jule," an old, pre-Christian bash, be celebrated with the new feast of Christmas. Anticipating the BYOB tradition, he also instructed each participant to bring a third of a barrel of beer for the guest's own consumption.

There is no record of what the king offered his guests in the way of snacks, but here's a simple and tasty hors d'oeuvre you can serve, whether your friends bring that third of a barrel or not.

2	ounces cream cheese
6	ounces Bleu cheese
2	tablespoons warm beer
3	ounces dried beef or prosciutto, snipped into tiny pieces

Mix cream cheese, Blue cheese and beer together to form a soft and smooth paste. Lay piece of dried beef on a flat surface. Spread generous smudges of cheese mixture evenly on slices. Roll into tight cylinders. Chill until firm. (Do not freeze them.)

Cut into small, bite-size pieces with a sharp knife. Either serve on crackers or thinly sliced toast, or spear with toothpicks. For a final pleasant note, pour a couple of special bottles of Pope's "1880" Beer to chat and sip over.

Makes some 40 fine nibbles.

A Boat We All Miss

The British Navy, those who manned England's indomitable "wooden walls," acquired a taste for good beer that still remains unslaked. In 1944, during the Second World War, the 13,000 ton mine-layer, <u>Menestheus</u>, was converted into a floating brewery. It took seawater, distilled it, and brewed 1800 gallons of beer a day, to the pleasure of allied serviceman stationed in the Pacific Theater.

Curb Your Enthusiasm and Hitch Your Pony

For those interested in making dramatic social entrances, be warned it's illegal to ride into a bar on horseback in the State of California.

Liverwurst Pâté

Serve this taste treat on crackers or bagel chips, or in a bowl beside some tortilla, corn, or potato chips. Made with a little less beer in it, this recipe becomes a true pâté and spreads nicely on fresh vegetables. It makes a fine celery stuffing.

1	pound liverwurst
8	ounces cream cheese
4	tablespoons melted butter
1	tablespoon instant minced onion
2	teaspoons dry mustard
2	teaspoons Worcestershire sauce
12	ounces warm beer or ale

Mix cream cheese, butter, and liverwurst with beer. Add minced onion, dry mustard, and Worcestershire sauce. Work spices into ingredients with a fork to form a nice creamy mess.

Chill in refrigerator for a couple of hours before serving. Or, if you're planning a party, make this the day before.

Because of its assertive flavor, choose a brew that is equal to it, maybe a German dark – a St. Pauli Girl or Löwenbräu, for instance.

Makes about 1 pint, enough for a dozen nibblers.

Olde Frothingslosh

Yes, Virginia, there is an Olde Frothingslosh, "the pale stale ale with the foam on the bottom." It all started in Pittsburg as a private joke between a local disk jockey and his audience. Eventually, it was produced and bottled by the Pittsburgh Brewing Company in the mid 1960s.

In 1969, not to be outdone by the then popular Miss Rheingold promotion, a special can was marketed extolling the virtues of the Rubenesque Miss Olde Frothingslosh, who had been "chosen on the basis of beauty, talent, poise... and quantity."

In an exclusive interview, quoted from the front of her favorite beer can, the current winner revealed her beauty secrets: "Fatima Yechburg, big winner of our Miss Olde Frothingslosh contest, hails from a small mining town on the outskirts of Pittsburg, where she always did what she wanted. 'I just like to eat,' explains the misty-eyed miss. She's an avid reader of comic books, race forms, cereal boxes and other stimulating things like that. Right now our winner is furthering her education by studying arc welding at night. By day, Miss Frothingslosh earns her daily bread, butter, steak, pastafazool, potatoes, corn flakes, pancakes, french fries, pies, and so forth as a trapeze artist."

Colorado Mushrooms

The lore of the ancients said mushrooms were the mystical offspring of lightning bolts. A few brave souls, Roman epicureans primarily, praised their delicate flavor when eaten. Unfortunately, because few then could distinguish the delightful from the deadly, mushrooms fell into disfavor. They eventually became associated with dark magic.

Not until the rise of Louis XIV, the Sun King, who reigned 1643-1715, did mushrooms make their long overdue return to culinary favor. It is hard to think of fine cooking today without this exquisite edible.

5	tablespoons *each* of wheat and white flour
¼	teaspoon *each* garlic and baking powder
1	dash *each* crushed red pepper and paprika
	salt and pepper to taste
1 ½	cups warm beer
1	pound medium size mushrooms
2	cups bread crumbs
	cooking oil for frying
1	cup Cheddar cheese, grated

Mix wheat and white flour, garlic, baking powder, red pepper, paprika, salt, and pepper. Add beer and stir mixture until batter is smooth.

Wash and drain mushrooms. Pat dry with a towel. Preheat cooking oil to 325 degrees in a frying pan or wok. Dip each mushroom into the batter till nicely coated, then roll each in the bread crumbs. Slide them into the hot oil. Use a large enough pan so you won't overcrowd them.

Fry mushrooms until they turn a golden brown. Do not overcook or they get tough. Drain on paper towels. Roll in grated cheese.

Next place the mushrooms on a baking sheet. Pop into a 350-degree oven until the cheese begins to melt and bubble.

Serve these little beauties by themselves as an appetizer, or as a noble companion fit for royalty to accompany char-broiled steak or fish. Sip a tall cold glass of Coors.

Makes 6 to 8 servings.

Old Time Beef Jerky

This frontier victual, probably borrowed from the Plains Indians, was a favorite way of preserving meat. The beef, venison, buffalo, elk, goat, or hooved whatever, was cut into thin slices, salted and hung out to dry in the sun.

On one occasion, the legendary mountain man Jim Bridger told how he was treed by a pack of wolves. The ravenous animals waited at the base of the pine for over two hours and then left, leaving one of the pack on guard. They soon returned and Jim thought his minutes were numbered, for they'd brought back a beaver to gnaw through the base of his refuge. Fortunately, he'd had the foresight to bring a handful of jerky with him. He simply dropped it among the beasts and as they chewed and chewed and chewed, he made good his escape.

Today, though we no longer require this trail ration to save us from predators, the savory flavor has not lost its appeal — especially with a good beer. The commercially prepared variety is expensive and somehow doesn't taste quite as good as homemade. When you consider how easy it is to make, the rationale for this recipe is obvious.

Make plenty! It has a habit of disappearing quickly.

4-5	pounds flank steak, top or bottom round, brisket or whatever
1	cup soy sauce
1	cup Worcestershire sauce
1	cup warm beer or ale
½	medium onion, diced
¼	teaspoon thyme or sage
⅛	teaspoon coarse ground pepper
2	cloves garlic, crushed
2	bay leaves
2	whole cloves

Place meat in the freezer compartment for ½ hour or until it becomes firm enough to slice easily. Cut into long, ¼ inch thick strips, going with the grain of the meat. Remove all excess fat and gristle; they can cause the jerky to spoil when stored. Mix soy and Worcestershire sauces with beer, onion and other spices in a large bowl. Place meat in marinade. Stir until it is all covered. Allow it to work overnight in the refrigerator, at least 10-15 hours. The longer you leave it in, the stronger the flavor.

Dry the strips of meat on paper towels to remove any excess moisture. Some experts advise using a rolling pin at this stage to squeeze the meat dry. Place evenly on metal racks so the strips do not touch one another. Slide racks into a warm oven, about 160 degrees. Allow to bake very slowly for 10-12 hours more, with the oven door ajar, until the jerky is thoroughly cured and dry. Turn once during this process. Store fresh jerky in an airtight container. No need to refrigerate! Makes 40-50 strips.

You can also experiment with other marinade ingredients. Try making some jerky using lemon juice, honey, or hot pepper sauce.

Another note: Beef jerky can also be made from ground beef. Marinate the meat the same way, then roll it into thin strips or patties before placing in oven. Because of the fat content in the hamburger, it's best to refrigerate or freeze the jerky.

Any nosh in this chapter might have slowed the effects of the practice described next.

Mugs and Muggling

To the word "muggle," Harry Potter is a latecomer, as you will see.

The word "mug" became a common name for a variety of drinking vessels, both decorated and plain, but has also had other meanings over the years. During the 17th century, when ale drinking was heavy in England, "mug" became a verb to describe the quaint pastime of "muggling." In this test of endurance a group of men would sit down and ritualistically drink themselves senseless.

The first of the group would chug a pint, while the others joked and waited their turn. The second would then match the first's pint and add one of his own. This meant that the third had to down three pints, and so on. The winner was the last survivor — the one who could match the total pints drunk before him and one pint more.

A description of this game is found in a moral treatise of the period entitled England's Bane. "I have seen a company . . . drinking for a muggle," the author, Mr. Young, explains. "Sixe determined to try their strengths. . . every man taking a glasse more than his fellows, so that he that dranke the least at the end of three rounds which was first, dranke one and twenty pints, and the sixth man thirty-six." There is no mention of what the prize was, but certainly all acquired a stupendous hangover — not surprisingly referred to, in those days, as being "kicked by the brewer's horse."

In the 18th century the word found a home in "mughouse." These establishments were gathering places of entertainers and the forerunners of the English music hall. Only ale or beer was served in mughouses, or "mugrooms," where one could enjoy the antics of variety performers, held in check by a master of ceremonies, who presided over the ruckus, sorting out songs, toasts, story-tellers, and political speech makers.

Saratoga Chips

Potato chips were invented at a fashionable resort in New York State, Saratoga Springs, about a hundred years ago, in a fit of anger. The master chef of Moon's Lake House had had an ongoing argument with a guest about the proper way to prepare French fried potatoes. Each time Chef George Crum sent the dish to the man's table the potatoes were returned with the message that they were not sliced thinly enough.

Finally, his patience gone, the chef cut the potatoes paper thin before dropping them into the hot oil. Not surprisingly, when the dish was served the patron loved it, and so have generations of chip eaters ever since. It would be nice if we knew the name of the stubborn customer. Shouldn't he really be given partial credit for the invention?

3-4	raw potatoes, sliced very, very thin
2-3	cups of cooking oil
12	ounces of beer or ale

Wash and slice potatoes (peeling is optional). Allow them to soak in cold beer – enough to cover them completely – for 2 or 3 hours.

Pour off the liquid. Dry slices thoroughly. Any drops of water will cause the hot oil to splatter when deep frying. You can use a pan or deep fryer to prepare the potatoes. Heat oil to 390 degrees. Drop chips in, a few at a time. Turn until brown and golden on both sides.

Drain on paper towels or shake in paper bag. Sprinkle with salt. For a real treat, serve while still hot with any cold beer.

Makes 3 to 4 servings.

Hail to the Queen!

During the reign of Elizabeth I of England, whenever "good Queen Bess" traveled to distant parts of the realm, she sent special couriers ahead to sample the ale. If it did not pass the test, arrangements were made immediately to see that her favorite London ale arrived before she did. Reportedly she knocked back two full tankards, every morning, with breakfast.

We can only infer that she learned these habits from her father, Henry VIII. He shocked most of Europe in the mid-15th century with his immoderation – with ladies and with beer. At court each lady-in-waiting was allowed a gallon of beer every morning to accompany her breakfast. That would start the day with a smile!

Toad in the Hole

This is a variant of an old English favorite.

12	Vienna sausages or cocktail franks
1	cup flour
1	cup warm beer
2	eggs, separated whites from yolks
½	teaspoon salt
	dash of nutmeg and pepper
	cooking oil for frying sausages

Mix sifted flour with warm beer, nutmeg, and salt and pepper. Add egg yolks and beat well. In another bowl whip egg whites until they are frothy and stiff. Fold into batter.

Dry the outsides of the sausages. Dip sausages into batter. Drop gently into well-heated oil, about 400 degrees. Turn until they are a nice brown. Be careful not to overcook.

Drain on paper towels. Serve while still warm with a full-bodied English Ale, such as Watney's or Fuller's.

Makes 4 to 6 servings.

Hate to Pick a Favorite Beer, But . . .

After the Great Britain Beer Festival, in London, all the brewery presidents decided to go out for a beer. The CEO of Corona sits down and says, "Eh Señor, I would like the world's best beer, a Corona." The bartender selects a bottle and gives it to him.

The guy from Budweiser says, "I'd like the best beer in the world, give me 'The King of Beers,' a Budweiser." The bartender gives him one.

The guy from Coors says, "I'd like the only beer made with pure Rocky Mountain spring water. Give me a Coors." He gets it.

The Guinness exec sits down and says, "Give me a Coke." The bartender thinks "Huh?" but gives him what he ordered. The other brewery presidents look over at him and ask, "Why aren't you drinking a Guinness?" The Guinness president replies, "Well, if you guys aren't drinking beer, neither am I."

CHAPTER TWO

SOUPS, SALADS, DRESSINGS

Yankee Tavern Soup

Sausage and Bean Soup

Cheddar Bisque

Stone Soup

Danish Beer Soup

Baked Onion Soup

Red Cabbage Salad

Sesame Seed Dressing

Old World Potato Salad

Hot German Potato Salad

Caesar Salad

Pennsylvania Slaw

California Salad

Four-Bean Salad

Yankee Tavern Soup

This tasty soup was heralded by the blast of coach horns, when hungry, tired and thirsty passengers were at the venal mercies of coachmen and innkeepers. According to one story teller, it was common practice in less reputable places to charge guests for a meal and then stall until just moments before the coach was ready to load and depart. When the horn sounded, customers only had a minute or two to wolf down a couple of bites – and the owner made a handsome profit with little outlay.

One day, a Yankee peddler who was familiar with this custom stepped from the coach. He paid his fifty cents and waited patiently. The meal finally arrived, followed a short time later by a call to re-board. The man ignored the announcement and continued to eat. Even with the nagging of the other passengers and the publican, the stranger could not be dissuaded from finishing his soup, bread and ale.

The coach finally left, shy one passenger. At this time, he pointed out to the landlord that all the silver spoons were missing from the table. "Well," he drawled, "I guess them folks decided to get something for their money."

The owner rushed out, shouting "Stop, thief!" A half hour later, the coach was back – accompanied by the sheriff. The man was waiting at the door, picking his teeth. When asked who the culprits were, he sighed, "I calculate you'll find them spoons inside, in the coffee pot." He then climbed aboard and settled back comfortably beside his starving fellow passengers.

Make Yankee tavern soup for your friends, but give them plenty of time to relish it.

16	ounces milk
16	ounces warm dark beer
16	ounces cheese spread
½	cup crisp bacon, crumbled
½	cup flour
¼	cup melted butter
½	teaspoon salt

Heat the milk, beer and cheese spread in a sauce pan over low heat. Stir in bacon. Melt butter in a small pan. Mix in the flour to form a ball. Drop the butter ball into the cheese mixture. Stir constantly till the flour is all dissolved and the soup is hot and thick.

Serve with hot bread and lots of butter. If you're really into a coach mood, you might also want to mull a mug or two of ale.

Makes 5 to 6 servings.

Sausage and Bean Soup

In many western countries politicians have been called "bean eaters." This expression goes all the way back to ancient Athens, the cradle of democracy. There citizens used black and white beans, dropped into a jug, as their method of voting on issues and electing officials. Later, as the custom was refined, small balls, called *ballotas*, were introduced in Italy – hence words like "ballot" and "blackball." The winner of an election, then, was the one who "ate the most beans," or, in a pejorative sense, the candidate who expeditiously disposed of any evidence of election-fixing.

This hearty English recipe combines white beans, bacon, and sausage to create a soup that will win votes in any election. It can't be a coincidence that one of the favorite dishes served in the dining room of the United States Senate is – bean soup.

½	pound sliced bacon, fried
1	pound dried white beans
24	ounces warm beer
4	cups beef broth
1	large onion, chopped
1	pound Italian sausages
¼	teaspoon hot pepper sauce
½	tablespoon parsley, chopped
1	bay leaf
	salt and pepper

Wash beans and remove any bad ones. Drain and place in a 4- or 5-quart pot. Add beef broth, beer, bay leaf, chopped onion and hot sauce. Cover and bring to boil. Reduce heat and let mixture simmer for 2 or 3 hours, or until beans are soft. Take 3 cups of bean mixture and puree it in a blender until smooth. Return it to pot and stir in thoroughly.

Place sausages in a large frying pan. Add ½ inch of water. Cover and simmer for 10-15 minutes. Set sausage aside. Discard water and dry the pan. Place bacon in pan and fry over medium heat until crisp. Drain and crumble bacon into bits. Save about 2 tablespoons of drippings. Return sausages to pan and fry until golden on all sides.

Stir sausages and crumbled bacon into bean mixture. Add water if desired, to thin the soup to preferred consistency. Salt and pepper to taste. Remove bay leaf. Cover pot and simmer another 10 to 15 minutes to blend flavors. Spoon off any excess fat before serving.

Garnish with chopped parsley. Serve as a first course, or by itself as a light meal with hot rolls and cold Double Maxim.

Makes 6 to 8 servings.

Cheddar Bisque

The primary ingredient for this smooth and soothing dish is Cheddar, America's favorite cheese. It was first made in the village of Cheddar, Somersetshire, England, during the 16th century. It didn't find its permanent home on these shores until 1851, when the first Cheddar factory opened in Rome, New York. The sharp variety, called for here, is regular Cheddar that has been aged for up to a year.

2 ½	cups sharp Cheddar cheese, grated
1	small onion, chopped fine
2	small carrots, chopped fine
½	cup celery, chopped fine
⅜	cup flour
3	cups cream
2	cups warm beer
4	egg yolks, beaten
1	cup sour cream
¼	cup chives, chopped
1	dash *each* salt and pepper

Melt butter and sauté onions, carrots, and celery until just golden. Stir in flour until mixture is smooth. Gradually add cream and beer, stirring constantly. Add Cheddar cheese and stir again, until melted.

Remove from burner and beat in egg yolks. Return to heat and season to taste with salt and pepper. Do not allow to boil.

Pour into serving dishes and garnish with a dollop of sour cream and a few chives. If you want your guests to be more inventive, supply them with bowls of other drop-ins, such as strips of green pepper or pimiento, toasted almonds, crumbled bacon, or even popcorn – popcorn is a Pennsylvania-Dutch additive to soups.

As you dip into this treat, you may also be inspired to raise a chilled stein of Löwenbräu to toast St. Boniface (ca. 680-754 A.D.), the patron saint of brewers and beer lovers.

Makes 12 servings.

Take It to the Judge

In Algeria those found guilty of misdemeanors can pay off court fines in beer. How civilized is that!

Stone Soup

Soup was a mainstay in early America. Iron kettles simmered in village inns and rural kitchens alike. It was easy to make, sitting there on the corner of the hearth, steaming all day. It tasted great, and it was economical – the cook simply dropped in whatever leftovers there were and then added a few bits of this and that to create a hearty meal.

The Pennsylvania Dutch praised it in the saying, "You don't have to have teeth to eat soup." They had more varieties than Mr. Heinz because they claimed to be able to make it out of practically anything, even rocks.

According to their telling, this dish was discovered during the time of Napoleon, when two hungry soldiers wandered into a small town in southern Germany. First, they engaged in a bit of noisy ballyhoo to raise a crowd and then offered to teach the local residents how to make the most economical dish known, Stone Soup.

While one soldier set a pot of water to boil, the other carefully selected and washed two large cobblestones. A bit later, even as the mixture began to simmer, one of the soldiers asked a woman, "Do you have an onion? It's not strictly needed, but it *will* improve the flavor."

As she reached into her market basket to accommodate him, his partner cajoled a farmer, for the same reason, for a morsel of meat, and another bystander for a few potatoes, a carrot or two, a leek and, of course, a few spices. Soon the soup did, indeed, begin to smell tasty. After another hour or two, the two strangers carefully fished out the stones, threw them away and sat down to enjoy a meal that might better have been called "gullible stew."

3-4	medium leeks
1	pound meaty ham bone or ham hock
1	pound knockwurst, casings removed, sliced
1	medium onion, chopped
1	stalk celery, chopped
1	medium carrot, chopped
1	medium potato, cubed
2	tablespoons butter
1	12-ounce package green split peas
12	ounces warm beer
1	teaspoon marjoram
6	cups water
¼	teaspoon ground allspice
⅛	teaspoon cayenne pepper
1	tablespoon white vinegar
¼	cup chopped parsley
2	clean stones (optional)

Cut leeks lengthwise. Separate leaves and wash thoroughly. Slice the white and light green sections thinly. Discard the tough, darker leaves.

Melt butter in a heavy kettle or Dutch oven. Add leeks, onion, celery, and carrots. Sauté until the onion is limp, stirring as necessary. Add potato cubes, peas, beer, water, marjoram, allspice, cayenne, and ham bone. Bring liquid to a boil. Reduce heat. Allow to simmer for 2 ½ to 3 hours, or until ham and peas are tender.

Remove the ham bone from the soup. Cool for a few minutes and strip off the meat. Discard the bone, fat and stones (if you had to use them). Break the meat into chunks and return it to kettle. Add slices of knockwurst, vinegar and parsley. Simmer for another 15 minutes.

This soup is extra good if made a day ahead of time. Cool, cover, and refrigerate overnight so all the flavors have plenty of time to blend. When it's time to reheat it, you may want to add a little more water if it seems too thick.

Serve with fresh rye bread, lots of butter, a simple green salad and some fresh fruit.

Makes about 3 quarts.

Tipping a Yard

A classic English yard of ale is served in a long-necked glass usually accompanied with a special stand to hold it when resting. The "yard" has a tall slender neck, a flared lip on top and a round, bulbous bottom thirty-six inches below. Rather cumbersome to tip and sip, it was designed this way to be handed up to coach drivers, allowing them refreshment without having to dismount.

Since then, it has become an ongoing practical joke to trip the unwary.

If one simply raises the jar and slowly tips it back while drinking, a moment will come when the air in the stem reaches the bulb full of beer. The foam tends to hide impending doom from the drinker. The ensuing gush, as the air breaks through, douses the drinker's face and body, if not his or her spirits.

The secret is not to tilt the glass too steeply or drink steadily. In other words, give the air a chance to displace the beer and enter the lower section smoothly. Some recommend swirling or twisting the glass as you get close to the bulb. For the less heroic drinker there is a "half yard" which is just as dangerous, but possibly better to practice on.

Speed-drinking competitions draw major crowds eager to applaud the skillful and see the unsuccessful wearing a lot of beer. One winner, Bob Hawke, drained a yard glass in 12 seconds and went on to become Prime Minister of Australia.

Danish Beer Soup

The idea of combining a bit of day-old bread, beer, and a squeeze of lemon seems to have developed in three countries well-noted for both their cooking and their fine beers, Denmark, Germany and Austria. These are traditional recipes and may seem bland to American palates; they are definitely an acquired taste.

In Denmark, where this soup is called *Øllebrod*, this soup is topped with whipped cream. Children, on their birthday, are given a spoonful for each year of their age.

6	slices dark bread, rye, or pumpernickel
16	ounces warm beer or ale
16	ounces water
1	small fresh lemon - the juice and the grated peel
½	teaspoon sugar
	whipped cream (optional)

Break bread into small pieces and soak in beer 4 hours or overnight. Either light or dark beer or ale can be used.

Pour mixture into a sauce pan. Add water. Simmer for 15 minutes. Stir occasionally as bread disintegrates and soup thickens. If desired, use blender to increase smoothness, then continue heating.

Grate the lemon peel, avoiding the bitter white inside rind. Squeeze the juice from the lemon and remove the seeds. Combine sugar, juice, and grated lemon peel. Pour into soup.

Serve hot with whipped cream topping.

Makes 4 servings.

The Germans and Austrians also make a similar dish called *bierkaltschale*. To prepare it combine

16	ounces of beer
1	cup of soaked currents
4	ounces of bread crumbs
1	teaspoon of lemon juice
1	stick of cinnamon
½	cup of sugar

This is a cold soup, so do not heat the mixture. Mix thoroughly. Allow to stand for ½ hour. Serve quite chilled.

The Skinny on Low-Cal Beer

Can beer lovers enjoy themselves without the telling side (and front) effects of excess poundage? Low-cal beer is the way to beat beer bellies without being reduced to diets or abstinence.

Light beer, low calorie beer, has for a long time been an option to brewers, tapsters and consumers alike. The calories are based on the ratio between additives, alcohol and water. The formula was even found in the lyrics of an old folk song which has the refrain, "I am the man, the very fine man, who waters the workers' beer." This simple formula — adding water — reduced calories and increased profits.

Isn't this like calling for a beer with a water back? No, our kindly brewers do better by us: Ever since the 1960s, light beer has had another difference, an enzyme called amyloglucosidase.

Simply stated, this enzyme converts more of the beer's starchy ingredients into alcohol, giving light beer about 1% more alcohol by volume. Since light beers don't contain the dextrins regular beers have — they're converted by the amyloglucosidase into alcohol — low-cal brews are more readily absorbed into the body. Quicker inebriation and 50 fewer calories, for less money? Are we in Heaven?

No. Brewers' goal is to produce a lower-calorie but not a more potent product. So they add water back in, and lower the alcoholic content to an acceptable level.

The light beer you buy does have fewer calories. It is also less filling because it has less body — body comes from those ingredients that amyloglucosidase converts into more alcohol. For those same reasons, light beer is paler than regular beer and, by the time it reaches your emporium, contains about half a percent less alcohol than traditional American lagers.

So Can Beer Help Me Lose Weight?

There are claims made about beer diets. Most of them read like something between an urban legend and a wish upon a star.

About the only hope is that beer is a diuretic. If your exercise is limited to the knee-bending and straightening that gets you out of a chair and running to the head, though, nope, sorry, that won't do it.

Still - 12 ounces of an ordinary U.S. pale lager actually has fewer calories than the same amount of 2 percent milk or apple juice.

Baked Onion Soup

Originally this hearty favorite came to this country from France. Once arrived, it traveled quickly. A number of gastronomic centers, notably New Orleans, New York and San Francisco, have developed their own versions.

This one still has its Gallic accent. Enjoy it as everyday fare or when entertaining guests who appreciate fine flavor and a touch of panache.

3	large Spanish onions, sliced very thin
3	cups hot water
8	ounces warm beer
½	cup butter or margarine
2	tablespoons instant beef bouillon
½	teaspoon garlic salt
1	tablespoon sugar
1	teaspoon Worcestershire sauce
2	cups Monterey Jack cheese, shredded
¼	cup Parmesan or Romano cheese, grated
4-6	slices French bread, sliced very thin and buttered

Sauté onions in butter in a heavy skillet until they just start to brown. Do not overcook. If sugar is used, add it to the onions here for flavor and color.

Combine the hot water, warm beer, Worcestershire sauce, onions, and garlic salt in a large pot. Bring to a boil. Simmer for 30 to 40 minutes. If you're short of time, you could serve it now, but why not go all the way?

Ladle the soup into 4 to 6 oven-proof serving bowls. Sprinkle about ½ cup of Jack cheese into each bowl. Place a slice of French bread on cheese. Top bread with Parmesan or Romano cheese and the remaining Jack.

Bake in a hot oven, 450 degrees, for 10 minutes or until the cheese is bubbly.

Turn on the broiler and heat another couple of minutes until cheese is golden and brown. Watch closely to avoid burning.

Serve hot from the oven with a green salad and tall bottles of Anchor Steam beer.

Makes 4 to 6 servings.

Red Cabbage Salad

Cabbage salad, in various forms, has been an American favorite since it immigrated to this country with settlers in the early 18th century. Its history, though, has not been without travail. In 1918, for example, owing to the bitterness of the First World War, anti-German sentiment in the United States led to rejection of sauerkraut as a symbol of the hated enemy.

Patriots tried in vain to rename this old standby "Liberty Cabbage." These efforts were about as successful as the attempt to rename French fries "Freedom Fries" or to call frankfurters "Victory Sausage."

1	small head red cabbage, shredded
½	cup salad oil
½	cup olive oil
½	cup vinegar
1	teaspoon honey
½	small onion, sliced thin
2-3	tablespoons warm beer or ale
2	tablespoons lemon juice
	sprinkle of coarse ground pepper
	salt to taste

Core and shred cabbage very fine. Peel onion and slice very thin. Combine vegetables in large mixing bowl with salt and pepper. Toss. Add olive oil and salad oil and toss again until cabbage and onions are well coated. Pour in vinegar, lemon juice and honey and toss once more. Serve now, or marinate in refrigerator for a couple of days if you like.

Makes 6 to 8 unbeatable servings.

The Conversion of Hathor

In old Egyptian lore, Ra, the supreme god of the heavens and earth, one morning chose to amuse himself by observing the daily activities of men. He was angered by what he saw, and as he beheld, his wrath grew beyond bounds. He caused the bovine war-goddess Hathor to wreak vengeance on all sinners. Unfortunately, once started, she so warmed to her task that not even Ra, when he cooled down, could deter her. She loved the blood. She killed and killed. Finally, to everyone's relief, he hit on a plan.

He brewed a special beer, blood red in color, and poured it on the ground directly in front of Hathor. She hesitated on seeing her reflection in the smooth surface. She paused, drank deeply, and "recognized man no longer."

Such actions did not pass unnoted by the decimated population. Gratefully they made the goddess, in turn, a venerated Egyptian deity of intoxication, then of joy and love, and, eventually, of music, dance and song.

Sesame Seed Dressing

In ancient Rome, about the time of Emperor Augustus, elaborate banquets combined feasting, enthusiastic drinking and entertainments of all kinds. These were sometimes gentlemen-only and sometimes women-only affairs. Because banquet guests almost always discussed political, business and social topics, the thoughtful host had a servant place a rose on each table just when the first salad was being served.

This floral signal meant that nothing discussed would be repeated later. The custom led to the expression *sub rosa*, beneath the rose, which we still use to mean "entrusted, secret" or "in confidence."

This dressing might have adorned that first salad course:

2	tablespoons sesame seeds
1 ¼	cup salad oil
2	tablespoons soy sauce
2-4	tablespoons rice wine vinegar or white wine vinegar
2	cloves garlic, minced
½	teaspoon thyme leaves
¼	teaspoon dry mustard
2	tablespoons warm beer

Melt butter in a heavy frying pan over medium heat. Cook sesame seeds slowly, stirring, until they turn a light brown. Allow to cool. Crush seeds with a mortar and pestle or the flat bottom of a glass.

Mix sesame seed paste thoroughly with salad oil, soy sauce, vinegar, garlic, thyme leaves, dry mustard, and warm beer. Chill. Shake vigorously before serving.

Apply to any crisp vegetable or tossed green salad. Chill all ingredients before mixing. To avoid sogginess, use only enough dressing to moisten and not drown other vegetables – unless, of course, you have a yen for a marinated salad.

Makes about 1 ¾ cups.

Three Cheers for Uncle Sam! And Some of His Beery Relatives

The United States produces 23 million kiloliters of beer annually. China produces more – almost 25 million kiloliters. We're second. Germany is third. and then Brazil and Russia.

Americans drink about 24 gallons of beer per capita. Germans drink more than 38 gallons per person. We're not trying hard enough.

30

Old World Potato Salad

The potato is from Peru, where, according to ancient legend, a powerful earth goddess gave it to inhabitants to protect their lands from invasion. When the natives planted it, beautiful plants sprang forth, but, when the enemy soldiers ate them, they became sick and died.

The goddess next instructed the inhabitants about unseen treasures. She told her people to dig up the roots and eat them. When they did, they became strong and quickly defeated the remaining invaders.

Surely this simple story predates the arrival of the Spanish. They not only ate the potato but carried it, with their gold and silver spoils, back to their homeland. Potatoes eventually became associated with any number of traditional European dishes. This is a deluxe version of the classic German salad, which has the advantage of serving all seasons, hot or cold.

6	cups potatoes, boiled, peeled and cubed
¾	cup chopped green onion (about 1 bunch)
1	cup celery, chopped
½	pound bacon, fried crisp
¾	cup mayonnaise
¾	cup sour cream
¼	cup warm beer
1	tablespoon salt
¼	teaspoon coarse ground pepper

Combine potatoes, onion, celery, and drained and crumbled bacon bits. For those with a stronger palate, ½ cup of chopped raw onion can be substituted for the green onions.

Blend mayonnaise, sour cream, beer, salt and pepper in a second bowl. Mix dressing thoroughly. Pour over potato cubes. Stir together until vegetables are well coated, being careful not to break the potato cubes.

Cool in the refrigerator for a couple of hours before serving alongside a couple of six-packs of Heineken.

Makes 6 to 8 servings for your next picnic or barbecue.

Hot German Potato Salad

If the weather outside is frightful, you won't have to wait until the snow clears to enjoy a potato salad. The Germans don't. They enjoy potatoes as an important part of every large meal, summer and winter alike. Try familiar ingredients to create this traditional hot salad, called *kartoffelsalat*.

Prepare the salad as described in the preceding recipe, but leave out the mayonnaise and sour cream. In their place, add 1 additional cup of chopped celery and

½	cup vinegar
2	tablespoons flour
2	tablespoons brown sugar
3	chopped, hard-boiled eggs
½	cup chopped pimiento

Chop bacon. Fry in a large skillet until crisp. Add green onion. Sauté lightly. Stir in flour. Gradually add vinegar, salt, pepper, brown sugar and beer. Reduce heat to low. Stir continuously, until mixture thickens slightly.

Add potatoes, chopped egg, celery, and pimiento to pan. Heat everything thoroughly. Transfer salad to an ovenware bowl. Store in a low oven, about 275 degrees, until ready to serve.

This version goes very well with knockwurst or bratwurst and a seidel or two of Beck's.

Indoor Beer Gardens

Germans immigrating to this country during the mid-1800s brought with them a love of good beer and conviviality. To enjoy these amenities during inclement weather, they developed huge indoor beer gardens, the most famous of which was the Winter Garden, located on the Bowery in New York.

These festive halls were described by a visitor in 1868 as an "... immense building, fitted up in imitation of a garden.... They will accommodate from four hundred to twelve hundred guests. Germans carry their families there to spend the day, or an evening.... Beer and other liquids are served at a small cost.... The music is a great attraction ... exquisite in some places."

Although none of these survived as beer gardens, the Winter Garden (actually the New Winter Garden) enjoys a second life today as a Broadway theatrical venue.

Caesar Salad

The Ancient Egyptians discovered the pleasure of mixing garlic and oil. The Romans improved on it by adding egg yolks to bind them together. The French followed and included lemon to create their tasty aioli, traditionally served on Christmas Eve.

From these beginnings an innovative Mexican chef at Caesar's Restaurant in Tijuana – where during Prohibition many famous gringos came to drink away the 1920s – added anchovies, cheese and a few spices. He tossed it all into one of the classic salads of modern times.

1	egg, coddled
4	small heads Romaine lettuce
8	tablespoons olive oil
4	tablespoons lemon juice
4	tablespoons warm beer or ale
1	cup garlic croutons
2	cloves garlic
8	tablespoons Parmesan cheese, grated
1	avocado, peeled and sliced (optional)
1	tablespoon anchovy paste
¼	teaspoon fresh ground pepper
2-3	dashes grated nutmeg
	salt to taste

Rub the entire inside surface of a large salad bowl with garlic and sprinkle with a little salt.

Wash Romaine. Dry thoroughly. Tear into bite-sized chunks. Combine olive oil, lemon juice and beer in bowl. Add Romaine and toss until the leaves are nicely coated. To coddle the egg, crack it and put it into a small microwave-safe bowl. Heat in the microwave about 15 seconds. This will slightly cook the egg, but it will still have a runny consistency. Then beat it slightly with the pepper, add it to the salad, and toss again. Top with grated Parmesan cheese, croutons and anchovies. Toss one more time.

Serve "as is" for a traditional Caesar. If you want to be fancier, garnish with avocado slices dipped in lemon juice.

Makes 8 to 10 servings. The beer? The fine Mexican beer Superior, of course! *Salud, amigos!*

Pennsylvania Slaw

Cabbage comes in at least seventy varieties and is, next to the potato, the most widely consumed vegetable in the world. This has led to literally thousands of dishes, from soups to salads to main dishes. A standard summertime dish, coleslaw, whose name is derived from the Dutch *kool* (cabbage) and *sla* (salad), is appropriate any time of the year.

For a Pennsylvania Dutch harvest party, try it with cold sliced ham and a platter of boiled potatoes with butter. Set out a large jar of prepared mustard, apple dumplings, and cold beer or cider. Add a few good friends and enjoy!

6	cups cabbage, shredded
1	cup mayonnaise
2	teaspoons onion, minced
½	cup warm beer
⅛	teaspoon coarse ground pepper
¼	teaspoon dry mustard
1	teaspoon celery seeds
1	teaspoon salt
½	cup green pepper, finely chopped (optional)

Mix shredded cabbage with celery seeds, minced onion, dry mustard, salt and pepper. Blend mayonnaise with beer until smooth. Pour dressing over cabbage and toss until coated.

Chill in refrigerator until serving time. Allow a couple of hours for the flavors to blend nicely.

Makes 5 to 6 servings.

A Friend Indeed

The sturdy Quaker founder of the Commonwealth of Pennsylvania, William Penn, after fleeing injustice in England, was given power by Royal Charter to make laws with the consent of the freemen under his jurisdiction.

In his efforts to make his colony a "Holy Experiment," he was instrumental in introducing brewing to the region. His decided preference for beer rather than stronger refreshments is found in his ordinances supporting the infant brewing industry. He carried his convictions further still when he built one of the first colonial breweries near his own home of Pennsburg.

California Salad

Many states in the U.S. have breweries, but California is *serious* about beer. The Golden State took 38 medals in the 2005 Great American Beer Festival, which was attended by about 30,000 people. Colorado was second with 29 medals. No other state was even close.

Any golden ale works in this salad, but why not use a California microbrew?

1	large head Romaine lettuce, torn
8	ounces fresh bean sprouts
4	ounces sunflower seeds, shelled
1	16-ounce can garbanzo beans
1	bunch green onions, chopped

Tear lettuce into chunks. Rinse garbanzo beans. Mix in a large bowl with lettuce, onions, bean sprouts, and sunflower seeds. Drain excess water. Chill an hour before adding dressing.

½	cup extra virgin olive oil
1	clove garlic, crushed
3	tablespoons warm beer or ale
¼	teaspoon salt
3	tablespoons vinegar
1 ½	teaspoons chili powder

Combine oil, vinegar, beer, crushed garlic, chili powder, and salt in a jar with a tight-fitting lid. Cover. Shake thoroughly to blend ingredients. Chill. Shake again, just before serving time. Pour enough over vegetables to coat them and toss well.

You can also vary the greens with chicory, escarole, endive, kale, spinach, dandelion greens, watercress, Chinese cabbage, or plain old iceberg lettuce.

Makes enough salad for 6.

Record of Hops' Value Comes from Dark Ages Abbess

Hildegarde von Bingen, born in 1098, was a Benedictine abbess and one of the few women of her time about whom we know anything. Centuries before the invention of printing, she was a book owner. Almost no one, man or woman, owned books, most people were illiterate, and it was a rare woman indeed who could read and write. She wrote poetry. She wrote music that is still played today. She analyzed scripture, advised Emperor Frederick I Barbarossa, wrote on science and medicine, and was the first person to write about the value of hops in brewing: "[Hops], when put in beer, stops putrefaction and lends longer durability." She drank beer regularly and lived to the astonishing (for the time) age of 81.

Four-Bean Salad

Beans and beer have always been buddies. Beer adds an earthy taste dimension to beans, and both are natural sources of great nutrition. Beans bring complex carbohydrates, iron, protein, calcium, and soluble fiber into a diet, and beer is like wholesome bread-in-a-bottle.

1	16-ounce can kidney beans
1	16-ounce can cut green beans
1	16-ounce can garbanzo beans
1	16-ounce can pinto beans
1	medium chopped onion
1	chopped green pepper
1	bunch green onions, chopped
½	cup salad oil
¼	cup spiced rice vinegar (find it in the Asian food section at your market.)
3	tablespoons warm beer
1	tablespoon sugar
1	teaspoon salt
¼	teaspoon coarse ground pepper

Mix vinegar, sugar and salt in a small sauce pan. Heat gently until sugar dissolves. Cool and blend the oil, warm beer and pepper.

Open and drain cans of beans to remove excess liquid. Mix all the beans with onions and green pepper in a large non-metal bowl. Toss gently until all ingredients look lightly oiled. Refrigerate for several hours or, even better, overnight. Stir occasionally.

Makes a quick, easy, and substantial addition to any picnic or potluck dinner. How about a LaBatt's with that?

Serves 8 to 12 people.

Whistle-Belly Vengeance

Descriptions of many Colonial-Period taverns in this country, the inns where travelers sought victuals and accommodations, were often more spartan than picturesque. No one having the price of lodging was turned away, but a full house might mean sleeping several to a bed — or on a table or the floor.

There was no menu or bill of fare; people ate what they were served. And drinks, though ample (possibly as a recompense for lack of privacy, selection and comfort), could be less then genteel. One such beverage, called Whistle-Belly Vengeance, was made from bitter beer, sweetened a bit with molasses, sprinkled with toasted corn bread crumbs, and served in a two- or three-quart tankard.

CHAPTER THREE

BRING ON THE MEAT!

Beer-Braised Pot Roast of Beef

Seaman's Beef

Texas Flank Steak

Vampire Steak

Mushroom Steak

Steak Iberia

Corned Beef Brisket

Shish Kebabs

Humbles and Onions

Chops and Kraut

Carnitas Jalisco

Gypsy Steak

Smuggler's Ribs

Baked Polish Sausage

Bratwurst and Sauerkraut

Beef Rolls de Paris

Beef Stroganoff

German Meat Balls

Danish Meat Balls

International Meat Loaf

Baked Ham

Latin Pochero

37

38

Beer-Braised Pot Roast of Beef

To brighten the hours of bored drinkers, Gretz Brothers once produced beer labels with the words of old favorite songs printed on them. Dubbed "Tooner Schooners," these aids to the sing-along were hits in their own right.

This beer-braised pot roast will be at the top of your charts, also.

3-4	pounds boneless chuck roast, whole
4-6	slices of bacon, cut into small pieces, fried crisp, and drained
1-2	tablespoons oil - or use a couple of tablespoons of the bacon grease
2	medium onions, quartered
1 to 2	tablespoons brown sugar
8-12	ounces sliced Portobello mushrooms
¾	cup flour
½	teaspoon pepper
1	teaspoon salt
1	teaspoon allspice
¼	cup vinegar
1	10-ounce can beef broth
1	cup warm beer

Sauté onions in the oil. Sprinkle them with the brown sugar, cook till they begin to brown, then remove from pan and set aside. Sauté the mushrooms in the onion-oil pan, adding oil if necessary to prevent from burning. When soft, remove mushrooms and set aside.

Mix flour with salt, allspice, and pepper. Roll the roast to coat with the flour and spice mixture. Sear the meat on all sides. Place the roast in a large pan with a lid. Place diced bacon, onions and mushrooms over the roast.

In the skillet, bring the vinegar, beef broth and beer to a boil. Cook about 3 minutes to blend the flavors; then add to the pot with the meat and vegetables.

Cover and simmer for about 2 to 3 hours, or until meat is tender.

This recipe works well in a crockpot too. Cook on high for 4 ½ - 5 hours or on low for 8 - 10 hours.

Serves 4 to 6. A fine creamy Guinness Stout compliments the beef!

Seaman's Beef

During the great days of the Empire, British fighting ships carried a complement of marines to handle the hand-to-hand fighting that so often took place when the great combat vessels locked together. Since most of the marines were recruited for their brawn, rather than their wit, regular sailors soon came to look down on them. Now, all sailors enjoy a good story to ease the idle hours, but when someone's bragging became too preposterous, his messmates would advise him to "go tell it to the marines!" – the assumption being that sailors aren't that gullible. Today's U.S. Marines are different – just as tough but much harder to fool!

One of the most incredible tales told was of a fantastic voyage on which the crew always enjoyed excellent meals. This was, of course, impossible due to the problem of keeping food fresh when at sea for months at a time. Things must have been better in the Danish Navy, though, where this simple recipe, called *skipperlabskovs*, is said to have originated. Also keep this one in mind for those "what do I do with this" leftovers that clutter refrigerators.

1 ½	pounds sirloin tip, cut into ½-inch strips
3-4	onions, sliced
4-5	potatoes, sliced
2	cups beef broth
¾	cup warm beer
3	tablespoons butter
1	tablespoon chopped parsley
¾	teaspoon salt
¼	teaspoon white pepper

Slice meat into strips. Salt and pepper the strips. Brown in a heavy skillet using half the butter. Set meat aside. Sauté onions in the remaining butter until they are just tender. In a 4-quart casserole dish, layer half the meat, half the potatoes and half the onions. Repeat with a second layer using the remaining ingredients. Pour in beef broth and beer. You may want to add a little more salt and pepper at this time.

Bake in a 350-degree oven for 1 hour. Garnish with parsley just before serving. Serve with hot bread, a tart salad and cold bottles of Tuborg or Carlsberg beer.

Makes 6 servings.

But Mr. Tax Man, It's Almost the Same as Bread

Beer has been taxed just about as long as there has been beer. Ancient Egypt taxed beer. The only up side is that quite a few improvements and advances in brewing have come about as brewers have tried to figure out ways of making beer that could be taxed at a lower rate. The "sin" tax always catches up. That really sticks in a person's throat!

Texas Flank Steak

Looking at current meat prices in the market, it's hard to believe that shortly after the Civil War, Texas longhorns wouldn't even bring a dollar apiece. Of course, back then, the interminable cattle drives to the distant railhead made the range-fed beef even tougher. At least the trail-riders occasionally got beef to eat along the way, resistant though it was to their dinner knives. Secret recipes such as this one saved many a belly-robber (as chuckwagon cooks were lovingly called) from abuse at the hands of hungry cowboys.

If you are looking at economical cuts of beef, consider flank steak, tenderized and marinated in beer. When prepared properly, it is as tender as more select meat, it has very little waste, and it offers a pleasant breather for the budget.

1 ½	pounds flank steak
¼	cup warm beer
1	clove garlic, minced
1	bay leaf
½	teaspoon *each* dry mustard, oregano, basil, thyme and pepper
1	teaspoon salt
2	tablespoons lemon juice
¼	cup cooking oil

Prepare marinade by combining beer, cooking oil, garlic, lemon juice, bay leaf, dry mustard, oregano, basil, thyme, salt, and pepper. Pour mixture over steak and place in refrigerator overnight, or for several hours. Give the marinade enough time to break down the tough fibers in the meat.

Pan fry or broil steak 5 to 6 minutes on the first side, a little less on the second. Your guidelines are the heat of the pan or fire and, of course, how rare you like it. Cut meat diagonally, across the grain, into thin slices. Serve on a wooden platter. Offer wild rice, fried green tomatoes, fresh vegetables and long-neck bottles of Lone Star.

Makes 4 servings.

Happy Birthday, Granddad

The oldest operating brewery in the United States is Yuengling of Pottsville, Pennsylvania. It's been satisfying customers since 1829. Plaudits for the oldest in North America, though, go to the Molson Brewery. They have been ministering to the croaking pleas of dry-throated Canadians continuously since 1786.

Vampire Steak

Throughout man's history, garlic has been associated with strength and magic. The Egyptian slave masters who supervised the construction of the pyramids fed it to their charges to ensure strength. Roman nobility, though not partaking of the "crude herb" themselves, made certain their legionnaires did, for endurance and courage.

Of course, no film buff worth a crumpled popcorn sack would accept a version of the Dracula myth without a necklace of garlic to protect the heroine.

There are probably more legends and folklore associated with this common herb than any other food in our menus. Fortunately, in all the superstition and tales of the evil eye, garlic is our protector. We also have not forgotten that it is one of our most bewitching flavors.

1 ½	pounds flank steak
2	tablespoons vinegar
3-4	slices chopped bacon
½	cup flour
1	teaspoon dry mustard
4	cloves garlic, minced
12	ounces warm beer
1	tablespoon cornstarch
	salt and pepper to taste

Score meat with a sharp knife in 1 ½-inch squares. Make cuts shallow. With the edge of a heavy saucer or cup, pound as much flour into the steak as it will hold. Spread the meat fibers with one hand and drive in the flour with the other. Keep going; it will hold more than you might think. Don't be concerned if the steak spreads out; it will shrink back to size while cooking.

Cut bacon into small pieces. Fry. Remove from pan and set aside. Brown steak on both sides in a heavy skillet or Dutch oven, using the bacon drippings or butter. Cover with warm beer. Add vinegar, dry mustard, bacon, minced garlic, salt and pepper. Simmer for 1 ½ hours with the lid on. Add a little more beer, if necessary.

When tender, slice into ¾-inch strips across the grain. If gravy is too thin, mix a little cornstarch and water. Pour into the sauce. Stir and heat until mixture thickens nicely.

Serve with mashed potatoes, a bucket of gravy, buttered string beans and cool bottles of Pilsener Urquell.

Makes 3 to 4 generous servings.

Mushroom Steak

This recipe is based on an old German dish *rindfleisch gedampet in bier*, which includes celery, parsnips and carrots to make a complete one-dish offering.

2	pounds round steak, cut ½ inch thick
2	large onions, sliced
2	cloves minced garlic
8	ounces beef broth or hydrated bouillon – more might be needed later
12	ounces warm beer
¼	cup catsup or steak sauce
1	cup flour
¼	cup cooking oil
8	ounces fresh mushrooms – or use a 4 ½-ounce can mushrooms – or a comparable amount of dried mushrooms, re-hydrated
1	bay leaf
	salt and pepper

Cut meat into serving-size pieces. Use the edge of a cup or a plate to pound as much flour as you can into the meat. Use your fingers to spread the meat while whacking it; it'll take in more flour and be more tender. Heat oil in a heavy skillet. Dust meat once more with flour. Brown on both sides. Set meat slices aside when done.

Add flour and garlic to meat drippings in pan – it may take a little more oil too. Heat until onions begin to turn golden. Set them aside with the meat. If using fresh mushrooms, sauté them lightly in the oil and set them aside. If using dried mushrooms, rehydrate them in bouillon. (Keep the bouillon when you drain them to add to the pot at gravy-making time.) Pat them dry and sauté them.

Add other ingredients, beef broth, beer, catsup, bay leaf, salt, and pepper, to drippings. Layer slices of meat, onions, and mushrooms in pan. Cover with a lid. Simmer for 1 to 1 ½ hours, or until meat is fork-tender.

Remove meat, onions and mushrooms to a platter. Keep hot for a few minutes. Eyeball the drippings/broth in the pot. You want about 2 cups of gravy when done, so you might need to add more bouillon at this point. Dip out approximately a cup of the drippings and mix in 3-4 tablespoons of the flour till smooth. Pour into pan. Stir well. Heat to boiling. As the gravy thickens, continue to stir.

Serve meat with noodles. Offer hot sauce.

Will take the chill off 6 people on winter evenings.

Steak Iberia

In the latter sections of *Don Quixote*, Sancho Panza becomes the governor of an island. In this role, he finds himself burdened with the assistance of an officious doctor who allows him to eat no meat or any dishes that are "too hot or over-flavored with spices." Happily, Sancho's intuitive judgment prevails; he fires the meddling physician halfway through his first official meal.

This recipe is of Spanish origin and is similar to the hearty entrees the wise Sancho, or, at least, his author Cervantes, enjoyed.

1 ½	pounds blade steak, ¾ inch thick
1	medium onion, sliced
1 ½	cups julienned celery
1	16-ounce can pinto beans
1	large green pepper, seeded and sliced
2	tablespoons cooking oil
½	teaspoon *each* salt, sugar and chili powder
⅛	teaspoon *each* pepper and savory
¼	cup warm beer

Get out the Dutch oven or a heavy skillet with a lid. Brown the meat in a little oil. Pour off any excess.

Mix dry spices: salt, sugar, chili powder, pepper and savory. Pour about half over the meat. Add warm beer. Cover with lid and simmer for 45 minutes to 1 hour. Turn meat once. Add remaining seasoning, beans, celery and onions. If you like dishes a bit hotter, a few chopped chilis are in order, too. Cover and cook another 30 minutes.

Add green pepper to stew. Cook 15 minutes more, with the lid on, or until both the meat and the vegetables are done.

Serve with a crisp green salad, buttered noodles and some Spanish San Miguel beer.

Makes 4 to 6 nice servings.

A Noble Compliment

After the King of Bohemia drank two tankards of Penarth beer in Berlin, he exclaimed, "Your beer is so good it almost glues one's mouth open."

Corned Beef Brisket

The word "corn," as used in corned beef, has nothing to do with maize or melted butter. In the years before mechanical refrigeration, meat was preserved either by salting or pickling in brine. Salt meat was prepared by sprinkling or embedding individual pieces or chunks of salt in it. At that time the Old English word "corn" had about the same meaning as we apply to "grain" as a unit of measure. They spoke of a "corn of salt" the way we speak of a grain of sand.

You don't have to be concerned about this recipe being too salty. It doesn't call for any corns of salt. Do be sure to lay on a supply of processed grain – in the form of fresh rye bread and beer – so you can enjoy corned beef or Reuben sandwiches the next day.

1	tablespoon flour
3	pounds corned beef brisket
1	onion, sliced
1	stalk of celery (with leaves), sliced
1	small carrot, chopped
8	ounces warm beer
2	tablespoons pickling spices

Pour a tablespoon of flour into a plastic baking bag and shake, to protect against bursting while cooking. Place bag in a 10 x 6 x 2-inch baking pan or dish.

Slide corned beef and vegetables into bag. Add beer and spices. Close with a twist tie. Make about six 1-inch slits in the top to release steam pressure.

Bake in a 350-degree oven for 3 hours or until meat is thoroughly baked.

Serve with a snappy mustard, braised cabbage, small boiled potatoes rolled in butter and chopped parsley, and cold mugs of Molson Ale.

Makes 4 to 6 servings.

Hot Beer

During the Middle Ages, as cities grew in number and importance, they often vied with one another for markets and power – at times engaging in violent military conflicts. Once, while the city of Hamburg was under siege, the local brewers supplied the defenders with 10,000 liters of beer. Some of the beer was used to fortify the soldiers. The remainder was boiled and poured over the heads of the attackers.

Shish Kebabs

It's difficult to say with any certainty where this succulent dish originated. Armenia, Greece, Lebanon, Romania, Russia, and Turkey all lay claim to the "original" shish kebab. It is certainly the product of a nomadic people, blazing campfires and naked swords. Its primitive quality, when contrasted to our present freezer-to-microwave cooking, may be why the kebab still has such a basic appeal to so many of us today. This, combined with the fun of "building your own," makes kebabs a natural for parties and other festivities.

1	medium onion, sliced
2	tablespoons curry powder
2	cloves garlic, minced
½	cup warm beer
1	tablespoon salt
¼	cup *each* salad oil and malt vinegar
2 ½	pounds lean beef (or lamb), cut into 2-inch cubes
	assorted vegetables (see below)

Mix beer with onion, curry powder, garlic, salad oil, vinegar, and salt. Pour over meat chunks. Marinate it at least 4 hours – better still, overnight in the refrigerator.

Thread meat on skewers with your favorite vegetables or fruits. Save remaining marinade to baste kebabs while cooking. Grill kebab skewers over hot barbecue coals. Baste regularly until done. HINT: Rub heated barbecue grill with olive oil before starting the fire to keep meat from sticking.

If you are planning a cookout away from home, pour all the ingredients into a heavy-duty sealable plastic bag. Shake well and keep in a cool place. A camp cooler, containing a good stock of beer as well as the meat, will allow you portability, convenience, and refreshment.

Makes 6 to 8 servings.

NOTE: Any of these, in 1-2-inch chunks or pieces, are good on kebabs. Use your initiative. If you can cook it and thread it on a skewer, it's a prime candidate for your next cookout.

Large whole mushrooms	Green tomatoes	Sweet red peppers
Sweet onions, quartered	Prunes	Eggplant, parboiled
Okra pods, parboiled	Corn on the cob	Peaches
Apple sections	Zucchini	Nectarines
Orange sections	Pears	Cold cuts
Apricots	Pineapple	Ham
Kiwi fruit, peeled	Green peppers	Sausage
Small or medium onions	Cherry tomatoes	

Humbles and Onions

During medieval times in Europe, it was the custom for the lord of the manor to take the best of everything for himself, allocating whatever was left to servants and serfs. There was no better example of this than the division of meat killed in the hunt. When a fat boar or stag was brought to earth, the lord and his peers kept the best meat and left the innards to the peasants. Ever innovative, even though at the bottom of the pecking order, they soon learned to make do with what they received, called the "umbles" or edible insides.

From this "humble" beginning, cooks devised many fine dishes, from bone soup to "humble pie," which in the modern lexicon refers to what the meek and modest eat – to the most noble of all, liver and onions.

1	pound calves' liver
½	cup flour
2	medium onions, sliced thin
8	ounces warm beer
3-4	tablespoons butter
6-8	strips lean bacon
2-3	dashes garlic powder
	salt to taste

Cut liver into serving pieces. Place in a shallow dish, cover with beer, and let stand at room temperature for 1 hour. Fry the bacon slowly until crisp. Drain and set aside in a warm oven. Save the drippings to fry the liver.

Sprinkle liver slices with garlic powder, salt and pepper. Coat both sides of liver slices with flour. Slip into skillet with hot bacon drippings. Fry, turning once. Do not overcook, or meat will become tough. Liver should be served pink in the center. When meat is nicely browned, remove to oven with the bacon. Keep drippings to make gravy later.

Clean skillet and melt butter. Drop onion slices into butter. Heat until golden brown. Turn once or twice to keep from sticking. When they are soft, pour 4 tablespoons of beer into skillet. Cover with a lid for just a few minutes to steam. The ideal onions are brown and tender. Use leftover drippings from the onions, liver, and bacon to make a brown gravy. Mix liquid with a thin paste of flour and water. Heat until it thickens. If there is no residue left, it's all right to use a packaged brown gravy mix.

Serve liver with heaps of onions on top, bacon on the side, a green vegetable, mashed potatoes with lots of butter, and Yuengling or Sierra Nevada Porter.

Makes 3 to 4 servings.

Chops and Kraut

Just as the Pharaoh fed his pyramid builders onions and garlic to make them strong, the ancient Chinese relied on cabbage and rice for their laborers when constructing the Great Wall – still the only manmade structure visible from space.

During the winter, cabbage was laced with rice wine to preserve it. The dish, simply called sour cabbage, was still quite popular a thousand years later when Genghis Khan, the Prince of Victory, wrested control of half the known world for himself and his descendants. When he sent his armies west, into eastern and western Europe, they carried sour cabbage with them as a staple – but, by that time, salt had replaced rice wine in the recipe. And so the Bulgars, Magyars, and Poles learned from their ruthless enemies, the Tartars, how to preserve cabbage. In Austria, the new food was christened "sauerkraut" and has been known by that name throughout most of the world ever since.

1	pound sauerkraut
6	smoked pork chops
1	medium onion, chopped
$\frac{1}{2}$	medium potato, grated
$\frac{1}{4}$	apple, peeled and grated
5	whole pepper corns
1	whole bay leaf

Wash sauerkraut in cold water to remove brine. Drain. Mix with beer, potato, apple, pepper-corns and bay leaf in a large pan. Place meat on top. Bring mixture to a boil. Reduce heat, cover and allow to simmer for several hours (at least two) or until meat is thoroughly cooked and tender. Or, if you don't want to watch a pot, bake in a 350-degree oven for 1 $\frac{1}{2}$hours.

Serve chops individually on a bed of sauerkraut, with fresh hunks of dill bread and cold Dortmunder beer.

Makes 6 servings.

Mind Your P's and Q's

This warning dates back many centuries to English tavern keepers' custom of collecting payment for drinks only once an evening from each patron. They kept track of everyone's consumption by simply drawing tally marks beside the person's name on a handy slate. Thus, guests were admonished, for good reasons, to keep an eye on the number of "pints" and "quarts" beside their own name.

Carnitas Jalisco

A controversial beer debuted in Mexico in summer 2008. Malverde Beer is named after Jesús Malverde, a Robin Hood-style figure who is revered by some in western Mexico. The outlaw may or may not have ever existed, but his legend places him in the late 1800s in Sinaloa, where he robbed from the rich and gave to the poor during the reign of dictator Porfirio Díaz. Minerva Brewery in Guadalajara makes the brew and donates 1 percent of its profits to Malverde's chapel in Culiacan. Now, Malverde is no saint in the Church's eyes; yet drug smugglers or "mules" pray to him, carry pictures of him, and leave offerings at his chapel asking his protection. The sales slogan of Malverde Beer is "A hero, a legend, a beer."

But a completely legal high is available to you here. If you are a little tired of tomato barbecue recipes for pork ribs, and have ever snitched the crispy brown pieces from a hot pork roast, or tasted carnitas in Mexico, this is a dish for you.

4-5	pounds lean pork ribs
12	ounces warm beer or ale
2	cups water
1 ½	tablespoons malt vinegar
1	tablespoon salt
¾	cup dark corn syrup
1	clove garlic, crushed
2	tablespoons prepared mustard
	Tabasco sauce to taste

Mix water, beer, crushed garlic and salt in large sauce pan. Bring to a boil and add ribs. Reduce heat, cover and simmer 1 hour. Remove ribs from water and arrange on a rack, over a foil-lined broiler pan, so they are not touching one another.

Strain the broth from the sauce pan and skim off any grease. Pour ¼ cup of stock into a smaller saucepan. Add corn syrup, vinegar, mustard, and Tabasco sauce. Bring mixture to a boil and simmer for 5 minutes. Pour sauce over each rib carefully, or use a small paint brush to coat them. Be generous and make sure all sides are well coated.

Slide the ribs under the broiler for 5-10 minutes to brown. Turn once or twice as necessary. When ribs are brown, bake them in a 350-degree oven for another 20-30 minutes to crisp them. If you like moist ribs, reduce the baking time; if you want them crisper, leave them in even longer. Check once or twice for doneness while baking.

Enjoy with rice, refried beans, warm corn tortillas, some hot salsa and chilled glasses of Dos Equis, Superior or Carta Blanca. Malverde may or may not be available!

Makes 4 to 6 servings. *Salud!*

Gypsy Steak

A hungry man was late getting to a restaurant. There was nothing left that was on the menu and nothing left in the kitchen itself except for some meat and some sauerkraut. He said, despairingly, "Please, just mix them." He ate.

He was elated with the combination, and so have all kraut fans been, ever since!

A folk tradition says eating pork and sauerkraut together on New Year's Day brings wealth and luck all year – something about cabbage resembling money. Add some caraway (keeps things from getting lost or stolen) and paprika (has healing abilities and keeps vampires away just as well as garlic does), and you have a delectable dish as well as guaranteed good fortune. Russian gypsies end these kinds of tales with "Such things do happen, you know."

1 ½	pounds pork steak
1	medium onion, chopped
12	ounces warm dark beer
1	pound sauerkraut
2	tablespoons butter
½	teaspoon *each* caraway seeds, salt, and Hungarian paprika
¼	tablespoon white pepper
	dash of garlic powder

Rub pork thoroughly with paprika, garlic powder, salt and white pepper. Brown the meat in a heavy skillet. Cover with water and simmer until pork separates from the bones, about 1 hour. Remove meat from pan, discard bones and pour off liquid and fat.

Wash skillet. Melt butter and sauté onions lightly. Drain sauerkraut and rinse in cold water. Add onions and sauerkraut to meat. Also add caraway seeds and beer. Simmer mixture, without a lid, until meat is tender and liquid is almost gone, about 45 minutes.

This same recipe works well with Kielbasa, or other quality sausage. Just remember to pour off the rendered fat in the first step after browning.

Serve with small, boiled potatoes, rolled in butter and chopped parsley, a pot of sharp mustard, crisp pickles, and cold bottles of St. Pauli Girl dark beer.

Makes 2 to 3 servings.

Smuggler's Ribs

Prior to the American War for Independence, taxes were the single most important issue for the colonies. While some men complained and others sought political remedies, not a few chose more direct methods. Smuggling was a frequent alternative to almost any English tariff or unwelcome restriction. Colonial mariners caught with rum or tea had little in the way of defense. But those who were bringing in sheep, to compete with the famed British wool industry, often escaped fines and imprisonment by innocently claiming the animals were aboard to supply the crew with fresh meat.

From this start as contraband, sheep soon became an important part of American farming and ranching, supplying both wool and meat. This very simple recipe combines the best attributes of baking and steaming lamb. It removes all the excess fat from the riblets and makes them quite tender. Give yourself enough time; it takes nearly 3 hours from start to finish.

3-4	pounds lamb riblets or shanks
1	teaspoon garlic powder
1	teaspoon seasoned salt
½	teaspoon black pepper
2	tablespoons lemon juice
2	medium onions, sliced
1	tablespoon beef flavor base
16	ounces warm beer

Trim meat to remove any fat. Place riblets in a large roasting pan, bone side down. Sprinkle with garlic powder, salt, pepper, and lemon juice. Preheat oven to 375 degrees.

Bake for 1 hour. Carefully pour off the drippings.

Slice the sliced onions and layer them on top of the meat. Reduce oven heat to 300 degrees. Bake another 45 minutes until the onions brown. Stir once in a while.

Add beef flavor base and beer to the pan. Cover tightly using a large sheet of aluminum foil to seal in the steam. Bake 1 hour more.

Serve with stewed tomatoes, steamed broccoli and some crisp Bass or India Pale Ale. Makes 5-6 servings.

Baked Polish Sausage

No one knows when the sausage was invented, but it was already known during the time of Homer. In the *Odyssey*, when the wandering Odysseus comes home to Ithaca and his wife Penelope, he finds the house full of insufferable suitors, all seeking his wife's hand and his wealth and meanwhile stuffing themselves with his food. He considers their fate "as when a man near a great glowing fire turns to and fro a sausage . . . anxious to get it roasted quickly; so to and fro Odysseus tossed and pondered how to lay hands upon the shameless suitors."

To the north of Greece, the Hungarians, Germans and Poles discovered that beer and sausage are more than sufferable companions. Here is a proven way to prepare one with the aid of the other.

2	1-pound Polish sausages or kielbasa
4	whole peppercorns
12	ounces warm beer or ale

Place sausage, beer and peppercorns into baking dish with cover. Bake in a 350-degree oven for 25 minutes.

Serve with hot potato salad, sauerkraut or baked macaroni and cheese and cold steins of Zywiec or Krakus beer, both of which are exported internationally.

Makes 4 servings.

A New Nation's First Brewery

One of the misconceptions many of us share is that the early American colonists, particularly the Puritans of New England, were against drinking. They were definitely not prohibitionists in that sense.

Miles Standish, for instance, who figures in Longfellow's story of John Alden's and Priscilla Mullins' romance, was a cooper by trade. His duties were to make beer and water barrels. Governor Bradford, shortly after landing, complained about the scarcity of beer in the new colony. In fact, after colonists imported their brew from England for only a few years, the first brewery was constructed by a Captain Sedgewick in Massachusetts. The city was Boston, the year, 1637.

Bratwurst and Sauerkraut

In Germany, where good sausage is a way of life, this dish is called *bratwurst mit sauerkraut und apfel.* Its restorative powers, especially noted on cold wintry days, are legendary. In fact, if more of this had been served in ancient times, the tragic events surrounding Siegfried and Brunhilde would probably have turned into a domestic farce and the Lorelei would be remembered as a sweet-tempered ale wife.

8	bratwurst
12	ounces beer or ale
2	tablespoons spicy mustard
1	teaspoon Worcestershire sauce
2	1-pound cans sauerkraut
3	crisp apples

Brown sausages lightly in a large, heavy skillet. Add beer, mustard and Worcestershire sauce. Bring to a simmer. Cover with lid. Allow to cook until almost all the liquid is gone.

Wash and drain the sauerkraut. Peel and core the apples. Cut them into sections.

When the meat is done, remove it from the skillet. Keep these little brats warm in the oven. Add sauerkraut and apples to pan juices. Simmer for 10 minutes.

Place the sauerkraut and apple mixture on a hot serving plate. Surround with bratwurst. Serve immediately with a pot of mustard, some hot potato salad and a mug or so of St. Pauli Girl. This would also be a good time to take those lidded German steins off the shelf and put them to use.

Makes 4 hefty servings.

The Ubiquitous Church Key

The American Can Company designed and introduced a special "quick and easy" opener for their newly patented beer cans in 1936. The older models, with a bottle opener at one end and a cork screw at the other, were functionally obsolete. Some brewers, though, uncertain of the intelligence, ingenuity or memory of beer drinkers, printed instructions on how to open beer cans on the new opener for the next ten years.

Now these "church keys," as they affectionately came to be known, have faded, too. With the introduction of the tab top, they became rust-prone curiosities. Some of the "keys" have become collectors' items. You can view them now in antique shops or, if you know what you're about, make a lucky find at a swap meet or garage sale.

Beef Rolls de Paris

Making inexpensive meats tender and tasty is the genius of good cooking. For years bottom round steak, sliced thin and pounded into submission, has been masquerading in fancy cookbooks under the titles *paupiettes*, *roulades* or *oiseaux sans têtes*. This preparation is unusual and will keep your fame in the kitchen on a roll.

1½ - 2	pounds top round steak, tenderized (have the butcher tenderize the meat.)
8	half-slices of bacon
1	medium onion, sliced lengthwise
1	carrot, chopped
1	stalk celery, chopped
1	dill pickle, sliced lengthwise
8	teaspoons prepared mustard
½	cup flour
8	ounces warm beer
3	tablespoons cooking oil
1	tablespoon corn starch
8-10	shakes meat tenderizer
1	cup water
	salt and pepper

Cut the meat into about 8 slices – the number will vary depending on the original size. Remove any excess fat. Use a blunt instrument to give each piece a number of good wallops – the edge of a heavy saucer works well. Pummel the pieces until they are thin and submissive – bottom round can take it! Sprinkle each slice with a shake or two of tenderizer and spread about 1 teaspoon of mustard over it.

Partially cook the bacon in a heavy pan.

Now to roll them neatly. Place a long slice of onion, pickle and bacon on the edge of a meat slice. Roll it up tightly, so nothing falls out, and tie with a couple of pieces of white cotton string. If you're having company, you can do this part the day before.

Mix flour, salt, and pepper and coat the beef rolls well with the dry mixture.

Heat oil in a heavy iron or electric skillet. Brown the beef rolls on all sides. Reduce heat. Add carrots, celery and beer. Cover and simmer for about 45 minutes, or until meat is tender. Turn rolls once or twice while cooking. Have a bit of water on hand to add if things start looking too arid.

Remove rolls and set aside in oven. Strain remaining liquid and return it to pan. Mix corn starch in 1 cup of water. Pour enough into the pan to thicken the gravy. Pour gravy over meat rolls. Serve with parsley potatoes, buttered asparagus, and Oranjeboom beer.

Makes about 8 beef rolls or 4 servings.

Naval Secrets Revealed

One of the major concerns Captain Cook noted in his diary was that he could carry only a limited amount of beer. When he departed Plymouth Harbor on August 26, 1768, he carried supplies of beer for "only one month." On September 27, he noted, "Served wine to the ships company, the Beer being all expended to two casks which I wanted to keep some time longer." The question, then, is how did he manage to complete his circumnavigation of the globe, a voyage that lasted some three years longer?

The secret was revealed some years later by Sir John Dalrymple, a Scottish scientist, in a pamphlet entitled "Three Addresses," dated 1808:

> The immortal Captain Cook, on a voyage round the world of three years and thirteen days, lost only one man to disease. Sir John Pringle, in his discourse to the Royal Society, upon preserving the health of seamen, ascribes this singularity to the use of malt, which Captain Cook carried with him, and from which he made [beer]... on which account Sir John Pringle, and all navy people, agree, that the seamen never lose their health as long as the beer lasts.

Dalrymple modestly takes the credit for the discovering the process of brewing at sea, an invention that, he asserts, would "be of more benefit to the seamen than any discovery since the Mariner's Compass."

Cook continued brewing, until his last fateful voyage, on which he aroused the ire of the South Sea Islanders, possibly because he would not share his secret.

Old German Proverbs

"He who does not become handsome before twenty years of age, strong before thirty, wise before forty, and rich before fifty, on such a man malt and hop is altogether lost."

They also say, "Drink and you die. Don't drink and you die too."

Beef Stroganoff

Catherine the Great, like many heads of state before and since (Elizabeth I of England and Winston Churchill come to mind), liked strong beer. Heeding the dietary advice of a wise Scottish physician named Dimsdale, Catherine caused a special Imperial Russian Stout to be brewed in England for her private consumption. She and subsequent Rulers of All the Russias imported this special brew to their tables in St. Petersburg for nearly 150 years. The 1917 Revolution abruptly closed the market.

Imperial Russian, first made by Anchor in the 18th century and now by Courage, is in the "barley wine" category and is comparable to the German *doppelbocks*. It is noted for its fruity flavor and its potency – far above that of regular stouts, porters, ales, and fruit wines. In fact a "nip" bottle has more alcohol in it than two pub-measures of Scotch. Be warned, *tovarich!*

The 19th century Russian gentry, despite their country's earlier altercation with Napoleon's armies, were strongly influenced by the French in matters of art, manners and culture. This classic dish, named for the famed diplomat Count George Stroganoff, combines a Russian sour cream sauce with a French preparation.

2	pounds sirloin, round or flank steak, cut in ½-inch strips across the grain
1	cup sour cream
2	medium onions
3	ounces fresh mushrooms, sliced
10	ounces warm beer
1	teaspoon Worcestershire sauce
2	tablespoons cooking oil
2	tablespoons flour
¼	teaspoon Hungarian paprika
	salt and pepper to taste

Heat oil in a heavy skillet. Season beef strips to taste with salt and pepper and brown the beef. Remove meat. Set aside. Sauté onions and mushrooms together, with a cover on the pan, until soft – do not brown! Remove vegetables. Set aside with meat.

Mix flour and paprika with pan drippings. Add beer and Worcestershire sauce. Blend smoothly. Simmer until mixture thickens. Return meat and vegetables to sauce. Stir in sour cream. Cook slowly until all ingredients are well heated. Don't boil!

Set the stew in the center of the table in a chafing dish, warmed by low flame. Invite guests to serve themselves and heap stew over buttered egg noodles or rice. Add some French green beans and bottles of Imperial Russian Stout – still brewed in England.

Makes 6 to 8 servings.

Russians Take Beer Seriously

In Soviet times a Russian high court found Galina Nikita, the chief barmaid at a cafe in Moscow's Gorky Park, guilty of diluting customers' beer with tap water. Investigators from the Moscow Department of Struggle Against Embezzlement of Socialist Property testified that the culprit and her co-conspirators not only watered the beer, they upgraded its price and pocketed all the money from the sale of potato chips. After a severe warning to all from the bench, the judge sentenced Ms. Nikita to fifteen years in a Siberian labor camp.

Spring Cleaning Myth

The most insidious and prevalent bit of folklore one hears about bock beer — in fact, it has even made its way into some encyclopedias, whose editors should know better — is that it's concocted from leftovers, when the brewers clean their vats. With press like that, no wonder it's not a best seller. Who wants to sip sludge and dregs?

But the report is false. First, a tour of any brewery will demonstrate to the greatest skeptic that brewers meticulously clean their equipment, including the vats themselves, after every run — not once a year. Secondly, bock gets its characteristic color, as do all beers and ales, from the malt used; in this case, a malt that is richly toasted to start. Bock is also brewed longer than lagers, about six weeks, which, added to the greater amounts of ingredients necessary, makes it a more costly product than regular beer.

So next time someone tries to tell you bock beer is a "slush" associated with spring cleaning, remind them that in Germany brewers rise and fall on the success of their bocks. Customers tend to remain loyal throughout the year to the brewmaster who offers them the tastiest bock each spring. You can also point out that one of the world's strongest beers, 13.2 percent alcohol by volume, is a Bavarian doppelbock named Kulminator — about three times stronger than American beer — and you certainly don't make that with leftovers.

Beer in Politics

Russia has an official Beer Lovers Party, registered in 1994. It hasn't won any seats in the Duma, but the Polish Beer-Lovers' Party won no fewer than sixteen seats — 3.5 percent of the seats in their Sejm — in 1991. Unaccountably, the Polish Beer-Lovers' Party has gone inactive. Norway has its Beer Unity Party. Belarus's Beer Lovers Party is described as "liquidated in 1998." Germany's Deutsche Biertrinker Union is still extant.

The United States, shamefully, has no Beer Drinkers' political party, though it does boast a Guns and Dope Party and a Surprise Party. Great Britain has no Beer Drinkers' political party but mustered a Death, Dungeons, and Taxes Party and a Monster Raving Loony Party, whose goals are painting the White Cliffs of Dover blue for the sake of camouflage and getting rid of the number thirteen because of its unlucky associations.

English-speaking beer drinkers have no political representation. How can right-thinking imbibers allow this travesty to continue?

German Meat Balls

The first beer in the city of Munich was brewed by monks of the Tegnersee monastery in the Middle Ages. From that beginning, the city achieved two unique claims to fame for beer lovers around the world. First, they originated the idea of the *brauhaus*, the brewery-operated tavern, and, as if that were not excuse enough to drink their fine products, they also introduced the Oktoberfest. This celebration, begun in 1810 to commemorate a royal wedding, is still staged each year for increasing numbers of visitors. Today the festivities honor the arrival of the first *Märzenbier*, March beer, from the taps during the last two weeks in September.

If you decide to stage your own Oktoberfest, here's a good German dish to go with it.

1 ½	pounds ground beef
¾	cups soft bread crumbs
2	cups onion, sliced
1 ¼	cups cold water
8	ounces warm beer
1	egg, beaten
4-5	tablespoons butter
1 ½	teaspoons sugar
1	teaspoon vinegar
1	teaspoon flour
1	bay leaf
¼	teaspoon thyme
1	teaspoon salt
¼	teaspoon ground pepper

Beat egg in ¼ cup of cold water, until smooth. Mix with ground meat, bread crumbs, and salt and pepper. Shape into about a dozen 1 ½-inch meat balls.

Melt 2 tablespoons of butter in a deep skillet. Brown meat balls evenly. Remove and set aside. Pour off about half the drippings. Add remaining butter. Sauté onions, until just soft. Blend in flour and 1 cup each of water and beer. Increase heat. Stir mixture until it just begins to boil. Reduce heat. Return meat balls to pan. Add vinegar, sugar, bay leaf and thyme.

Cover pan. Simmer over low heat for 45-60 minutes. Season with salt and pepper to taste. Serve with braised cabbage, boiled potatoes, buttered corn niblets, and some Kölsch or Spaten beer from Germany.

Makes 3 to 4 servings.

Danish Meatballs

Historically, the Danes have not been not wine drinkers. The national beverage, from olden times, has been beer. In Viking mythology, brave warriors, after death in battle, were carried to the famous banquet halls of Valhalla. There, served by the beautiful Valkyries, the maidens of Odin, they dined with the gods while consuming great horn cups of gushing ale, from the udder of the mighty goat Heidun.

There is no record of what the mighty feasted on, but these traditional *frikadeller* would not have been long ignored.

1	pound lean pork, ground fine
1	pound lean chuck, ground fine
1	medium onion, chopped
1	egg, well beaten
1	cup flour
1	cup milk
12	ounces warm beer
¼	cup bread crumbs
3	tablespoons butter
1	tablespoon lemon juice
¼	teaspoon *each* nutmeg and pepper
1	teaspoon salt

Melt butter in heavy skillet. Brown onions lightly with a little salt.

Combine onions and ground meats in a large bowl with flour, beaten egg, nutmeg, pepper, and a teaspoon of salt. Add milk, a little at a time, while kneading mixture thoroughly. When all ingredients are blended together, shape into small balls, about walnut size. Roll in flour.

Brown meatballs in skillet with butter. Pour in beer and lemon juice. Cover with a tight lid. Simmer for 30 minutes.

Sprinkle with bread crumbs. Serve hot with plenty of potatoes, creamed spinach, stuffed tomatoes, fresh bread, and butter. A couple of bottles of cold Tuborg, Giraf or Carlsberg will round out the occasion.

Meatballs also make delicious canapés. To serve them this way, drain on paper towels, spear with wooden toothpicks, and offer in warm chafing dish.

Makes 4 to 6 servings.

International Meat Loaf

Meat loaf probably started with a Baltic favorite. The inhabitants of Estonia, Latvia and Finland enjoyed finely chopped meat, mixed with salt, pepper and onion juice, and eaten raw. Tartar steak (Steak Tartare on the menus of fancy eateries) came to Hamburg aboard merchant ships.

From there the recipe took two directions: One to New York City, where it evolved into the ubiquitous American hamburger, and the second to the dish known almost everywhere as meat loaf, which is just an overgrown hamburger with a little class. The universal appeal of this dish is why wise cooks start out with a plan to make too much: Any leftovers, served up hot or cold, make great day-after sandwiches. Remember too that if time is crucial, this recipe can double nicely for quick meatballs.

1	pound ground beef
1	package spaghetti sauce mix
½	cup bread stuffing mix
1	tablespoon instant minced onion
½	teaspoon garlic powder
½	cup warm beer or ale
2-3	strips bacon

Combine meat, spaghetti sauce mix, bread stuffing mix, instant minced onion, instant green pepper, garlic powder and warm beer or ale. Mix them thoroughly; then shape into a loaf. Place in a greased, shallow ovenware dish.

Bake in a 350-degree preheated oven for 1 hour. After 30 minutes, top with bacon strips. When done, pour off excess fat. Allow to cool for about 10 minutes, so it will slice without crumbling.

Serve with potatoes au gratin, Harvard beets and a "shout" or two from "down under." Some of the better Australian beers, most of which can be purchased as "Darwin stubbies" (24-25-ounce cans or bottles), are Tooth's KB Lager or Cooper's Real Ale.

Makes 3 to 4 servings.

Kaiser Bill

Before World War I, Kaiser Wilhelm of Germany made this remarkable statement: "Give me a woman who likes beer, and I will conquer the world." The Allied Forces made him take back his boast. Maybe more of our women liked beer, and liked it better.

Baked Ham

The most famous hams in history come from the area surrounding Smithfield, Virginia. The reasons for this were twofold: Pigs there were raised on a diet of acorns and peanuts, which gave the meat its magnificent flavor, and processors used a secret method, strongly influenced by the Chinese, that allowed hams to be cured and shipped without refrigeration.

In the 18th and 19th centuries Smithfield hams traveled the world. Queen Victoria's standing order brought six hams to Buckingham Palace every week of her long reign.

1	half or whole ham
½	cup dry mustard
1	cup brown sugar
12	small bay leaves
¼	teaspoon celery seeds
16	ounces warm beer or ale
1	handful whole cloves
4-6	ounces water

Wash ham. Remove most of the fat. Score the outside of the ham into traditional diamond pattern with a sharp knife; stick a clove in the center of each diamond.

Mix sugar, celery seeds, and dry mustard with enough water to make a thick paste. Brush mixture generously over ham. Use toothpicks to fasten the bay leaves to meat.

Place ham in a roaster with a lid. Pour the beer in. Cover. Bake in a 450-degree oven 20 minutes per pound. Remove ham from oven. Discard bay leaves. Carve into thick slices.

Moosehead goes well with the excellent flavor of baked ham.

Eric the Red and Greenland Ale

While living in Greenland, the legendary 10th century Norseman, Eric the Navigator, more popularly known as Eric the Red, was visited by a number of his countrymen who planned to spend the winter. In part, a record of their conversation includes these lines: "I fear it will be said that never have you passed a worse Yule than . . . in Greenland."

"Not so," replied one of the new captains, "for we have on board malt and meal and corn for Yule, which was sent to you to make the feast your generosity requires." Thus, with the ingredients on hand, even though it lacked but a few weeks to Christmas, the winter brewing was assured, particularly since the Norsemen were noted for their preference for _aul_ (from which English speakers get the word ale) that was both young and strong. Skoal!

Latin Pochero

Originally bananas were probably native to India – though some argue Africa. We know the fruit arrived in the New World in 1516. It is interesting too that bananas were once forbidden in their homeland: According to Hindu tradition it was the banana, and not the apple, that caused the greatest pratfall in history, Adam and Eve's expulsion from the Garden of Eden, which supposedly was located on the island of Ceylon.

Today there are over thirty different varieties of the "Fruit of the Tree of Paradise" available to be enjoyed *au naturel* or cooked, as in this lovely Latin stew.

2	pounds beef top sirloin, cut in 1-inch cubes
2	bananas or plantains
1	medium onion, chopped
½	medium-size head cabbage, quartered
2	medium potatoes, peeled and quartered
½	pound green beans, cut in 1-inch pieces
½	cup cooked garbanzo beans
2	5-ounce cans Vienna sausage
1	clove garlic, minced
16	ounces warm beer or ale
½	cup tomato sauce
1	cup water
2-3	tablespoons cooking oil
½	cup flour
	salt and pepper to taste

Heat oil in heavy skillet. Roll beef in flour. Brown on all sides. Add beer to pan. Bring to a boil. Reduce heat. Allow meat to simmer in beer for 1 hour, or until tender.

In another pan, sauté garlic lightly. Mix in onion, tomato sauce and heat thoroughly. Add cabbage, potatoes and green beans to tomato mixture. Pour in 1 cup water. Simmer until potatoes are easy to pierce with a fork. If the vegetable sauce starts to get too thick, add a little more water.

Add garbanzo beans and Vienna sausages. Cook for another 15 minutes. Add salt and pepper. Stir in vegetables. Cut plantains/bananas in diagonal slices. If using plantains, add them 25 minutes before serving; for bananas, add to stew about 10 minutes before serving.

Serve over rice, with lots of gravy on the side and a good Latin beer, such as Nationale or Salva Vida, from Honduras, or Belikin, from across the border in Belize.

Makes 6 to 8 servings.

CHAPTER FOUR

Entrees, Stews, Meat Pies, One-Dish Meals

Flemish Carbonnes

Hungarian Goulash

Uncle Sam's Barley Stew

Doughboy Stew

Steak and Kidney Pie

Hearty Steak and Guinness Pie

Polish Delight

Mexican Lamb Stew

Pork Chili Verde

Pecos Chili

Bartender's Chili

Chili Azteca

Spaghetti with Meat Sauce

Stuffed Green Peppers

New England Baked Beans

Beef Canton

Pork and Apple Ragout

Flemish Carbonnes

"Carbonnes" refers to meat chunks grilled over hot coals, which is probably the oldest method of preparing this classic dish. Bless the invention of cooking pans: Carbonnes don't have to get carbonized now, and no cook need scorch any fingers in making this widely known Belgian recipe.

Belgium is also renowned for its Abbey beers (top-fermented ale-type beers called Trappiste), brewed by Cistercian monks since the Middle Ages. Today these popular offerings, some of which approach 12% alcohol by volume, not only pay for the Order's expenses but produce enough revenue for philanthropic work as well. Obviously this can only mean that you're helping your fellow man if you sit down and enjoy this tasty dish with a couple of siedels of Abbey brew. Remember, it's in a good cause.

3	pounds chuck, cut in 1 ½-inch cubes
¼	pound lean ham, cut in 1-inch cubes
6	large onions, peeled and quartered
1	10 ½-ounce can beef broth
2	cloves garlic, crushed
12	ounces warm dark beer
1	cup flour
½	cup butter
3	tablespoons cooking oil
2	tablespoons wine vinegar
2	teaspoons salt
1	teaspoon fresh ground pepper
1	tablespoon sugar
1	small bay leaf
½	teaspoon thyme

Cube meat. Roll in mixture of flour, salt and pepper. Heat oil in Dutch oven or heavy sauce pan. Brown beef evenly. Add ham and brown it. Remove the meat from pan. Set aside. Brown onions and garlic ever so lightly in half the butter. Set aside with meat cubes.

In the pan melt the remaining butter and add about 3 tablespoons of flour. Stir over low heat until blended smoothly. Pour in beer. Bring to boil while stirring slowly. Reduce heat. Return meat and onions to pan. Add sugar, bay leaf, thyme and beef broth.

Cover with a tight lid. Simmer at low temperature for 1 to 1 ½ hours, or until beef is tender when pierced with a fork. Stir occasionally. Add a little more beer, if necessary, to keep stew from sticking to the pan. Just before serving, be a nice person and remove the bay leaf.

If you prepare this recipe in a slow cooker or crock pot, cook the stew on low for 6-7 hours or until beef is tender. Twenty minutes before serving, dip out about half a cup of the stew's liquid. Mix 2-3 tablespoons of flour into it and stir it back into the pot. Turn heat to high and cook until gravy thickens.

Carbonnes are traditionally served with boiled potatoes, but if you prefer, rice, hominy grits, or polenta (corn meal mush mixed with Parmesan cheese) will also go well. Dill pickles seem to have an affinity for this dish, as do cold steins of the aforesaid Belgian beer — sometimes referred to as "the Burgundy of Belgium." Consider Rodenbach, a red ale that is aged two years in oak barrels.

Makes 4 to 6 servings. *Prosit!*

Only the Yeast Knows!

The traditional difference between beer and ale has been so diluted by time as to be almost lost. Originally, beer contained hops and ale did not — it was "bittered" slightly with acorns. Currently this distinction is shadowy, for many brewers now add hops to their ale. The only thing, then, that makes the two dissimilar is the yeast used. Beer is made with "bottom" fermenting or lager yeast, which settles out of the brew. Ale is a product of "top" fermenting yeast, which rises and must be skimmed off the surface of the wort.

Some argue that ale is heavier, stronger or higher in alcoholic. These distinctions, however, are not generic. They reflect the preference of the individual brewers. Yes, some ales have a smarter kick than beer, but beers can go that way too, as the German doppelbocks and British barley wines show.

Why We Drink – It's the Longevity

The Horse and Mule live thirty years,
Yet nothing know of wines and beers.

Most Goats and Sheep at twenty die,
And never tasted Scotch or Rye.

A Cow drinks water by the ton,
And at eighteen is mostly done.

The Dog in milk and water soaks,
And then in twelve short years he croaks.

Your modest sober, bone-dry hen,
Lays eggs for Nogs, then dies at Ten.

All animals are strictly dry,
They sinless live and swiftly die.

But sinful, Ginful, beer-soaked men,
Survive some three scores years and ten.

While some of us, though mighty few,
Stay sozzled till we're ninety-two.

— Origin Unknown

Hungarian Goulash

"Herdsman's meat" is what *gulyas*, which we call goulash, means in Magyar. It is an ancient dish that harkens back to the iron kettle days when Hungarian peasants set stews to simmer all day over an open fire. The dish was so tasty and convenient that it soon spread throughout middle Europe. Today travelers find many and various versions of this savory stew.

When preparing goulash, try to find Hungarian paprika. The Spanish variety, so common in this country, by comparison merely colors the food. If your market doesn't have the Hungarian available, you can make a passable substitute by adding a dash of cayenne pepper to the Spanish paprika.

2-3	pounds stew meat, cubed
3	medium onions, coarsely chopped
1	10 ½-ounce can beef stock
8	ounces warm ale
6-8	slices bacon
2	ounces butter
½	cup flour
4-6	tablespoons cooking oil
1	tablespoon paprika
5	tablespoons tomato paste
2	tablespoons vinegar
2	lemons, juice only
2	tablespoons lemon rind (yellow part only)

Mix flour and paprika in a bowl. Cube meat and remove any excess fat. Heat oil in a heavy skillet. Roll meat in flour. Brown on all sides. Place in a Dutch oven with beef stock, ale, tomato paste, vinegar and lemon juice. Bring mixture to a simmer.

Brown chopped onions in skillet with butter. Add to stew. Cover. Simmer for 2 ½-3 hours, or until meat is good and tender.

Just before serving, cut bacon into 1-inch pieces. Fry until crisp. Mix lemon rind and 1 teaspoon of butter into bacon a few minutes before done. Stir lemon-bacon mixture into goulash and serve stew with buttered egg noodles or spaetzle. In the old country, spoonfuls of cool sour cream are sometimes heaped on the steaming stew at serving time.

Since this is an international recipe, you can accompany the meal with any robust beer from Germany, Austria, or Czechoslovakia. You might try a Hungarian beer, though Hungary is better known for its wines.

Makes 6 to 8 servings.

Uncle Sam's Barley Stew

Who was the original Uncle Sam, did I hear you ask? And what did he have to do with the American beef industry? The story starts during the War of 1812, in Troy, New York, when a well-known meat packer, Samuel Wilson, received a contract to supply the Army with kegs of cured beef. Each wooden barrel was stamped "US," meaning "United States."

Soldiers, knowing that Wilson was called Uncle by many of his friends, began telling recruits that the "US" meant that the meat belonged to Uncle Sam.

Later, actors and itinerant entertainers, always looking for new characters, added Yankee trader characteristics and, finally, the red, white and blue patriotic costume to complete a series of events that began with a keg of beef, probably destined for somebody's stew.

2	pounds beef, cut in 1-inch cubes
2-3	cups water
12	ounces warm beer
1	6-ounce can tomato paste
½	cup barley
1	envelope onion soup mix
2	cups *each* carrots and celery, sliced
¼	cup flour
1	small bay leaf
¾	teaspoon salt
¼	teaspoon pepper

Cube, dry and flour meat. Brown in a heavy skillet. Combine with water, beer, tomato paste, barley, onion soup mix, bay leaf, salt, and pepper in a large sauce pan or Dutch oven. Stir ingredients thoroughly.

Bring to a boil. Reduce heat. Cover with a tight lid. Simmer on low heat for 1 ½ hours, or until meat is tender. Add carrots and celery. Continue simmering another 30 to 40 minutes, or until vegetables are done. Check progress now and then. You may have to add a little water during cooking.

In some parts of this country, stew is served over fried bread, or you may accompany it with a large green salad, cheese bread and frosty pitchers of Budweiser.

Makes 6 to 8 servings.

Doughboy Stew

Dumplings are an international accompaniment to meat dishes. Probably devised by the Chinese, they are also basic fare on German, Russian, Hungarian and Italian menus. The lowly dumpling had a special appeal to cooks at sea (the marine sea, not the confused variety), because they required no extra pans in a space-restricted galley.

American sailors enjoyed a doughnut-like dumpling served with hash called a "doughboy," probably invented earlier by mariners on the Spanish Main as a respite from the standard-issue, tooth-chipping hardtack.

During the Civil War the name became associated with the large brass buttons worn by the military, and, eventually, in the First World War, "Doughboy" became a nickname for the American foot soldiers in France.

Doughboy Stew is also known as "slumgullion," a messy word coined by American whaling crews to describe shipboard stews. During the California Gold Rush, Mark Twain commented on the excesses of "whatever stew" in *Roughing It* when he speaks of eating this stew "with too much dishrag, sand and old bacon rind . . . in it." Later the term was applied to attempts by AEF troops in World War I to doctor up the ubiquitous canned corned beef hash, by making crackers into biscuits or doughboys.

With this sort of heritage, there is no true recipe for this dish, so feel free to improvise, guided by your imagination and whatever you have on hand.

2	pounds stew beef, cut in 2-inch chunks
8	ounces sliced mushrooms
6	small whole onions, peeled
6	ounces warm beer
2	strips bacon, fried
¼	cup flour
½	teaspoon *each* sugar, pepper and vinegar
¼	teaspoon *each* oregano and marjoram
1	bay leaf
1	teaspoon paprika
1	tablespoon salt

Mix flour, paprika, salt and pepper in a paper sack. Cube the meat, dry it, and shake it in the sack with flour mixture until evenly coated. Brown meat in a heavy skillet or Dutch oven. Add onions, bacon, and mushrooms. Mix beer with sugar, vinegar, oregano, marjoram, and bay leaf and pour into stew. Cover and slide into a 175-degree oven for 6 to 8 hours, or until meat is tender. Discard bay leaf prior to serving.

This recipe works well in a slow cooker or crock pot. Cook on low for 8 to 10 hours or till meat is tender when prodded with a sharp fork.

If you want an all-in-one-pot dinner, about 15 minutes before serving time, drop spoonfuls of dumpling dough into the boiling stew and cover with a tight lid.

For the Doughboy Dumplings,

¼	pound unsalted crackers
1	tablespoon nutmeg
½	teaspoon salt
3	eggs, beaten
⅓	cup warm beer
2	tablespoons chopped parsley
1	tablespoon melted butter

Rolls crackers into fine crumbs. Mix thoroughly in bowl with dry ingredients. Stir in beer, butter and eggs.

Drop mixture into boiling gravy. One tablespoon makes a nice sized dumpling. Cover. Allow to cook at a slow boil for about 10 minutes or until dumplings are done.

Serve up the stew and dumplings in large bowls, accompanied with a light salad and tall glasses of Rolling Rock beer.

Expect about 6 to 8 servings.

A Noggin of Old Rattle Skull

Prior to the advances in modern brewing methods, the taste of the average beer and ale was a hit-and-miss process at best. Some beers, of course, were noted for their consistency and quality, but many were merely adequate and quite a few were barely palatable. Probably for this reason, in old documents one finds mention of tavern and inn beverages employing spices, honey, liquor, and sometimes a red-hot poker to make their less felicitous brews drinkable. A few of the picturesque names give an idea of their popularity and impact.

We find Rattle Skull, Lamb's Wool, Auld Man's Milk, Bellows Top, Black Jack, Colonel Byrd's Nightcap, Early Birds, Dog's Nose, Jehu's Nectar, Wassail, Mother-in-Law, Rumfustian, Shandy Gaff, Yard-of-Flannel, Splittin Headache, Gossip's Cup, Braggart, Caudle, Black Velvet, and for the devout, Abbot's Flip, the Bishop, the Cardinal, and the Pope. Many of these exotic concoctions have been lost in time. We no longer even know what they mixed with their beer or ale, let alone the proportions.

Steak and Kidney Pie

Traditionally, the English have been fond of pies and pastries. But in the olden days, few people had the means to prepare them – almost no cottage boasted an oven, and even if it did, fuel was expensive. Public bakers were essential during the Medieval Period; in their shops patrons could buy a "pasty" or an elegant meat pie for a few pence.

Public bakers in London date back to the 12th century, where they enjoyed a place in the workaday world until the early 1800's, when the first affordable kitchen stoves, invented by one Count Rumford, were marketed widely.

The great Dr. Johnson, according to his faithful Boswell, enjoyed steak and kidney pie, baked in a public oven, every Sunday. "Thus, the advantage is obtained of not keeping servants from Church to dress dinners."

When you make this dish, don't be concerned about leftovers. Be guided by the old admonition, "the more you warm it, the better it tastes."

2	pounds lamb or veal kidneys
2	pounds beef chuck, cubed
1	large onion, diced
12	ounces warm dark beer
2	cups beef bouillon
2	tablespoons Worcestershire sauce
1	bay leaf
12	ounces small mushrooms
	flour for dredging beef chunks
½	cup butter
1	teaspoon prepared mustard
	paprika to taste
	cornstarch as needed
	salt and pepper to taste
2	prepared pie crusts

To prepare the kidneys, wash, split and devein them. Remove any fat and cut into very thin slices. Cover with 1 cup of beef bouillon in a bowl. Allow kidney pieces to stand 1 hour.

Cut beef into ¾-inch cubes. Dry the meat chunks. Flour the beef pieces and let stand.

Sauté onions in butter in a large skillet or Dutch oven until transparent, and set aside. Sauté mushrooms briefly in butter, stirring in mustard. Set aside.

Dredge beef in flour again. Dust lightly with paprika. In the skillet, brown beef in remaining butter. Set beef aside. Deglaze pan with a little water and reserve the drippings and fried bits.

Drain bouillon from kidneys, discarding bouillon. Dry kidneys, then brown lightly in skillet, adding a little more butter if necessary.

Return onions and beef (with drippings) to skillet with kidneys. Add the beer, 1 cup beef bouillon, the Worcestershire sauce, bay leaf, salt, and pepper. Cover. Simmer for about an hour, stirring frequently to check consistency. If after about 45 minutes the stew has not thickened enough, mix ⅛ cup of cornstarch with some of the hot stew liquid and add gradually back into the simmering stew till you have the desired consistency. Remove from heat and take out bay leaf. Add mushrooms to stew.

Get out a 9- or 10-inch diameter deep-dish pie plate. Roll out pie crust to about 13 inches diameter and carefully drape it into the pie plate. Spoon the stew into the crust. (Don't overfill; any extra gravy can always be offered at the table.) Roll out second pie crust to about 12 inches diameter. Cut steam slots in crust, lay carefully atop the stew, and brush with milk. Roll and crimp edges to seal, and trim off excess dough. Bake in a 450-degree oven for 15 minutes (if edges start to burn, take some strips of aluminum foil and cover the edges loosely). Reduce heat to 350. Bake another 20 minutes, or until crust is golden and crisp.

Serve with small green peas, and onions sautéed in butter. For liquid back-up, we return to Boswell, who called Belhaven of Scotland the "best small beer" he'd ever tasted. Lastly, fresh pears soaked in port wine make a superb dessert. Should you travel in Great Britain you'll find steak and kidney pie a "pub grub" standard, to be enjoyed with a pint of bitter.

For a variation, make a one-crust pie using a round of puff pastry (thawed and cut to fit your pie pan), available in the frozen-foods section of your supermarket.

Makes enough for 4 to 6 servings. Cheerio, old thing!

In Vassar Halls

Matthew Vassar was a successful brewer when he decided to endow a college for women in Poughkeepsie, New York, in 1865. He stated that women should have "the same right as men to intellectual culture and development." From that time forward, this school has been noted for high standards of scholarship; and, through all these years, the ladies have not forgotten their benefactor, as this old Vassar song explains.

> *And so you see, for old VC*
> *Our love shall never fail.*
> *Full well we know, that all we owe*
> *To Matthew Vassar's ale.*

Hearty Steak and Guinness Pie

Gerry, an Irish-American, was traveling with friends around Ireland and enjoying the inimitable Guinness on tap. He was interested in all things Irish, and he'd read about brewing, top fermenting and bottom-fermenting, and all those grand things. He ordered his third Guinness and the barkeeper said, "Give us a minute; I'll just get you some from the new keg." "What's the difference between the old keg and the new keg," Gerry asked. The bartender looked thoughtful and then told him, "The new keg's got beer in it."

This recipe is great if you don't want to mess with kidneys, and Guinness stout raises this meat pie high above mundane meat pies. The Stilton in the crust does no harm either.

½	cup olive oil
1	pound mushrooms, sliced
2	cups frozen pearl onions, thawed
	salt, to taste
3 ½	pounds thick beef sirloin or chuck steak, cut into 1-inch cubes
1	cup flour
3	cloves garlic, minced
3	tablespoons tomato paste
2	cups Guinness stout, room temperature
1	cup beef broth
1	pound carrots, cut in chunks
1	tablespoon chopped fresh thyme
¾	teaspoon fresh coarsely ground pepper
½	teaspoon cayenne (red) pepper
2	frozen deep-dish pie crusts, thawed
4	ounces stilton cheese, crumbled
1	egg, beaten with 1 teaspoon water

In a skillet, heat 2 tablespoons of the oil. Brown the mushrooms and onions, and salt and pepper them. Transfer them to a stewing pan that holds 6 or 7 quarts.

Season the beef with salt and dredge it in flour. In same skillet, heat 2 tablespoons oil. Sear a third of the beef cubes (takes 5-7 minutes); transfer to stewing pan. Deglaze skillet (that is, add about ½ cup water to skillet and loosen any fried bits left in the pan); pour water and bits into stewing pan. Repeat twice with the rest of the beef.

Return skillet to medium-high heat. Add garlic and tomato paste; stir 30 seconds. Transfer it to the stewing pan. Add the stout and the broth. Add carrots and seasonings; bring to boil.

Cover. Simmer over medium-low heat, stirring occasionally, for 3 hours. If it begins to stick, add a little more broth.

After that you'll need your Dutch oven. Most of them are 5 ½ quarts. Put as much of the stew into the Dutch oven as will fit. Don't overfill; allow for some bubbling in the oven. You can enjoy any extra stew as a great leftover later in the week.

Lay out one of the pie crusts. Sprinkle the crumbled Stilton cheese on it. Lay the other pie crust on top of this, then press them down and roll the Stilton-filled crust out big enough to cover the Dutch oven.

Preheat oven to 400 degrees F. Brush rim of Dutch oven with water. Carefully transfer pastry to top of meat pie; it's fine if it droops down onto the filling. Trim dough to 1 inch; crimp to seal. Brush with egg mixture. Cut a few slits to allow steam to escape. Bake 35-40 minutes or till pastry is golden brown.

Serves 8-10.

Gin Lane

Gin, synonymous with our picture of the English good life, was not well accepted when it was first introduced. In the 17th century, the king, William of Orange, needed money to finance his military campaigns in Ireland, so he taxed, my god of all things sacred or profane, beer. In fact, he taxed it so smartly that it became prohibitive for most folks to buy. As a result, still thirsty, they turned to gin, which had recently developed as a medicine in the Lowlands.

The new beverage became the rage. It was so widely guzzled, in fact, that in most social critics' minds the problem of alcoholism was endemic. By the time the government realized its mistake and the taxes were reduced, the English were accustomed to hard liquor. Beer and ale rebounded, of course, but they never regained their position as the universal, wholesome, have-it-every-meal beverage.

William Hogarth, the satirist, immortalized the dubious nature of the dispute in his famous companion sketches, "Gin Lane," a place of moral degradation, and "Beer Street," where all was well, comely, and in good order.

Polish Delight

For those who like plain food and don't want to spend too much time preparing it, this combination should fit both requirements nicely. Also keep it mind if you are ever called upon to feed an army – it goes a l-o-n-g way.

1	pound ring of kielbasa sausage cut in 1-inch slices
1	small onion, cut in chunks
16	ounces warm beer
1	1-pound can sauerkraut
1	cup barley
2-3	cloves garlic, crushed
3	cups water
1	sweet red pepper, cut in strips
½	teaspoon caraway seeds
1	small bay leaf
2	tablespoons cooking oil
	hot pepper sauce, to taste
	fresh ground black pepper

Heat oil in a large skillet. Lightly brown crushed garlic. Add onion and sauté until soft. Pour water, warm beer and barley into pan. Drop in bay leaf. Bring to a boil. Cover. Reduce heat. Allow barley mixture to simmer 1 hour, or until the barley is tender and all the liquid is absorbed.

Add undrained sauerkraut, sausage slices, sweet red pepper strips, and caraway seeds to barley. Stir in black pepper and a dash or two of hot pepper sauce to taste. Heat another 10 to 15 minutes with a lid on. Remove bay leaf prior to serving.

Serve with parsley potatoes, fried green tomatoes, and that fine Polish beer Piwo.

Makes 4 to 6 servings.

Tepache

A less well-known native beer of Mexico is made from sugar, barley and pineapple. It is served throughout the Republic on feast days, but if you are impatient, it can be found daily in the plaza of Cuernavaca.

Mexican Lamb Stew

There are many variations of basic lamb stew. Some use fresh lamb; some leftover roast. This one calls for lots of different vegetables. So, depending on the extent of your larder, you can use them all or whatever's available. For example, pinto beans or rice can be substituted for the potatoes. Only the lamb and onions are essential.

This version is called *cazuela de cordero* in Spanish. A *cazuela* is a dish or a large pot used for cooking. In this case it also refers to the time this stew sits on the fire and slowly gathers its flavors.

2	pounds lamb stew meat (or cubed leg of lamb, lamb chops or shanks)
2	tablespoons cooking oil
1	teaspoon paprika
1	onion, peeled and chunked
6	medium potatoes, peeled and chunked
3	medium carrots, peeled and chunked
2	stalks celery, chunked
1	green pepper, seeded and chunked
½	pound zucchini, chunked
½	cup fresh or frozen peas
1	pound frozen whole-kernel corn, thawed
2	tomatoes, peeled, seeded and chunked
1	clove garlic, peeled
2	cups warm beer
4	cups water
1	tablespoon chopped parsley
⅛	teaspoon oregano
¼	teaspoon thyme
1	tablespoon cornstarch
	salt and pepper to taste

Coat the inside of a Dutch oven or heavy 5-quart pot with oil. Dust the lamb pieces with paprika. Brown the lamb thoroughly on all sides. (If you are using fresh meat, coat the pieces lightly with flour before browning.) Add onions and garlic. Sauté until soft, but not brown.

Pour in beer and water. Bring to boil. Add oregano, thyme, salt, and pepper. Reduce heat. Cover. Simmer undisturbed for 1 hour.

Add potatoes, carrots, celery and zucchini. Check level of liquid. Cover. Simmer another ½ hour. Stir occasionally.

76

Add green pepper, peas, corn, and tomatoes. Check level of liquid. Cover again. Simmer another ½ hour. Stir occasionally. Poke vegetables with a sharp fork to check doneness. Mix cornstarch with a couple of tablespoons of cold water. Stir slowly into liquid to thicken. Garnish stew with parsley.

If you like hot dishes, this one can be turned explosive by adding a can of drained green chilis, some dried New Mexican chilis and a few dashes of picante sauce – *muy fuerte*.

This lamb stew is truly a one-dish meal – everything good is already in the pot. Serve it hot in bowls with hard rolls and butter on the side. An additional touch would be to garnish each plate of stew with some grated cheese and sliced black olives.

Also don't forget to include a fine light Mexican beer. Pacifico makes an excellent accompaniment to this *cazuela*.

Makes 6 servings.

I Think He Liked the Beer

In his novel <u>The Trumpet Major</u> *(1880), Thomas Hardy describes the beer of Casterbridge with words that would make an advertising copy writer salivate:*

> *It was the most beautiful colour that the eye of an artist in beer could desire; full in body, yet brisk in volcano; piquant, yet without a twang; luminous as an autumn sunset; free from streakiness of taste; but, finally, rather heady. The masses worshipped it, the minor gentry loved it more than wine, and by the most illustrious country families it was not despised. Anybody brought up for being drunk and disorderly in the streets of its natal borough had only to prove that he was a stranger to the place and its liquor to be honourably dismissed by the magistrates as one overtaken in a fault that no man could guard against who entered the town unawares.*

What more elegant tribute to a famous, truly classic brew?

A special commemorative brewing of Thomas Hardy Ale was prepared in 1968. In 1980 a single bottle was offered at auction; the starting bid was $1,000.00.

Thomas Hardy Ale was unavailable for a number of years, but there's great news: English brewers and U. S. importers are bringing it to you again.

Pork Chile Verde

When Cortez arrived in Mexico in 1519, he had no way of knowing that a number of events were conspiring to ensure his conquest of the vast and warlike Aztec Empire. Native soothsayers had predicted the arrival of strange, bearded gods from the east, men who would follow the sun and be able to call fire and lightning from the blue sky.

The Conquistadors' guns, their horses (which the natives thought at first were four-legged monsters with men sprouting from them), and the Spaniards' arrogance carried them to the capital city of Tenochtitlan in just twenty days. There they discovered a splendor and magnificence that boggled their most outrageous expectations. Thus the historical stage was set for a tragedy we find incredible today – the rape and destruction of an entire empire by invaders who were outnumbered ten thousand to one.

Fortunately, portions of pre-Columbian culture escaped the ravages of the Army of God. Among them was a small sweet pepper used extensively to spice the dishes served to the Aztec leader, Montezuma. The Spanish mistook the word *chile* or *chili* to mean the entire family of peppers. Later *chili* came to refer to only the hottest of these *diabolitos*.

3	pounds pork roast or shoulder, cut in 1-inch cubes
4	yellow chilis
4	tomatoes, peeled and seeded
1	medium onion, chopped
1	6-ounce can tomato paste
1	8-ounce can tomato sauce
1	clove garlic, minced
1	7-ounce can diced mild green chilis
3	cups water
8	ounces warm beer or ale
	salt to taste

Cut tomatoes into chunks. Traditional Mexican cooking removes the seeds as well. Remove stems and seeds from yellow chilis. Boil both in 3 cups of water until tender. Drain. Pulse tomatoes and chilis in blender a few times. Do not puree.

Cut meat into cubes, trimming off as much fat as possible. Brown in Dutch oven or heavy skillet, without any cooking oil, until meat is well cooked and crispy. Drain any excess fat from the meat, leaving just a little in the bottom of the pan. Add salt to taste. Mix in tomato and chili mixture, green chilis, tomato sauce, tomato paste and 1 cup of beer. Cover pan. Simmer for 45 minutes or until meat is done and sauce thickens.

Chili verde is a versatile dish that can be served alone, over rice, as a side dish, in a burrito, as a taco, or with refried beans. A typical Mexican accompaniment to this lively plate would be grilled corn on the cob, doused with mayonnaise and chili powder, and a fresh salad of avocado, tomato and jicama slices.

However you array your chili verde, have on hand some products from the Montezuma or Cuauhtemoc Breweries. Cuauhtemoc was the last Aztec emperor, after Montezuma's death. Considered a great hero in Mexico, he led the battle against the Spanish and, when captured, refused to tell Cortez the hidden location of the Aztec treasure

Makes about 8 entree servings.

Tavernkeeper's Verse

Mine host, at an 18th-century inn, had the same balance to strike as today's barkeepers do. Tapsters still strive to keep patrons coming, to keep patrons drinking, to keep patrons in good order, and to collect what's owed on the tab.

This was a genial landlord's appeal to his patrons:

> All you that bring tobacco here,
> Must pay for pipes as well as beer;
> And you that stand before the fire,
> I pray sit down by good desire;
> That other folk as well as you
> May see the fire and feel it too.
> Since man to man is so unjust,
> I cannot tell what man to trust:
> My Liquor's good, 'tis no man's sorrow,
> Pay to-day, I'll trust to-morrow.

Bartender 'Bot

Some German computational linguistics students at the University of Saarland have made a robotic bartender. Digital language technologies, combined with robotics, enable the 'bot to understand natural language. It can suggest drinks to you, take your order and tell you what the alcohol content is, mix any drink, make a new drink out of ingredients you select, and tell you jokes all the while from its substantial database of drink-specific jokes.

But it can't break up a fight, tell you there's lipstick on your collar, or field a phone call from your significant other. We were not informed what happens when you fail to tip.

Pecos Chile

Meat, beans and chilis were a mainstay on Texas cattle drives. On one occasion, a group of cowboys was sitting around the fire enjoying a particularly spicy chili dinner. Just then a tall man walked into camp and, without a by-your-leave, dipped his hand into the cooking pot and stuffed his mouth with the fiery fare. He followed this by picking up a boiling pot of coffee and drinking about half of it directly from the pot; next, he chugged five gallons of beer. Then, to the astonished eyes of those present, he reached over to a cactus and broke off a giant prickly pear to wipe his mouth. Satisfied, he turned and asked, "Who's the boss of this here outfit?"

A strapping, seven-foot cowboy laid aside the monte hand he'd been holding, stood slowly and replied, "I was, but you are now, stranger!"

The newcomer was, of course, the toughest cowboy that ever was, the true product of those evenings spent sitting by a fire, lyin' and spittin', none other than himself, in the flesh, Pecos Bill.

3	pounds boneless pork shoulder, cut in 1-inch cubes
2	1-pound cans tomatoes
¼	cup instant minced onion
¼	teaspoon instant minced garlic
	salt and red pepper to taste
½	cup salsa – your choice – mild, medium, or volcanic

Simmer for 2 – 4 hours, adding liquid if needed.

Yippie ti yi yo!

New Heights for Beer

Beer and the American serviceman are an inseparable item, but they were especially so during the Second World War, if these Navy stories are to be believed. According to a wholly unreliable source, one South Pacific squadron, to remain here unidentified, is supposed to have gone into combat with the ammunition storage area in the wings of the planes equally divided between belts of machine gun bullets and cans of beer.

On other occasions, when a celebration was in order, which it usually was, land-based pilots loaded their aircraft with cases of warm beer – always a problem in the tropics – and flew then into the blue yonder. There, high above the island heat, the brew quickly cooled in subzero temperatures, and, if the pilots dived for their bases quickly enough, the brew arrived at the party in lovingly chilled cans.

Bartender's Chili

Each year, in the far west, there's a World Championship Chili Cookoff. The event, now in its fifth decade, brings fanciers of the hot and spicy from all corners of the world, ready to tantalize judges with their secrets – some of which would raise a few eyebrows at a conclave of wizards and shamen. The only rules of the event are that the fare, baked, boiled or fricasseed, be prepared on an ordinary camp stove within a reasonable amount of time.

The entrants call themselves "chili heads," dress in fanciful attire, and gleefully add every imaginable spice and condiment to their pots in quest of the $25,000 prize. Usually there is no argument about "traditional" chili, as long as the final product is good – except on one point. Aficionados will debate endlessly whether or not chili should contain tomatoes. It's a mystery why this single ingredient, of all the thousands of "secrets" stirred into a chili pot, from possum meat to Aztec mummy dust, should be in contention, but it is. So be forewarned when discussing the merits of Texan and Mexican chili.

2	pounds beef stew meat, cubed
1	pound pinto beans
1	pound kidney beans
1	large red onion, chopped
1	small Bermuda onion, chopped
1	medium green pepper, chopped
3	New Mexico red peppers, chopped
1	quart ale
2	tablespoons margarine
4	ounces gin
2	ounces vermouth
1	12-ounce can stewed tomatoes
1	clove garlic, minced
1	small can Mexican salsa
2	teaspoons chili powder
1	tablespoon cornstarch or arrowroot
1/8	teaspoons *each* liquid smoke and Worcestershire sauce
1/2	teaspoon powdered cumin
1/4	teaspoon celery flakes
1	dash Angostura bitters
8	ounces sharp Cheddar cheese, grated

Pour dried beans into a large pot. Rinse with water. Drain. Cover with ale. Bring to a boil and cook for 3 minutes. Remove from heat. Let stand in ale 1 hour.

Chop onion, garlic and peppers. Sauté in the margarine till soft. Add meat and brown it. Add the bitters. Cook for another 5 minutes. Remove onion and meat mixture from pot and set aside. Return beans in ale to pot.

Simmer beans and ale over low heat. Add chili powder until beans begin to darken. Stir in cumin, Worcestershire sauce, celery flakes, gin, vermouth, and liquid smoke. Cover. Reduce heat to allow ingredients to just barely simmer. Cook another 20 minutes.

While beans are still firm, add stewed tomatoes and salsa – tomato paste can be substituted for the salsa, if you don't want things to get too hot. Add a few red peppers. Be discreet! These little devils can fool you. Wait about 15 minutes to taste-test for potency. Add more, if you want a four-alarm chili. Salt to taste.

Simmer another 10 minutes, or until beans are just right. Return meat mixture to pot. Stir well. If chili looks too thin, add a little cornstarch or arrowroot mixed with water, to thicken.

Remove chili pot from heat. Allow to cool. Place in refrigerator for a few hours, preferably overnight. Good things do come to those who wait.

Reheat and serve. Garnish with more chopped onion and shredded Cheddar cheese. Serve with hot biscuits and chilled bottles of your favorite fire extinguisher.

Makes enough good stuff for trail boss and 6 to 8 hungry hands.

And Speaking of Heat

Who was to blame if your latest batch of beer went sour? In old Switzerland the culprit, often as not, was a beer witch, who spitefully cast spells on brews. These devil's disciples were dealt with summarily by the inhabitants. The last known beer witch was burned at the stake in St. Gallen in 1581.

Chili Azteca

A great one-dish meal that requires little time or attention, this chili will be a hit at any pot-luck dinner, barbecue or gathering when you want to spend more time enjoying your friends than watching pots. It's attributed to the Aztecs, probably because the major ingredients, corn, tomatoes and chilis, were served on the beach to the Conquistadors when they landed. And you can believe that!

1 ½	pounds ground beef
1	medium bell pepper, chopped
1	medium onion, chopped
1	15-ounce can tomato sauce
1	15-ounce can kidney beans, drained
1	15-ounce can whole kernel corn, drained
6	ounces tomato paste
8	ounces warm beer
2	tablespoons butter
1 ½	teaspoons New Mexico chili powder
1	dash cayenne pepper
	salt to taste

Brown beef in a large skillet. Pour off the fat and set the meat aside. Sauté onions and chopped green pepper in butter. Add cooked beef, chili powder, tomato sauce and paste, corn, kidney beans, beer, cayenne pepper, and salt.

Simmer, uncovered, over low heat for 30 minutes. Stir once in a while.

Put a good mariachi recording of "Guantanamera" on the player. When the mood is right, serve up the chili with warm flour tortillas and Carta Blanca beer.

Makes 6 long-to-be-remembered servings.

Blue Ribbon Tweak

When Captain Frederick Pabst was engaged in making beer and guiding the industry into the twentieth century, he and all other brewers were continuously beleaguered by prohibitionists such as Susan B. Anthony and her Blue Ribbon Committee for Temperance. To show his own feelings clearly to the world, the waggish Captain labeled his newest creation Pabst Blue Ribbon Beer.

Spaghetti with Meat Sauce

The Chinese, reportedly, have eaten macaroni products since 5000 B.C. Here, though, is a fanciful story that places the discovery of spaghetti considerably later. When Marco Polo was visiting the Orient in the 13th century, one of his men, less interested in the historical import of their venture, spent most of his free hours courting a maiden whose job was to prepare bread for the court.

One afternoon, during their dalliance, some stray leaves blew onto the neglected dough. The gentleman, to assist his love and save her from a birching for neglect, picked up a convenient wicker basket, and, using it as a sieve, forced the dough through it to remove the offending leaves. Fascinated by the outcome, she, in turn, allowed the long strings to dry in the sun and presented them to the amoretto. Later, aboard ship, he cooked the strings and so brought a courtly gift to his native land.

What a pity this charming legend is specious, for noodles had been enjoyed in Italy, too, for centuries, and nowhere in his Travels does the great Marco (not noted for modesty) claim the breakthrough as his own.

Spaghetti as most of us know it today, however, was not an immediate application of the noodle principle. The Italians and the world had to wait a few more centuries for tomatoes to arrive from the opposite direction, the New World.

1	pound lean ground beef
1	large onion, chopped
1	clove garlic, minced
1	8-ounce can tomato sauce
1	12-ounce can tomato paste
2	1-pound cans tomatoes
12	ounces warm beer
1	tablespoon brown sugar
2	tablespoons olive oil
1	4-ounce can mushrooms or ½ pound fresh mushrooms
2	tablespoons parsley, minced
2	tablespoons beef flavor base
½	teaspoons *each* oregano and basil
4	ounces sliced ripe olives (optional)
	salt and pepper

Pour a little olive oil into a large, heavy skillet. Add ground beef, breaking it apart as it cooks. Sauté onion and garlic until soft. Cook, with onion mixture, until meat loses its redness and crumbles easily with a fork. Pour off any excess fat.

Drain juice from tomatoes. Cut them up, saving the liquid to add later if sauce becomes too thick. Add tomatoes, warm beer, tomato paste and sauce to onion and meat base. Stir thoroughly. Mix in remaining ingredients: brown sugar, basil and oregano, beef flavor base, salt and pepper.

Cover with a tight lid. Simmer slowly for at least 1 hour. Add mushrooms and any necessary liquid; the juice from the tomatoes is good for thinning the sauce. Simmer for another 30-40 minutes.

Prepare your favorite pasta. Add a few drops of olive oil to the water to reduce sticking and boil-overs. Heap hills of pasta on plates and ladle the spaghetti sauce liberally. Garnish with parsley and chopped olives.

Serve with a large tossed salad, hot, fresh Italian bread, some crisp Peroni or Moretti beer, and, for dessert, fresh pears and Provolone cheese.

Makes 6 hearty servings. Also remember that this sauce will taste even better the next day, so plan for some leftovers.

Stone Street

It's hard to imagine New York City as a small Dutch village, surrounded by peaceful little farms and woods, but that's what it was when it was called New Amsterdam. Many of the inhabitants, including the colonial governor himself, Peter Minuit, considered it too rural. Whenever it rained, the streets became treacherous quagmires, impeding almost all travel and commerce.

Many complained, but it was the governor who finally took action. Since Minuit also owned a brewery, one of the first in colonial North America, it was his responsibility to see that his barrels of beer were delivered promptly. Pairs of porters, hauling huge casks between them on stout poles, made their rounds — unless they became mired in the mud. It was bad enough that patrons could not travel to the various inns and taverns in the hamlet, but undeliverable beer was intolerable.

Serious problems demand drastic actions. Being a practical man with political power, Minuit had the main street paved with cobblestones. Stone Street, located just below what is now Canal Street, had the honor of being the first paved road in the country. Subsequent reports assure us that beer then reliably reached the thirsty without major incidents, allowing them to become as stoned as they wished.

Stuffed Green Peppers

In 1493, Peter Martyns wrote of a new vegetable brought back by Columbus: "a pepper more pungent than that from the Caucasus." From first notice in this obscure footnote, green peppers spread throughout the Mediterranean area and the Near East to become a much enjoyed staple in most lands. This recipe, one that should delight the fussiest appetite, calls for the sweet variety, the bell pepper.

4	medium bell peppers
1 ½	pounds ground beef
¾	cup Cheddar cheese, grated
1	cup boiled rice
2	6-ounce cans tomato paste
1	cup chopped onion
1	clove garlic, minced
8	ounces warm beer
1	tablespoon *each* of sugar and flour
1	teaspoon salt
¼	teaspoon ground pepper

Combine flour, tomato paste, half the beer, and the sugar. Mix until smooth and set aside. Brown beef in skillet. Add onion and garlic. Cook until onion is transparent. Remove from heat. Drain off excess fat. Stir in grated cheese, rice (day-old rice is great), ¼ cup tomato sauce, salt, and pepper. Mix thoroughly.

Cut peppers in half, lengthwise. Wash and remove seeds. Drop halves into hot water, almost boiling, for about 5 minutes. Remove from water while still firm; do not fully cook or boil. Fill each half pepper with generous mounds of meat mixture. Mix remaining beer and tomato sauce. Shake a little flour inside each of two plastic baking bags. Pour about half the sauce into each baking bag and place them in a 10x16-inch baking dish. Slip peppers carefully into the bags. Ladle some of the sauce over each one. Close and seal bags with tie-wires. Make about six ½-inch steam slits in the top of each bag.

Bake in a preheated 350-degree oven for 30 to 40 minutes, or until peppers are tender. Open plastic bags carefully so you can save the sauce to spoon over the peppers when serving. Watch out for hot steam!

Note: these tender beauties freeze well and make great lunches when reheated. You may want to make enough for multiple meals.

Serve with fresh succotash, mashed potatoes and tall, slender bottles of Moosehead.

Makes 4 servings.

The Agony of Prohibition, from a Cockroach's Point of View

Newspaper columnist Don Marquis (died 1937) published in 1927 a series of poems and commentaries, written at night by Archy, a literate cockroach, and "found" by Marquis in his typewriter in the morning. Archy wrote by leaping mightily from key to key (you couldn't expect caps and punctuation under the circumstances). Prohibition, 1919-1933, troubled all right-thinking people and cockroaches and even the mummy of the Pharaoh in the Metropolitan Museum, whom Archy interviewed as follows:

on what are you brooding
with such a wistful
wishfulness
there in the silences
confide in me
my imperial pretzel
says i

i brood on beer
my scampering whiffle snoot
on beer says he

my sympathies
are with your royal
dryness says i

my little pest says he
you must be respectful
in the presence
of a mighty desolation
little archy
forty centuries of thirst
look down upon you
oh by isis and by osiris
says the princely raisin

and by pish and phthush and phthah
by the sacred book perembru
and all the gods
that rule from the upper
cataract of the nile
to the delta of the duodenum
i am dry
i am as dry
as the next morning mouth
of a dissipated desert
as dry as the hoofs
of the camels of timbuctoo
little fussy face
i am as dry as the heart
of a sand storm
at high noon in hell
i have been lying here
and there
for four thousand years
with silicon in my esophagus
and gravel in my gizzard
thinking
thinking
thinking
of beer

When Archy breaks the news that this is a beerless land, the despairing Pharaoh crumbles into dust.

New England Baked Beans

The history of this world classic is a portion of the story of the Pilgrims' progress. During the time of earliest western European immigration to this hemisphere, the Puritans celebrated the Sabbath, the day of rest, from sundown Saturday to sundown Sunday. One of the practical problems that had to be solved was eating – more specifically, how to prepare meals without working.

Finding a practical solution, they came to rely on kettle dishes, like Indian baked beans, that could be made in advance and then set beside a banked fire to simmer, long and slow, all the next day.

After a time, the local tavern keepers became a part of this folk ritual. They would keep a fire going so the local wives could bring their beans to the inn early Saturday and leave them there. The next day, the publicans would return the meal with a little brown bread added as lagniappe to encourage future patronage.

½	pound salt pork, cut in chunks
1	pound small dry white beans or navy beans
1	medium onion, chopped
½	cup dark molasses
3	tablespoons light brown sugar
2	quarts warm beer or ale
½	teaspoon dry mustard
1	teaspoon salt
⅛	teaspoon pepper

Pour dried beans into a large bowl. Clean the beans and remove any bad ones. Soak beans overnight in about a quart of beer

Drain beans, rinse with water. Pour into a sauce pan, cover with water and bring to a boil. Cover pan. Simmer until beans are cooked but still firm, about 30 minutes. Drain off liquid. Put beans in a 3-quart lidded oven dish, casserole, or bean pot.

Scald pork in boiling water to drive off excess salt. Remove any hard rind and cut the pork into chunks. Brown the onion lightly in a separate pan. Add salt pork and onion to beans. Combine mustard, brown sugar, salt, pepper, molasses, and 1 quart of beer. Pour mixture over beans. Stir gently.

Cover dish. Bake slowly in a 250 to 275-degree oven for 6 hours. Stir beans every hour or so, so they will cook evenly. If they become too dry while baking, add a little water – no more beer, though.

This recipe can also be prepared in a crock pot or slow cooker. It's a little easier, but you'll have to plan well in advance, for it takes from 10 to 12 hours this way. You may also notice the beans will lose some of their baked flavor. Compensate with a few drops of liquid smoke.

Should you feel an urge for Boston Baked Beans, use ½ cup of maple sugar or syrup instead of the molasses and sugar in the recipe above. (If this sounds like too much sweetness to you, cut the proportions of the two sweet ingredients in half.)

Baked beans go well with knockwurst, Polish sausage, or frankfurters and some fresh and lusty mustard. The easiest way to prepare a meat accompaniment is just to drop it into the bean pot about an hour before serving. If you want to be more traditional, serve the beans without meat, but do remember they also like a plate of sliced brown bread with lots of butter. Save any leftover beans for reheating. Have them as is, or on bread for a hearty baked bean sandwich.

What beer, you ask? Why not try something on the dark side, maybe Henry Weinhardt, Heineken or Dos Equis?

Makes 6 to 8 servings.

Go to Bed, Tom, Drunk or Sober

These words are part of an old English rhyme based on a barracks ballad. In it, Tom, a British soldier, is advised to stop drinking when he hears the drum signalling all the troops to return to camp. The military word for this is "tatoo," derived from the Dutch word taptoe, which literally means to shut off the tap on a keg. According to orders issued by Colonel Hutchinson in 1644, "If anyone shall bee found tiplinge or drinkinge in any Taverne, Inne, or Alehouse after the houre of nine of the clock at night, when Tap-too beates, hee shall pay 2s. 6d."

Beef Canton

Of the major contributors to international cuisine, the far-wandering Chinese have had widespread influence. There are few places in the world one does not find their restaurants serving hot bowls and platters of Cantonese, Hunan, Szechuan, Fukien, Shantung, Peking or Shanghai style dishes. The following recipe, *chi chow*, shows its Cantonese origin in the word *chow*, which means stir-fried. To make this, seek out the freshest vegetables possible.

1 ½	pounds sirloin or round steak, cut in 1-inch strips
½	pound mushrooms, sliced
8	ounces bamboo shoots
8	ounces water chestnuts
1	medium onion, cut in wedges
½	cup green onions, sliced diagonally
½	cup condensed beef broth
8	ounces warm beer
½	cup soy sauce
1	tablespoon sugar
5	teaspoons cornstarch
2	tablespoon cooking oil
1	teaspoon salt
	dash ground ginger

Prepare meat by partially freezing and then slicing as thinly as possible across the grain – this greatly enhances tenderness. Trim off any excess fat.

Heat oil in a deep skillet or wok. Brown the beef slices. (If you really want to get into the mood, use chop sticks to add, stir and serve.) Add mushrooms, bamboo shoots, water chestnuts, onion wedges, green onions, beef broth, beer, sugar, and salt. Mix thoroughly. Cover. Simmer for 5 minutes. Watch cooking time carefully. Woks get very hot and the secret to most Chinese cooking is not to overcook things. The vegetables are best when the crunch is still evident. Blend cornstarch with soy sauce. Stir into mixture and cook, continuously stirring, until sauce thickens and begins to bubble.

Serve over hot steamed rice, topped with a dash of ground ginger, and tall glasses of Tsing Tao beer. Chinese beers, that is, those from the People's Republic, are usually named after the province where they are brewed.

Makes 4 to 6 servings. *Wen lie! Gom bui!* (Cantonese) or *Gan bei!* (Mandarin)

Pork and Apple Ragout

A *ragout* is a pinky-up French word used to describe a spiced stew made with meat and vegetables or fruit. This one has a mild sweet-and-sour flavor that's not overpowering.

3	pounds boneless pork, cubed
12-18	small boiling onions
3	red delicious apples, peeled and cored, one of them grated, two quartered
6	carrots, peeled and cut in chunks
24	ounces warm beer
1	clove garlic, minced
3-4	tablespoons cooking oil
½	teaspoon *each* oregano and thyme
¼	cup flour
1	teaspoon salt
¼	teaspoon fresh ground pepper

Cut pork into bite-sized cubes. Remove any excess fat. Heat oil in a heavy skillet or Dutch oven. Brown meat well on all sides. Add salt and pepper to taste. Remove pork and set aside. Add onions and garlic to pan. Sauté gently until onions just change color. Remove and set aside with meat. Sauté carrots lightly. Pour off all but 3 tablespoons of remaining oil.

Mix flour and beer together until smooth. Add to pan. Heat slowly until thick. Return pork, onions and carrots to pan. Add oregano, thyme, and grated apple.

Cover tightly with lid. Bake in 350-degree oven for 1 ½ hours. Add apple wedges and bake another 30 minutes.

Serve with asparagus spears, hot croissants and butter, and some crisp Kronenbourg beer from the province of Alsace.

Makes 6 to 8 servings.

Indestructible Guinness

The early days of the 20th century were punctuated by many exciting and dangerous expeditions to the earth's poles. One group, having to lighten their loads or die, and, after a long debate, finally left a case of Guinness behind. Eighteen years later, after the Great War, it was found, frozen solid, and in perfect condition.

CHAPTER FIVE

FROM THE AIR AND THE WATER

Barbecued Chicken

Irish Chicken Cretloe

Flemish Chicken

Hoosier Game Hens

Chicken Ecuador

Baked Curried Chicken

Chicken Stuffed with Rice

Spanish Paella

Fish and Chips

Canadian Salmon Steaks

Rolled Sole with Peanuts

Dixie Fish Turbans

Texas Gulf Shrimp

Asparagus and Shrimp

Barbecued Chicken

The ancient Greeks wrapped shrimp in fig leaves to bake them by an open fire. The practice can be found in most corners of the globe. From Russia, to the Mediterranean, to the jungles of South America, the broad and accommodating leaves of cabbages, grape vines, banana plants, and other vegetation play an integral role in cooking and blending seasonings – and sometimes just holding things together. Although not as whole-earthy as the methods just described, we can now use aluminum foliage to make fish and chicken tasty and convenient.

2	broiling/frying chickens, cut in pieces
1	medium onion, chopped fine
8	ounces warm beer
¼	pound butter or margarine
¼	cup vinegar
¼	cup Worcestershire sauce
2	cloves garlic, minced
1	teaspoon *each* dry mustard, celery seed, sugar, salt, and pepper
1	12-ounce bottle catsup
⅛	teaspoon Angostura bitters

Combine onion, beer, butter or margarine, vinegar, Worcestershire sauce, garlic, dry mustard, celery seeds, sugar, salt, pepper, catsup and bitters in a sauce pan. Bring to a boil, stirring; then reduce heat and simmer till thickened, stirring occasionally to avoid scorching.

Generously blanket chicken pieces with sauce. Wrap individually in foil packets. Place over a charcoal fire. You might open foil packages periodically and baste – carefully – they get hot! Turn the packets a couple of times. To test for doneness, pierce with a sharp fork. When they're done, and just before serving, turn the pieces out of the foil and let the skins brown.

For a complete outdoor dinner add potato salad, fresh sweet corn on the cob with lots of butter, sliced tomatoes, and a six-pack of good, amber Watney's.

Makes 6 servings.

Sign of Prohibition

During the "dry years" in this country, when the Volstead Act was federal law, quantities of beer were illegally made to slake the undiminished American thirst. Advertising of one's products, though, was a risky proposition. Patrons of out-of-the-way cafes were often pleased to note this discreet legend on their tables.

NEAR BEER HERE!
REAL BEER NEAR HERE

Irish Chicken Cretloe

Sometimes just called Chicken in the Pot, this Irish dish also shows the influence of cooks from this country.

1	3-4 pound broiler/fryer chicken
½	pound smoked ham, cubed
8	green onions, chopped (include tops)
¼	pound mushrooms, sliced
6-8	ounces warm beer or ale
1	large clove garlic, crushed
2	tablespoons cornstarch mixed with
2	tablespoons water
2	tablespoons *each* salad oil and butter
1	teaspoon Old Bay seasoning
	salt to taste

Wash chicken. Cut into serving-size pieces. Remove large pieces of skin and fat and discard. Sprinkle lightly with salt and pepper. Heat 1 tablespoon each of oil and butter in a deep frying pan or Dutch oven. Brown chicken over medium heat. Set chicken pieces aside as done.

Add garlic, green onions and mushrooms to pan. Simmer slowly until mushrooms are limp. Return chicken to pan. Add diced ham, Old Bay seasoning (can substitute 1 bay leaf combined with ½ teaspoons each rosemary and thyme), salt – not too much if the ham is already on the salty side – and enough beer to half cover the chicken.

Bring to a boil. Allow to cook for 5-10 minutes. Reduce heat to a simmer. Cover and poach chicken gently for 1 hour or so, or until it's no longer pink next to the bone. Don't let it get to the point that the meat is falling off the bones. When done, place chicken on a large serving dish. Remove any fat from the surface of the pan liquid. Mix cornstarch and water. Add to pan. Increase heat until the mixture boils and thickens into a nice gravy. Pour sauce over chicken pieces just prior to setting out the platter.

Serve with brown rice, gravy, whole green beans, and Guinness Stout. If you find the Guinness too robust, you can mix it half-and-half with a lager beer to make mugs of black-and-tan.

Makes 4 to 6 servings.

Flemish Chicken

In the province of Flanders and the Nord Department of France dwell the Flemish, a Germanic people known for their enjoyment of exceptional cooking and beer. The city of Lille boasts a number of fine beers including, in an interesting mixing of business and culture, an Irish "top brewing" russet ale, brewed by Pelforth and licensed by George Killian Lett, who also has lent his name to Coors' Killian's Red.

This particular French brew, called Bière Rousse, draws on Gaelic legend to further its public image. According to Celtic mythology, the first King of Ireland, Brian Boru, was riding the moors one day when he was immersed in a dense cloud. There he met a goddess, a magnificent creature, who represented the independence of the land. To commemorate the event she gave him a foaming bowl of russet ale and imparted the magical secret of brewing the timeless elixir. Try it with this *coq à la Flamande*.

1	3-pound broiler/fryer chicken, cut into pieces
2-4	tablespoons butter or margarine
2-4	tablespoons salad oil
2	large onions
6-8	chives (including tops), chopped
1	tablespoon sugar
⅓	cup cider vinegar
1	herb bouquet (see below)
4	slices bread
½	teaspoon prepared mustard
1	12-ounce bottle beer
1	12-ounce bottle ale
	salt and ground pepper to taste

Wash chicken. Cut into serving-size pieces. Remove large pieces of skin or fat and discard. Sprinkle lightly with salt and pepper. Heat 1 tablespoon each of oil and butter in a deep frying pan or Dutch oven. Brown chicken over medium heat. Add more oil or butter as required. Set chicken pieces aside.

Sauté onions and chives in pan, adding butter and/or oil if needed. Add vinegar and sugar to onions. Heat. Return chicken to pan. Cover each piece with lots of sauce. Pour in enough beer and ale to cover meat.

Make an "herb bouquet" out of the following ingredients. Tie all ingredients into a piece of cheesecloth, and drop the bag into the pan.

½	carrot, chopped very fine
1	leek, chopped very fine

⅛	teaspoon thyme
2	whole cloves
1	sprig parsley
1	sprig celery (the top of a stalk, with leaves)
¼	bay leaf
⅛	teaspoon marjoram

Spread mustard generously on slices of bread. Place bread slices on top of chicken. Season with salt and pepper to taste. Cook slowly over low heat for 1 hour, or until chicken is tender or no longer red near the bone.

For a great dinner, serve with cream of asparagus soup, wild rice, and whole baby carrots, washed down with glasses of Irish Red Ale.

Makes 4 good-for-raves servings.

India Pale Ale

The year was 1822; the young man's name was Samuel Allsopp; and his challenge was to save the family brewery. His forefathers had been brewers in England since the time of the Crusades — Hugh de Allsopp fought with Richard the Lion-Hearted in the Holy Land.

Shrinking markets and high foreign tariffs on exported beer and ales were causing many English breweries to fail. Allsopp's efforts would decide the fate of the family's little enterprise. He had to find a new market within the boundaries of the British Empire.

His first good lead came from reports that English beers shipped out to India for His Majesty's troops acquired a distinctive, crisp flavor to the beer, evidently owing to a combination of a long sea voyages and wooden casks. So, armed with a few bottles that had made the passage and back, he enlisted the aid of the veteran brewmaster Job Goodhead — that was really his name. According to the story, after many unsuccessful tries, India Pale Ale was finally made ... in a teapot.

The popularity of the India Pale Ale surpassed Allsopp's fondest dreams. IPA became one of the most popular brews of the century and was the forerunner of Double Diamond Ale, one of Great Britain's Burton ales today.

Hoosier Game Hens

H. L. Mencken's *The American Language* (1937) is one of the 20th century's most remarkable books about American expressions. But even he admits that the origins of some words, such as "Hoosier" for Indiana natives, remain uncertain. Unable to resist offering some possibilities, he suggests, first, that it could have derived from the old Saxon word "hoo," which simply meant a rustic person. A more macho theory is that it came from the frontier word "husher," which referred to a brawny person who could "hush up" anyone with his fists. An even more whimsical suggestion is that people from the area are remarkably curious and cannot pass a house or an open doorway without saying "who's there?"

Regardless of where the name comes from, the inhabitants do enjoy this recipe, credited to Le Petit Cafe in Bloomington.

4	Rock Cornish hens, split in half
8	large shallots, minced
32	ounces warm beer
1	pound mushrooms, sliced
1	cup sour cream
3	ounces gin
2	tablespoons flour
½	cup unsalted butter
¼	cup vegetable oil
1	teaspoon crushed herbs (bay leaf, rosemary, tarragon and thyme)

Melt butter with oil in a large skillet. Brown birds evenly. Remove and set aside. Add shallots to butter mixture. Sauté lightly. Drain off all but 1 tablespoon of butter and oil. Return hens to skillet. Flame with gin – carefully! Remove hens and keep them warm in oven.

Stir flour into about ½ cup of beer until completely dissolved. Slowly pour into skillet. Stir. Add remaining beer and crushed herbs. Bring to a simmer. Return hens to skillet. Coat with sauce. Cover pan. Simmer for about 45 minutes or until birds are tender. Remove birds and return to oven to keep warm.

Turn heat to high. Cook till sauce is reduced by half. Stir occasionally. Reduce heat. Add mushrooms. Simmer for 10 minutes. Remove skillet from heat. Stir in sour cream. Return hens to pan once more. Coat generously with sauce.

Serve with a fresh gazpacho, scalloped potatoes, salad, and chilled steins of India Pale Ale.

Makes 4 servings.

Chicken Ecuador

If you are tired of the same old chicken recipes, try *pollo en cerveza*, from South America, smothered in sweet bell peppers.

1	3-4 pound broiler/fryer, cut in pieces
½	cup butter
4	medium green (bell) peppers, chopped
6	ounces warm dark beer
1	cup tomatoes, peeled and chopped (canned may be substituted)
1	tablespoon dry mustard
1	tablespoon chopped parsley
	salt and pepper to taste

Melt butter in Dutch oven or heavy sauce pan with a lid. Remove large pieces of skin or fat and discard. Brown chicken. Remove from pot. Sauté the 4 chopped peppers until tender. Add tomatoes, parsley, dry mustard, salt and pepper. Simmer mixture for 5 to 10 minutes to combine flavors.

Add beer and chicken to sauce. Cover with lid. Simmer until chicken is tender and sauce thickens – about 30 to 40 minutes.

Serve with mounds of creamy mashed potatoes, lots of extra sauce, chopped spinach with a splash of vinegar, and any dark, heavy bodied beer, called *obscuro* in Spanish. Carta Blanca Dark Export would cause no arguments.

Makes enough for 4.

Cone Mouth Beer Cans

Cone type beer cans were not, as folklore would have us believe, the earliest metal beer containers. The first beer cans were flat topped. The cone variety, similar in design to automobile brake fluid containers, was around from late 1935 to the mid-1950s. Brewers liked them because they could easily adapt regular bottling machines to handle them. The cones were closer in height to small bottles than the flat-tops were.

Another story, though, was heard from shippers, retailers and customers, who found these cans a nuisance to stack and store. After a battle that lasted some twenty years, cone-mouth beer cans succumbed to a wave of criticism. They've gained some recent popularity among beer can collectors because of their relative rarity.

Old World Connection

If asked where the first brewery was established in the New World, most beer lovers and history buffs, after a few sips and a moment of rumination, would answer New York, then called New Amsterdam. Right? Nice try, but no cigar.

True, the first brewery in what is now the United States was founded in that Dutch village in 1612. But on May 15, 1544, Alfonso de Herrera, in a report to Charles V, King of Spain, recounted that the Spanish viceroy of Mexico, Don Antonio de Mendoza, had among his many activities recently issued a permit to open the first brewing facility on this continent. In his missive, Herrera went on to describe the wide and enthusiastic acceptance of the new brew by both the Spaniards and the local Aztecs, who until that time had had only pulque to sip, a native beer, made from the agave plant, that proves its authenticity with a curled worm in each bottle.

Herrera also laments that the burgeoning facility was of limited capacity. It had difficulty meeting the demands for its product — a challenge Mexican brewers are still valiantly trying to meet.

Beer Comes to Japan

Beer was introduced to the Floating Kingdom in 1886 by an enterprising American, William Copeland, who opened a small brewery in Yokohama. In 1888, the Japan Brewery, as it was called, changed its name to Kirin, linking itself with a mythical creature that was half horse and half dragon.

The story of this wonderful beast has all the elements of good folklore, romance, fame, fortune and magic. It starts in China, as much Japanese culture does, long, long ago, about 550 B.C., with a beautiful young woman named En Chen Tsai. One evening, as she was strolling in her garden, she saw before her, framed in moonlight, a strange animal. She approached it and laid a thread across its horns, whereupon the kirin cloaked her with its sacred breath.

For three nights the two walked alone; on the third, the creature walked around her three times and vanished, never to return again. As a result of this encounter, the girl gave birth to a son, K'ung fu-tzu, whom Westerners call Confucius, the famed statesman and teacher.

From that time on, a kirin reportedly visited Chinese women prior to the birth of saints. Not surprisingly, it became regarded as a messenger of good fortune, a harbinger of happy events and a symbol of festivities in both China and Japan.

Today a stylized kirin prances handsomely across the label of its namesake Kirin beer, made in one of the largest breweries in the world.

Baked Curried Chicken

Although it does not look much like a world traveler, the lowly chicken has circumnavigated the globe. Originally from China, it first moved west to India. From there it trudged through barnyards in the near east and the Levant, to Europe, where, over many generations of breeding, it underwent numerous changes in size and plumage.

When Europeans, questing after the jewels and spices of Cathay and India, discovered the New World, chickens were probably in the holds of both Spanish and French ships, although the first official chicken arrived in Virginia in 1607.

These placid creatures, much prized for their delicately flavored meat, their eggs, and their feathers, continued to move west with various waves of settlers, until they met the barrier of the Pacific Ocean. The story would have halted here, if Oriental breeders hadn't requested American and European birds for their flocks. And so, in the last few years, the mild-mannered chicken completed its species' excursion around the world.

As the bird made its home in successive new lands, international cooks devised many variations of their favorite fowl dish. Among the more dramatic and pleasing are the curries from Southeast Asia and India, particularly the tandooris. Their interesting additives are mixtures of chilis and other spices. They can range from savory, to titillating, to tongue-blistering (but oh, so good).

4	plump chicken breasts
1	10 ¾-ounce can condensed tomato bisque soup
½	medium onion, chopped
1	cup mushrooms, sliced
1	clove garlic, minced
8	ounces warm beer
4	tablespoons Parmesan cheese, grated
4	tablespoons butter
1	teaspoon curry powder
4	tablespoons black olives, sliced
½	teaspoon oregano
	salt and pepper to taste

Sauté onions and garlic in 2 tablespoons of butter. Add mushrooms and cook a few minutes more. Stir in soup and beer. Add spices, curry powder, oregano, salt, and pepper. Simmer sauce another 10 minutes to blend flavors.

In a separate pan, brown chicken breasts in the remaining 2 tablespoons of butter till golden.

Arrange chicken breasts in a 2-quart baking dish. Pour tomato-beer sauce over them. Cover dish. Bake in a 350-degree oven for 30 minutes. Remove cover. Continue to bake another 25-30 minutes, basting occasionally.

To serve, place chicken pieces on plates. Drench with sauce. Top with grated Parmesan cheese and olive slices.

Serve with mounds of fluffy, steamed rice. Traditionally, small sides accompany curries: dishes of raisins soaked in brandy, chopped nut meats, desiccated and toasted coconut, sour cream or yogurt, and, of course, chutney — but watch these, for chutneys range from the mild mango variety to wild chili.

As to the beer, there are a number of choices. Try a beer from India — you might find some Flying Horse, Taj Mahal, or King Fisher. If not, try some Thai beer — Singha — or some India Pale Ale.

Makes 4 to 6 servings.

Rushing the Growler

In the forty years between 1880 and the beginning of Prohibition, among the working class in America, it was the custom to buy beer in bulk from the corner saloon. The transaction, carrying the empty pitcher or tin bucket to the saloon and bringing it back full, was called "rushing the growler."

Since children were often recruited for the chore, and as many of the growlers were made of metal, the canny customer smeared the lip of his or hers with butter. This kept the beer from foaming, so partially filled growlers, with lots of head, could not be sent back by unscrupulous bartenders. The term "growler" itself may have come as a reaction to customers who did not take kindly to this foul practice.

In the cities, where men were often working in crews, it was not unusual to see an enterprising boy, hurrying along the sidewalk carrying a notched broomstick, from which six or eight full growlers danced and sloshed. This was also a case of not sending a man to do a boy's job, for the older the "rusher," the more beer seemed to spill along the way, for mature runners tended to stop and ease their thirst with a sip or two from each bucket.

Today, we still enjoy sitting at home and schlucking the local brew, but now we buy our growlers by the six-pack and there is considerably less risk of loss in transit due to sloshing and sipping.

Chicken Stuffed with Rice

Poultry has been a part of the American scene since the time of the first settlers. Chickens, due to a lack of refrigeration, were a popular source of fresh meat, especially for those traveling. Many a chicken walked across the United States in those days, finding its own food in the great numbers of insects and seeds along the way. Roosters also doubled as rough-and-ready entertainment in the form of cock fights.

Prior to the Revolutionary War, a Captain Caldwell from Delaware was known throughout the Colonies for the prowess of two fearless fighting cocks. Whenever he was asked about their lineage, he simply stated that they were the off spring of his "old blue hen." When the war with England came, the patriots of Delaware boasted that they were as good soldiers as the Captain's brood were fighters. Thus Delaware became known as the Blue Hen State.

You won't want a tough old bird, though, to prepare this tasty dinner.

1	5-6 pound roasting chicken
3-4	ounces warm beer
1	7-ounce package chicken flavored rice with vermicelli
1	cup water
2	tablespoons butter
½	cup celery, chopped fine
1	tablespoon *each* instant onion flakes and poultry seasoning
	salt and pepper

Glaze
½	cup pineapple juice
½	cup warm beer
1	teaspoon curry powder

Prepare rice according to package directions using beer, water and butter. When tender, after liquid is absorbed, stir in celery, onion and poultry seasoning. Rub chicken, inside and out, with salt and pepper. Stuff cavity with rice mixture. Skewer or tie opening shut to ensure even cooking. Mix pineapple juice, warm beer and curry powder. Brush this all over bird before and during roasting to form a nice glaze.

Roast bird in a preheated 350-degree oven for 1 ½ hours or until done. To check if the chicken is ready, move a drumstick up and down. If it wiggles easily, it's cooked.

Serve with green bean salad, tiny green peas and mushrooms, plenty of hot gravy made from chicken drippings, and a lemon sherbet for desert. An offering from the Blue Hen State, maybe an Iron Hill beer out of Wilmington, Delaware, is also in order.

Makes 6 servings.

104

Spanish Paella

This Spanish classic has as many variations as cooks who serve it. True paella seems to exist only in the mind, like some Platonic ideal that can never be achieved. This version shows the influence of both the Creole and Black cultures, who developed close kin in Jambalaya and Hoppin' John – all simple rice and garlic dishes, much favored by people without much money who did not want to sacrifice taste to economy. Modern combinations of seafood and rice are more expensive than then 18th century counterparts, but with modern packaging, they can be prepared more handily – and of course you can toss in appropriate leftovers.

1	5-ounce package Spanish rice mix
1	10-ounce package raw frozen shrimp, peeled and cleaned if not already done
1	7 ½-ounce can minced clams
1	5-ounce can boned chicken
1	4-ounce can sliced mushrooms
8	ounces frozen lobster (optional)
1 ½	cups water
8	ounces warm beer
1	tablespoon butter
8	ounces frozen peas
¼	cup diced pimientos

Prepare rice according to package directions, using the beer, water and butter. When rice is almost tender, add chicken pieces to pan. Also stir in clams and mushrooms, including juice. Add frozen peas, shrimp and pimiento. Stir gently until well mixed.

Cover pan. Simmer for 15 minutes, or until peas and shrimp are done. A little more water might be required to keep the rice moist – no more beer though. If you want to be continental and keep your guests alert, use fresh shrimp, clams and lobster (cut into chunks), all in the shell.

Serve hot in soup bowls with lots of fresh baked bread and butter. On the side, add some cold asparagus with lemon butter, and a cold, crisp Pilsner-style beer, such as San Miguel from Spain or its premium version, Selecta XV.

Makes 4 to 6 servings.

Fish and Chips

The development of fish and chips is directly related to brewing. In the early 1850's, a Scot immigrant to Australia devised an improved ether compressor that made it possible to cool the wort during brewing – heat being a continuing result of fermentation. Thus brewers "Down Under" could make beer even during the hot summer months.

The invention was quickly applied to other uses, such as making ice, which was a boon to the fishing industry. (Prior to that time fishermen had to catch and sell their fish immediately. People living at a distance from the ocean ate few ocean fish. The poor in England's interior enjoyed only pickled fish, and only now and then.)

Sometime between the years 1864 and 1874, some genius in London, or Lancaster, or Dundee, opened a shop in which fresh frozen fish, dipped in batter and fried, was served with deep fried potato slices. Bundles of "fish and chips," traditionally wrapped in newspaper, entered the diet of average people. Unfortunately, since health officials persuaded legislators to outlaw newspaper-wrapped food, your fish and chips on the British scene now come in polystyrene boxes.

2-3	pounds bass, trout or catfish filets
3	whole lemons, sliced in wedges, or malt vinegar
1	cup packaged pancake mix
4	ounces warm beer
1	egg, beaten well
½	cup cooking oil
	salt to taste

Slice fish into convenient pieces. Sprinkle with lemon juice or vinegar. Let stand for 15-20 minutes. Dry with paper towels. Salt lightly to taste.

Prepare pancake mix according to instructions, but substitute beer for whatever amount of liquid is required. Add beaten egg to batter. Mix ingredients until smooth. Batter should be thick enough to stick well, but not so heavy it'll turn doughy when cooked. Dip fish into batter. Coat completely. Fry in hot oil until they turn a nice golden brown. Don't overcook.

Keep this recipe handy when going on a camping or fishing venture. It's great for a "catch 'em and fry 'em in a cast iron skillet" breakfast or dinner. This batter also enhances deep-fried shrimp, clams, scallops or abalone.

Drain fish and chips on absorbent paper. Serve with lemon slices or malt vinegar, French fried potatoes and seidels of cold Whitbread Pale Ale.

Makes 4 to 6 servings.

Fish 'n Chips Batter #2

Here's an even easier fish batter.

> 1   cup flour
> ½   cup real mayonnaise
> 1   cup warm beer

Prepare the fish as described in previous instructions.

Mix flour into mayonnaise to form a smooth paste. Add beer slowly, blending with a whisk.

Carry on cooking the same way as in the first Fish 'n Chips recipe.

Those of you with a quick eye can see why this second recipe works so well. Most of the ingredients omitted in the simplified list are found in mayonnaise. But be sure to use real mayonnaise in this recipe – other spreads won't work.

Porter: A Strong Man's Drink

An old custom in England is to mix beer and ale, the famous "half and half," or to blend two types of beer and ale, to make what was called "three shreads." In 1722, a brewer and publican named Howard or Harwood developed a drink that combined these ingredients in a single keg, an efficient time-saver for tavern keepers. He dubbed the new beverage "entire," or "entire butt," but it soon became popularly known as "porter." One explanation for this is that, when Howard had pints delivered his customers' lodgings, the carriers knocked on the doors and announced themselves as "Porters."

Modern, bottom-fermented porter is brewed more lightly than its predecessors. But it's still made from unmalted barley that has been well roasted prior to fermentation – this gives it its distinctive dark color and heavily bittered hop flavor.

Tip a Black and Tan

The "troubles" in Ireland have a long and tragic history. In the 20th century, between 1919 and 1921, a group of special constables recruited in England were sent to Ireland to "keep the peace." They were referred to as the "Black and Tans" because of the uniforms they wore.

Since their presence, by and large, was less than welcome, a disparaging remark about them in an Irish bar was often good for a free drink. The drink that came to be known as a black-and-tan is composed of equal parts of stout, preferably Guinness, and ale. It is really just another variation of a classic "mild and bitter" which mixes light and heavy ales.

Canadian Salmon Steaks

Salmon is found in the northern waters of both the Atlantic and the Pacific oceans. As an important food source of the Indians of the American Northwest, it became a part of their religious rituals and legends. In one of their tales, similar to the Bible story of Jonah and the Whale, a young brave is swallowed by, and later saved from, a giant salmon. Even though they don't grow them that big any more (contrary to some fisherman's reports), here's a salmon preparation that can certainly fulfill the biggest appetite.

6	salmon steaks, fresh or frozen
1	medium onion, chopped
4	tablespoons butter
16	ounces warm beer
1	tablespoon sugar
2	whole cloves
2	tablespoons parsley, chopped
1	lemon, wedged
2	tablespoons flour
1	medium cucumber, sliced
	salt and pepper

Wash and dry salmon. Rub lightly with salt and pepper.

Sauté onion in melted butter in a large pan. Add flour a little at a time. Stir until smooth. Slowly add beer, stirring continuously. When mixture reaches a boil, slip fish into pan. Add sugar and cloves. Cover. Reduce heat to low. Simmer for about 30 minutes.

Arrange steaks on serving platter. Circle fish with cucumber slices. Sprinkle with parsley. Save any remaining sauce in a small dish to pass at the table.

Serve hot with lemon slices, sauce, string beans and garlic bread. A smooth, full-bodied beer from Canada is also probably in order. Blue Pilsner, Moosehead or Molson will do nicely.

Plan on one steak per serving.

Drawing Straws

In Mesopotamia, in the Kingdom of Ur, some 4,000 years ago, the Sumerians drank their beer from large jars, set on the floor, through long metal straws. Archeologists have unearthed a number of golden tubes, about three feet long, that they believe Queen Shu-Bad used when sipping beer with her friends.

Rolled Sole with Peanuts

Peanuts, also called earth-nuts, goober-peas, ground-nuts, monkey-nuts, and pinders, were considered a curiosity prior to the American Civil War. They were grown in the South as fodder for pigs and food for the poor. Then, during the extended hostilities, soldiers from both armies, faced with short rations, discovered their nutritive value and unique flavor – especially roasted over a fire.

From that period, spurred by the imaginative research of George Washington Carver, peanuts became an international money crop. Their use in cooking is still rather limited here, although widespread in the Orient among the Chinese and Thai. Most Americans still look on the peanut as a snack food.

After trying them with baked fish and lemon, you may think of a number of other dishes that would be improved with a helping handful or two.

1 ½	pounds sole or flounder, about 6 fillets
¾	cup unsalted peanuts, chopped
⅜	cup onion, chopped
2	tablespoons cooking oil
¼	cup lemon juice
6	tablespoons pimiento, chopped
6	ounces warm beer
3	tablespoons parsley, chopped
½	teaspoon garlic powder

Sauté onion in oil in a large skillet. Add pimiento, peanuts and garlic powder. Heat briefly. Set aside.

Slice fillets in half. Spoon peanut and onion mixture onto the skin side of the fish. Press filling lightly to compact it. Roll each piece of fish tightly, starting at the wide end. Toothpicks are handy for holding it all together.

Place rolls, seam side down, in a shallow 2-quart baking dish. Pour beer and lemon juice over them. Sprinkle with parsley.

Bake in a 350-degree oven for 35-40 minutes, or until fish turns white and flakes when pierced with a sharp fork.

Serve with buttered rice, a green vegetable and Pabst Blue Ribbon beer, light or dark. Warn guests about toothpicks! For later, try a little Brie cheese on crackers, and coffee.

Makes 6 servings.

Dixie Fish Turbans

Southern cooking isn't limited to the varied and delicious fried dishes. The Gulf Coast, especially the City of New Orleans, boasts excellent French and Creole cuisines. The word "dixie" itself, long associated with the locale, comes to us from the French word *dix*, meaning ten. It first appeared on the backs of the ten-dollar bills issued by the New Orleans Creole Bank.

In the days before the Civil War (or the Second War for Independence, depending on your politics), when any bank could issue wildcat currency, "dixies" were much in demand because of the soundness of the bank. When an itinerant musician, Daniel Decatur Emmett, wrote the song "Dixie" in 1859, it quickly became so popular that it was the anthem of the Confederacy.

Fortunately, you don't have to hop the next stern-wheeler to the Crescent City to enjoy the subtlety of New-World French cooking.

6	large flounder fillets
1	6-ounce package long grain and wild rice mix
12	ounces warm beer or ale
1	tablespoon lemon juice
2 ½	cups water
6	tablespoons butter
1	egg, well beaten
1	¾-ounce package chicken gravy mix
½ - 1	teaspoon mixed dried herbs (dill, basil, parsley) or Italian seasoning salt and paprika

Sprinkle fish filets with salt and paprika.

Prepare wild rice according to package instructions but using 1 cup of beer, 2 cups of water and butter. When done, cool rice slightly. Stir in beaten egg.

Divide rice equally into 6 portions. Spread rice evenly on fillets and roll into "turbans." Secure each with toothpicks. Stand fish rolls upright in a well-greased baking dish. Dot tops of each turban with a little butter. Bake in a preheated 350-degree oven for 25 to 30 minutes, or until fish turns white and flakes easily when tweaked with a fork. Combine gravy mix and herbs with ½ cup water, ½ cup warm beer or ale and lemon juice. Heat mixture and simmer the sauce until it bubbles and thickens.

Place fish on serving dish and cover with herb gravy. Serve with lemon slices, glazed carrots, snow peas, and, for dessert, a bit of Gorgonzola cheese with crackers and coffee. The beer with the meal? Dixie, of course! Or, should you wish something with a little more body, some imported French Kronenbourg.

Plan one fillet for each dinner guest.

King Gambrinus

In folklore, the giant warrior, King Gambrinus, is to beer what Bacchus is to wine. Supposedly, besides engaging in great and heroic deeds, he taught man the art of brewing fine beer — with hops. One finds many stories of his exploits in northern European legends.

It is claimed by those with a penchant for the supernatural that his spirit can still be seen in company with his long-dead companions in two locations. The first is near Grafenburg, at a place called the Devil's Table, where the ghosts of the old Frankish kings attend a gala banquet each May Day eve.

Scholars, with their characteristic lack of romance and compulsion for accuracy (often at the expense of a fine tale), trace the King Gambrinus legend to a real man, Jan Primus, Duke of Brabant, a 13th century hero.

What's Behind the Clink?

When Caesar and his cronies attended a Colosseum event, they were treated to various exhibitions of martial skill. These events, performed by professional gladiators or condemned criminals, were also occasions for high-stakes gambling. Given this situation, it was not uncommon for a shady gambler to try to insure his sesterces by drugging or poisoning contestants.

To protect themselves against this form of hedging, gladiators, when drinking their traditional toast just before a fight, poured some of their wine into each other's cups. These efforts proved so successful that after a while only the ritual remained. In fact, it was reduced it to just a touch of cups and a wish of good health.

In medieval times, when men were more metaphysically oriented, many thought that both disease and drunkenness were caused by evil spirits that entered the body through the mouth while drinking. It was also known that these demons could be exorcised by a bell, a book and a candle. Since these items were not normally carried around while drinking, it became the custom to clink glasses — making a small bell sound — to drive off any lurking spirits.

The reasons behind this classic gesture may have been forgotten over the centuries, but certainly not the wishes of good health that follow the cue of glasses raised and tapped together.

Texas Gulf Shrimp

Near the Gulf of Mexico there's a variety of shrimp that should be known to all seafood lovers. This accommodating fellow hatches in salt water and then spends the remainder of its life in fresh; actually, it's a fresh water prawn rather than a true shrimp. The marvel of it has to do with its size and texture. Gulf shrimp have the flavor and consistency of lobster and grow very large. Fortunately for us, they also thrive in commercial aquatic farms. There is a special way the locals enjoy them.

You can use any fresh or frozen shrimp and still enjoy this recipe.

3	pounds fresh large shrimp, peeled and deveined
24	ounces warm beer
½	teaspoon thyme
1	teaspoon celery seeds
1	clove garlic, chopped
1	teaspoon salt
1	tablespoon parley, minced
1	tablespoon lemon juice
½	pound butter (optional)
	Tabasco sauce (optional)

Wash the shrimp in cold water. Pour beer into a large sauce pan. Add thyme, celery seeds, chopped garlic, salt, parsley and lemon juice. Bring to a boil. Drop in shrimp. Cook 3 to 5 minutes.

If serving them hot, drain shrimp and place in bowl. If serving them cold, refrigerate the shrimp in the beer broth – it makes them juicier when served. When it's time for the meal, drain shrimp and pile them into a serving bowl.

Accompany with cocktail sauce, chives and sour cream, mayonnaise, or melted butter mixed with a few drops of Tabasco for zing. If you like your shrimp sauce a little more *picante*, a teaspoon of Mexican *salsa verde* or horseradish in the butter should do the trick. Also have handy for the event lots of napkins and a tub of Lone Star on ice.

Makes 4 servings.

Here's a variation: By adjusting the spices, Texas Shrimp can be turned into a Danish delight. Leave out the thyme, celery seeds, garlic, salt, parsley, and lemon juice. In their place substitute 2 or 3 stalks of chopped celery, and one teaspoon each of dill weed and mustard seed (or 2 tablespoons of pickling spices). From this we learn that the spices are not as important to tasty steamed shrimp as the beer broth.

Asparagus and Shrimp

Asparagus is a member of the lily family and native to the Mediterranean area. It was cultivated by the Greeks and Romans, in spite of a 4th century warning that it caused blindness. It seemed to travel everywhere the Legions went, although it was often not popularized immediately.

Asparagus came to America with the early European settlers. Some referred to it as "sparrow grass," partially because it sounds like the original Greek word but mostly because of the large numbers of birds it attracted when it went to seed.

There's no record of the genius who first combined shrimp with this exotic vegetable, but with the general flow of food customs and people, a good guess would place its origin along the lower Mississippi river, probably in the Delta region.

1	pound shrimp, fresh or frozen
2	pounds fresh asparagus
½	cup warm beer
½	cup water
2	tablespoons salad oil
2	tablespoons cornstarch
4	tablespoons soy sauce
1	tablespoon brown sugar

Clean shrimp if not already done. Remove heads and veins. Sauté lightly in 1 tablespoon of salad oil. When just barely brown, add beer. Poach for 5 minutes.

Wash asparagus and break off the tough stem ends. Cut diagonally into 1-inch pieces. Sauté in 1 tablespoon of salad oil until lightly brown. Do not overcook.

Mix shrimp with asparagus. Add ¼ cup of water. Cover and steam for 5 minutes. If you prefer your vegetables crisper, in the Chinese stir-fry tradition, cook only 2-3 minutes.

To make the sauce simply push the fish and vegetables to the side of the pan. Mix cornstarch, soy sauce, and sugar with ¼ cup of water. Pour mixture into the center of the pan. Heat for another 5 minutes or until liquid thickens.

For a complete dinner, serve shrimp and asparagus with cups of cream of mushroom soup, a crisp watercress salad, and wild rice flavored with beef bouillon. The beer shouldn't be too heavy, so try a crisp, clear pilsner, like Budweiser or Pilsner Urquell.

Makes 6 to 8 servings.

CHAPTER SIX

FROM THE GARDEN: MEATLESS DISHES AND SIDE DISHES

Spanish Rice

French Fried Onion Rings

Succotash

Cabbage and Noodles

Braised Cabbage

Fried Green Tomatoes

Corn on the Cob

Frijoles Borrachos

Potato Casserole

Spuds Au Gratin

Oriental Fried Rice

Stuffed Tomatoes

Brussels Sprouts

Candied Sweet Potatoes

Mandarin Carrots

Baked Red Onions

Breaded Eggplant

Red Cabbage

115

116

Spanish Rice

In 1694, the captain of a square-rigger from Madagascar bound for England put into Charleston harbor for emergency repairs. The captain gave the colony's governor a handful of rice grains. From this handful came an industry: Just four years later the colony shipped 60 tons of the stuff to England for a very nice price, and thus rice became a diet staple and cash crop in the New World. Over the years many cooks experimented with various rice dishes. One of the most sturdy rice dishes is Spanish Rice, which isn't Spanish at all, nor Portuguese, or even Mexican; it was devised in the American South, possibly in the same city where rice first came ashore.

Whatever its nationality, this dish is an attractive combination of everyday foods that can be served alone or as a compliment-getting accompaniment.

1	cup rice, uncooked
4	green onions, including tops, chopped very fine
1	cup tomato juice
1	green pepper, seeded and chopped fine
1	cup Italian tomatoes, canned
2	tablespoons Parmesan cheese, grated
$\frac{1}{2}$	cup olive oil
$\frac{1}{2}$	cup warm beer or ale
$\frac{1}{4}$	cup water
1	tablespoon chili powder
1	sprig parsley, chopped
	salt to taste

Heat oil in a heavy skillet. Sauté onions and green pepper for a couple of minutes. Shake pan often while heating. Add rice. Fry everything together briefly, still shaking pan, until rice begins to color.

To the rice mixture add tomatoes, chili powder and liquids – tomato juice, beer, and water. Cover. Simmer, on low heat, until rice is tender. When done, liquid will be pretty well absorbed. If it starts to stick to the pan, add a little more water as needed. Sprinkle rice with grated Parmesan cheese and garnish with chopped parsley. Serve with pork dishes, ham or stews. A southern regional beer, like Dixie Lager, or any good German-style beer, would be a fine liquid accompaniment.

For a one-dish meal, similar to Louisiana Jambalaya, add $\frac{1}{2}$ pound of sautéed ham chunks and/or cooked shrimp and leave off the cheese. Very tasty, this, indeed!

Makes 4 to 6 servings.

French Fried Onion Rings

The onion, queen of vegetables, originated in the Orient before recorded time. It traveled along early trade routes through the Fertile Crescent to Egypt, where, because of its compound layers, it was venerated as a symbol of the universe and the glories of eternity – and eaten regularly by all. A typical meal in those days consisted of raw onions, bread and the national beverage in the Land of the Pharaoh, beer.

In addition to its pungent to sweet flavor, the onion has always been important in the world of superstition. Its powers will, some assert, protect you from witches and snake bite, reduce pain, and, according to *Present Remedies Against the Plague* (1594), guard against diseases of the most pugnacious nature.

As one commentator noted, "Onions are so valuable, that if they were not so common, they would be extremely expensive indeed."

A few hundred years ago, the French were credited with developing a deep frying method for preparing onions – although, to be fair to all nations, especially those who favor beer, there is equal evidence the process might have originated in Belgium.

2	large onions, sliced thick
1	egg, beaten well
8	ounces warm beer or ale
1-2	cups cooking oil
1 ½	cups flour
¼	teaspoon salt
1	teaspoon baking powder
1	tablespoon coarse ground salt (optional)

Peel onions. Cut into ⅜-inch thick slices. Separate into individual rings. Sift together flour, baking powder and salt. Add the beaten egg, 1 tablespoon of oil, and beer to flour mixture. Beat batter until smooth.

Dip onion rings into batter with a fork, coating each one thoroughly. Deep fry in hot oil, about 375 degrees, until nicely golden brown on both sides. Turn once. Drain excess oil on paper towels while rings are still hot. Sprinkle with coarse salt and serve.

Or – freeze them for reheating later. To freeze, spread the fried rings on a baking sheet so none are touching, and slide into your freezer. When they're frozen solid, package them in freezer bags for storage. When ready to use, spread frozen rings on a baking sheet. Heat in a hot oven, 400 degrees, for 5 to 6 minutes. Don't try to refry them! When hot and ready to serve, sprinkle with coarse ground salt.

Fried onions rings can be served as an appetizer that will make your guests' hands vanish in a blur of motion, especially at a well-stocked beer tasting, or as a great side dish with almost any meal from fish to fowl. Makes from 50 to 60 individual rings.

Beer Dreams Foretell Future

Dreaming of beer, to the ancient Egyptians, was a form of omen, and, with interpretation, a way of divining one's destiny. To dream of drinking sweet beer, for instance, was a very good sign, for it portended good fortune and rejoicing in the near future. To imagine bakery beer — that is, commercially brewed beer — indicated a long life, while dreaming about store beer was a certain indicator of health or healing.

In contrast, a dream of drinking warm beer meant suffering and ill fortune; a dream of making beer at home foreboded being turned out of a dwelling; and, finally, a dream envisioning the pouring of beer into a vessel or pitcher indicated the dreamer was going to lose something of value in his or her home.

Wet Your Whistle

This common phrase comes to us from Scotland. According to the story, many years ago an arrogant Danish chieftain was visiting the Highlands. His loud, insistent bragging about his capacity to drink more and longer than anyone else rankled his hosts. When the Scots could take it no longer, a noble proposed a contest between the overbearing visitor and one Sir Robert Lawrie. One of the two would receive a silver whistle if he triumphed in the bout.

The two men sat down to their task and began tossing off pints of ale. Three days and three nights they drank, till at the end of the third day the Dane silently slid beneath the table. Sir Robert, to prove he deserved the championship, rose, stepped over his opponent's form, and blew a shrill blast on the whistle.

The poet Robert Burns captures the pride of this moment in these lines:

> *I sing of a Whistle, a Whistle of worth;*
> *I sing of a Whistle, the pride of the North*
> *Was brought to the Court of our good Scottish King,*
> *And long with this Whistle all Scotland shall ring.*

Succotash

Succotash is an American Indian dish, originally made with corn, kidney beans and bear grease. It was one of the first dishes the Native Americans taught the Pilgrim settlers. The Europeans called it succotash because they had trouble with the original Narragansett name, *misickquatash*.

The recipe itself traveled widely, but, possibly because bears don't come around as much as they used to, the ingredients changed. Certainly we can still smell the pleasant northern origins in this South American dish called *locro do cholos*.

6	ears fresh corn
1	green pepper
2	tomatoes (optional)
1	medium onion, minced
1	clove garlic, minced
3	tablespoons chopped parsley
1	cup zucchini, cubed
1	pound fresh or frozen lima beans
3	ounces warm beer
3	slices bacon, chopped
1	tablespoon paprika
½	teaspoon sugar
	salt and pepper

Slice corn kernels from cobs. Include all excess pulp and milk with scrapings. Set aside. Roast green pepper over an open flame until it blisters. Peel and seed. Cut into strips. Do the same with tomatoes, if you include them. Peel, seed and chop into strips.

Fry chopped bacon until almost done. Add onion, garlic and 1 ½ tablespoons of parsley. Sauté until onion turns golden brown. Add paprika. Sauté another minute or so. Pour corn, green pepper and tomatoes into pan. Also stir in lima beans, zucchini, sugar, and beer.

Cover with tight lid. Simmer for 30 minutes, or until vegetables are tender. Uncover. Allow most of the remaining liquid to boil away. Season with salt and pepper to taste.
Top with chopped parsley. Serve as a side dish to enhance your favorite meat entree.

For a vegetarian version, leave the bacon out and use a little corn oil. Or, for variety, add a few slices of chorizo (Mexican beef sausage) and cook the meat with the vegetables. For an appropriate beer, you have the entire northern and southern hemispheres to wander through.

Makes about 8 servings.

Cabbage and Noodles

English legend has it that the moon is not made of green cheese, but is a cosmic cabbage. According to one ancient tale there was once a notorious thief who plagued farmers by stealing their crops. One night he was making off with a huge cabbage when he was apprehended by a mysterious boy dressed in white. In the altercation, the boy cast a magic spell that hurled the culprit from this world up into space, where he can be seen to this day as an example for miscreants. The cabbage, of course, became the lunar sphere itself, and the thief, the penitent face we view.

This dish, like many others successful recipes, has many origins – the English and Germans lay close claim by tradition. But it didn't come to American shores until after 1540, the date recorded by the famed Breton explorer Jacques Cartier when he planted the first New World cabbage in Canada.

½	head cabbage, shredded
2-3	cups cooked egg noodles
1	clove garlic, minced
4-6	tablespoons butter
8	ounces warm beer
2	tablespoons caraway, poppy or sesame seeds (optional)
	coarse ground pepper

Drop minced garlic into a skillet with about half the butter. If you use sesame seeds, add them also. Sauté until the garlic and seeds are golden brown. Add noodles. Continue to sauté until they, too, are brown. Stir frequently to prevent sticking.

In another pan, melt remaining butter. Add shredded cabbage. Sauté, stirring continuously, until cabbage turns limp, about 5 to 10 minutes. Add caraway or poppy seeds here, depending on your choice.

Add noodles and beer to cabbage. Stir together and simmer, letting most of the brew escape as steam. Serve with goulash or stew. It also makes a good companion for ham, sausage and pork dishes.

A good Canadian beer, in memory of Cartier, seems in order. Why not order up some Labatt's? After all, they've been there, brewing away in Canada West, now called Ontario, since 1828.

Makes 4 healthy servings.

Braised Cabbage

The Egyptians believed the substances found in the humble cabbage were strong enough to counteract the effects of alcohol. They recommended eating it to stave off the miseries of overindulgence. Greeks and Russians used cabbage or sauerkraut or its juice for this purpose as well. A cure for hangovers – what a godsend! As late as the 17th century, the curative powers of cabbage were mentioned by John Gerard, in his work *Herball* (1636). The reason, he said, was the contrary attributes of cabbage and grapevines. Anyone so foolish as to plant them together would see new grapevine shoots die and established ones grow in the direction away from the cabbage.

But the world of cabbage stories seems to know no time or geography. This account of "that tall cabbage," reported in the *Los Angeles Star* in 1861, would test the mettle of any Texan or Alaskan tale spinner. According to the printed account, one George Lehman grew a cabbage that was

> . . . fifteen feet tall and still growing. The cabbage was planted in 1856. Since that time George has gathered seed from it nine times, made sauerkraut forty times, coleslaw as often, and used it for salad for twenty-five occasions. It has numerous limbs in the form of a tree, all of which have heads of cabbage, which are from time to time taken off for use. It is in truth a vegetable curiosity, well worth visiting.

If old George and his marvelous cabbage were still around, he could add this to his Cabbage Recipe Book (which also seems to have disappeared).

4	pounds cabbage, shredded
16	ounces warm ale
3	tablespoons butter
1	tablespoon flour
½	teaspoon sugar
1	teaspoon salt
¼	teaspoon black pepper, fresh ground

Shred cabbage coarsely. Sauté in melted butter for 5-6 minutes. Stir frequently. Sprinkle in salt, pepper, sugar and flour. Mix well.

Pour in beer or ale. Cover with a lid and simmer for 10 minutes on low heat.

Serve with corned beef, boiled potatoes, and a seidel or two of German Dortmunder Union beer.

Makes a vegetable accompaniment to satisfy 4.

Fried Green Tomatoes

Mention fried green tomatoes to anyone who has had them and their eyes will cloud with nostalgia. For some reason, this simple dish has been virtually forgotten in this country, possibly because supermarkets insist on stocking only red tomatoes. So your first task, if you decide to accept this assignment, will be to find a couple of pounds of green fruit.

Once you do, and once you savor the results, you'll always have unripened tomatoes somewhere in the back of your mind when you shop for produce.

2	pounds firm, green tomatoes
2	teaspoons soy sauce
2	tablespoons beer or ale
½	teaspoon hot pepper sauce

Mix beer with pepper and soy sauces. Cut tomatoes into ½-inch slices. Marinate in beer mixture for an hour or so. Turn once or twice and spoon sauce over fruit to ensure equal flavor.

1	cup flour
¼	teaspoon Hungarian paprika
½	teaspoon chili powder
¼	teaspoon dry mustard
¼	teaspoon ground cumin
½	teaspoon Cayenne pepper
¼	teaspoon salt
⅛	teaspoon black pepper, fresh ground
4-6	ounces good olive oil

Combine flour, paprika, chili powder, dry mustard, ground cumin, Cayenne pepper, salt and pepper in a heavy-duty plastic bag. Shake ingredients together thoroughly. Drop tomato slices in and turn until nicely coated.

Heat oil in a frying pan or wok – use enough oil to cover the bottom. Fry tomatoes until they turn crisp and golden, turning once. Add oil if necessary while frying.

Serve as a side dish for any outdoor meal – especially good with chicken or fish.

Makes 3 to 4 servings.

Corn on the Cob

Americans are famous around the world for their tall tales. From Pecos Bill and Paul Bunyan of old to the modern urban legends, we love eye-opening stories. For instance, there was a young Kansas farmer who one day decided to climb a cornstalk, the better to view his crop.

But in the heat the corn was growing faster than he could climb down. He tried and tried, but finally, exhausted, he had to stop and rest. As the cornstalk rose into the sky, he thought of his sad future, dying of starvation long before he could be rescued. But then he noticed the abundant feast that surrounded him. He made a meal of raw corn. And then another.

Eventually, two weeks later, the plant reached maturity and stopped growing. The farmer, his overalls in rags, finally clambered to the ground. And what did he find? Forty bushels of dried cobs, the remains of his repasts while stranded aloft.

You can tell your friends this story while preparing them some fresh-picked sweet corn. A few beers might make the tale more digestible, too.

1 ½ -2	quarts beer or ale
12	ears of fresh sweet corn

Husk and wash corn. Bring beer to a boil. Drop ears into rolling liquid. Leave the heat on high; when the beer begins to boil again, about 5 minutes, the corn is done. The trick in preparing fresh corn is speed. Don't waste any time getting it from the pot to the table. Serve immediately with lots of butter and a little salt and pepper.

This recipe is excellent for those who brew their own beer and can afford to be profligate with it, for, like boiling shrimp or franks in beer, it can get expensive. For those who want to save money, use about half water and a stronger flavored brew, like Scotch ale.

Makes 6 servings.

London Beer Flood - Free Beer by Force of Nature

Ordinary thirsty folk may have gotten too much of a good thing on October 17, 1814. In the St. Giles district of London, fermentation weakened a huge brewery tank. The vast barrel snapped its hoops and 1,224,000 liters of porter under pressure blasted through the brewery's brick wall and gushed into the crowded slums. The wave demolished buildings and nine people actually died — but residents weren't willing to let the brew go to waste. They grabbed pots, buckets, pans, and even a few nose-bags purloined from astonished horses to scoop up the beer.

Many underestimated the strength of the flood. Those injured were carried to local hospitals. There, other patients smelled the air and immediately began to complain: Why are these new arrivals getting beer, and we aren't?

Frijoles Borrachos

Mexico has many fine ways to glorify the lowly bean. *Frijoles rancheros, frijoles a la charra, frijoles fronterizos* and this one for "drunken beans," are but a few forerunners of their world-famous *chili con carne*. This version is from the city of Monterrey, which also just happens to be Mexico's beer capital.

4	cups dry pinto beans
2	chopped onions
1-2	cups chopped tomatoes, fresh or canned
2	cloves garlic, crushed
6	slices chopped bacon
12	ounces warm beer
1	tablespoon soda
1	tablespoon salt
2	tablespoons chili powder
2	tablespoons chopped fresh cilantro
½	tablespoon ground cumin
½	teaspoon sugar
1	teaspoon oregano
	Tabasco sauce to taste

Pour beans into a large Dutch oven. Cover with water. Soak overnight. Pour off water. Rinse beans.

Pour in fresh water to cover them about an inch. Bring to a boil for 15 minutes. Reduce heat. Add soda slowly – it will foam. Stir for about 1 minute. Drain beans quickly by pouring into a colander, return beans to pot, and set aside.

Fry chopped bacon in pan. Sauté onions and garlic in bacon grease. Drain off fat. Add bacon mixture to beans. Pour in enough water to cover beans with about 2 inches of water.

Cover pot. Cook slowly over low heat for 2 to 4 hours, or until beans are tender. Add beer, tomatoes, sugar, salt, chili powder, cilantro, oregano, cumin, and Tabasco sauce to taste, about 30 minutes before serving.

Makes 8 to 10 servings.

A Pint and a Gill

To give "a pint and a gill" was the landlord's equivalent to the baker's dozen. A gill was four ounces; thus this kind of a good deal was equal to a "heavy noggin" or a 20 percent bonus.

Rally Round the Flagon

Mention oak ships, stout-hearted men and a bottle of rum and, automatically, our imaginations flash to the romance of great voyages of discovery, sea battles, and the Spanish Main, when Blackbeard, Kidd, Sir Henry Morgan, and their ilk plied their nefarious trade. But was their "Yo Ho Ho" always followed by a swig of rum? Not by a long shot from a short cannon. You can bet your scuppers that they guzzled lots of beer and ale.

Why beer? Because it was generally important to a sailor's health and well-being, be he pirate, privateer, merchantman, or regular Navy. As the days out of sight of land became longer, food and water became more critical, particularly water — which has a habit of spoiling quickly at sea. Many of the early skippers carried a good supply of liquor and wine for this emergency. But those who sailed under the Union Jack discovered the glory of beer at sea. It not only lasted longer than water, it was less lethal than rum and contained a number of good things to combat scurvy. Beer has a variety of nutrients beneath the foam: carbohydrates, proteins and minerals, as well as B-complex vitamins — riboflavin, niacin, pantothenic acid, and pyridoxine.

The First Bottle of Beer

According to English legend, the first bottled of beer was accidentally discovered by Alexander Nowell, the Dean of St. Paul's. The year, 1563, was during the period of bloody religious persecution waged between Protestants and Catholics in England as ruling sovereigns, each with a faith and accompanying politics, changed.

While on a fishing expedition, Nowell received word that the authorities were after him. Pursued by the Catholic Bishop Bonner, he embarked forthwith on an extended continental tour, forgetting his lunch and some ale had carried along in a tightly corked bottle.

Six years later, when he returned to that part of England and quieter times, he chanced upon the same bottle, where it had been languishing beside the river. Out of curiosity, he uncorked it. "No bottle, but gun," he later wrote, so great was the sound at the moment. Fortunately, his curiosity carried him further. Much to his delight, when he sipped the contents, he discovered that maturity had greatly enhanced the brew.

"Bottling," since this serendipitous moment, has been an established method for convenient transportation of the brewer's art. It is also noted for its ability to add flavor and froth to good ale and beer.

Gather friends, pop those tops, and salute the gun!

Potato Casserole

The potato was brought from ancient Peru to Spain and Italy in the 1500s. Once across the Atlantic, however, "earth apples" didn't spread far for almost two centuries, partly because of human prejudice against new foods, but primarily because cooking methods of the times didn't do potatoes any favors. Few folks were thrilled with the taste of potatoes steeped in red wine, or baked with spices, or stewed with sweet relish.

Gradually the spud moved northward to Germany and Belgium, then on to England and Ireland, and finally to France and the American Colonies. Its route traces the politics and economics of Europe as much as the eating habits of people. The way of the potato was a path of necessity, following war, famine, poverty, and other social cataclysm.

Then the tuber came into its own. According to the International Potato Center, the population explosion of the 18th century was due to the potato's introduction. "Production from a small plot of ground provided enough food for a family and usually a surplus to sell. This made the Industrial Revolution possible."

Surely, if this recipe had been around then, spuds would have moved more speedily.

4	large potatoes, peeled and sliced fairly thin
2	large onions, peeled and sliced
2	cups celery, chopped
1	cup warm beer
1	cup chicken stock
¼	cup grated Parmesan cheese
½	cup dry bread crumbs
¼	cup butter
¼	teaspoon garlic powder
1	teaspoon salt
¼	teaspoon white pepper
	paprika
	flour

After slicing potatoes, layer them with the onion and celery in a 2-quart casserole dish. Sprinkle a little flour between each layer of potatoes. Combine warm beer, chicken stock, salt, and pepper. Pour liquid over vegetables.

Cover dish and bake in a 375-degree oven for 45 minutes to 1 hour, or until potatoes are tender when pierced with a fork.

Melt butter in a saucepan. Stir in bread crumbs, garlic powder, and Parmesan cheese. Uncover casserole. Sprinkle bread crumb mixture onto potatoes and dust with a little paprika. Bake another 10 minutes or so, or until bread crumbs are golden brown.

Serve hot with your favorite roast or thick ham slices. Makes 6 to 8 servings.

A Mouthful of Beer Proverbs

Wine is but single broth.
Ale is meat, drink, and cloth.   English.16th Century

Good ale will make a cat speak.   English

The mouth of a perfectly happy man is filled with beer.   Egyptian

A fine beer may be judged with only one sip, but it's better to be thoroughly sure.   Czech

I fear the man who drinks water and so remembers this morning what the rest of us said last night.   Greek

When There WAS a Free Lunch

The free lunch was an American innovation, combining hospitality and shrewd business acumen, that reached its zenith during the final years of the nineteenth century. First introduced in the West, the custom traveled east, until by 1900 there was no well-frequented saloon that did not boast a lavish assortment of grand food – not merely the happy-hour snacks and tidbits found today. For the price of a beer, five cents, one could dine regally; in fact, some of the finest chefs of the period happily contributed superb cuisine to these gastronomic indulgences.

According to the New York Daily Tribune, in 1896, "Millions were annually expended in this seeming gratuity, and over fifty thousand regulars depend upon what they gather from our counters for their daily subsistence."

One observer described the victuals at the Hotel Vendome, in New York, this way:

At the extreme end of the room, and separated from the bar by twenty or thirty feet, stands the free lunch counter, built of African marble and Mexican onyx! It is loaded with the most tempting food cooked by master hands.

The bill of fare at the famed Palace of Art, for instance, included cracked Dungeness crab, thick slices of Smithfield ham, beef stew and a wide assortment of cheeses, breads and other treats. Sadly, these luxuries of the fin-de-siècle are gone, victims of the temperance movement, Prohibition, and economics. Today we can only lament the passing of an elegant tradition from a more leisurely time.

Spuds Au Gratin

Potatoes have a complex history. When the Spaniards found the Indians of Peru munching them, in 1553, they mistakenly thought they were related to the sweet potato, and called them by the same name, *batata*. Later, the English claimed the plant had been brought to Europe by Sir Walter Raleigh from Virginia in 1596. Raleigh, however, never visited Virginia, nor are potatoes native to the area.

Originally, the word "spud" did not designate the vegetable, but a narrow spade used to pry them from their beds. Despite all these confusions, potatoes have changed our eating habits and even history itself. During the devastating "potato famine" in Ireland, between 1845 and 1847, many families immigrated to the United States, where their labor and tenacity helped link the two seaboards of a new nation with iron rails.

This uncomplicated method of serving potatoes adds a French touch with its crust of toasted almonds.

1 ½	pounds of frozen shredded hash-brown potatoes
1	can Cheddar cheese soup
¼	cup warm beer
½	cup dry bread crumbs
½	cup blanched almonds, chopped

Break up frozen potatoes and put them into a baking pan. Pour the beer over the potatoes. Bake in preheated 400-degree oven for 20 minutes.

Top potatoes with bread crumbs and nuts. Bake 15-20 minutes more, or until top is golden brown.

Makes 6 to 8 servings.

Old Ben's Elbow

In the musical play, "Ben Franklin in Paris," our most practical-minded Founding Father's thoughts inspired the song "God Bless the Human Elbow." According to Dr. Franklin, the design of the human arm by its Creator was indeed providential:

". . . if the elbow had been placed closer to the hand, the forearm would have been too short to bring the glass to the mouth; and if it had been closer to the shoulder, . . . the forearm would have been so long that it would have carried the glass beyond the mouth."

Oriental Fried Rice

Rice is essential to daily life in the Orient. In Java it is referred to as the "perfect food," a gift of the Hindu god Shiva. In Old China, about 2,000 years before the first Christians, the Emperor personally plowed three rows at planting time to ensure a bountiful harvest.

Even as valued as it is, plain boiled rice day after day takes its toll. Imaginative cooks, using a few leftovers here and there, have been offering us blessed variations such as this fried offering from the Middle Kingdom. Today one finds the descendants of basic fried rice from India and Japan to San Francisco and Mexico City.

2-3	cups cooked rice
½	small onion, chopped
½	bunch green onions, chopped
1	clove garlic, chopped
6	strips crisp bacon, crumbled
4-6	tablespoons warm beer
1	egg, beaten
1	teaspoon soy sauce
1	tablespoon butter

Cut bacon into small pieces. Brown slowly in a heavy skillet. Drain bacon on paper towels and set aside. Save drippings in skillet.

Place boiled rice, preferably a day or so old, in skillet, covering the bottom evenly with grains to keep grease and hot rice from splattering. Heat slowly until rice turns brown and a bit crispy. Don't burn it, but don't worry about overcooking it. A little liquid will make it tender again. Add chopped onion and garlic. Heat until onion just begins to turn color. Return bacon to skillet. Drop in chopped green onions.

Beat egg with one tablespoon of beer. Heat butter in a large frying pan. Pour in egg mixture so that is forms a thin omelet. Turn once to cook the other side. Cut into thin strips. Turn gently into the rice.

Just before serving, mix 1 teaspoon of soy sauce with 2-3 tablespoons of beer. Pour over hot rice mixture. Stir thoroughly. When steam dissipates, the rice is ready to serve.

Part of the fun of this dish, just like jazz, is the endless opportunities for variations. Try pork or beef strips, ham, shrimp, chopped green peppers or celery, water chestnuts, bean sprouts, black mushrooms, and the list goes on. Use your imagination while at the market, or just inventory the leftovers in the fridge.

Depending on what you add to the basic recipe, this is either a side dish for a wide array of entrees, or a stand-alone meal. For an Asian flavor, try some Sapporo beer.

Makes 4 to 5 servings.

Scholars' Theory Gauls Germans

Ancient Gaul, encompassing much of the territory that is now France, underwent a traumatic experience in 92 AD. When the population displeased the Roman Emperor Domitian, he ordered the grapevines in the area uprooted and forbade the planting of any new ones.

For almost 200 years, until the arrival of a later edict from Emperor Probus in 280, little or no wine found its way to the tables of the thirsty region. This incident likely accounts for the establishment of beer and the spread of brewing among the Celts, particularly in the northern parts where grapes never did that well anyway. Some modern scholars, extrapolating from this event, contend that brewing was introduced to Germany during that time by, of all people, the French.

Three Sheates to the Wind

The Outer Hebrides are islands located in the North Atlantic Ocean northwest of Scotland. In ancient times, chiefs and leading men of these rocky islands would gather to celebrate a sheate, a festival dedicated solely to eating and drinking ale. Each guest was provided with a large shell goblet that never ran dry because of attentive cup-bearers charged with the duty of seeing that no one lacked liquid refreshment.

Since these fêtes were of indeterminate duration, two husky men stood at the door with a wheelbarrow. Whenever anyone came out reeling from the effects, they loaded him into the barrow and wheeled him to a sleeping place. A stipulation accompanied this muscular hospitality, for when the celebrant woke up, if the sheate was still in progress he was expected to return and begin again.

Stuffed Tomatoes

Tomatoes journeyed from the New to the Old World in the 15th century. Almost immediately they became the center of folklore and controversy. For several centuries, in civilized places like England and the American Colonies, this exotic fruit was shunned as inedible, even poisonous. Thomas Jefferson, it's said, shocked his contemporaries by actually eating one in public.

In the romance-language countries, though, the "love apple" was taken to heart, described as the favorite food of Aphrodite and consumed (optimistically) as an aphrodisiac.

There is no record of who first decided to stuff a tomato, but the idea is highly civilized.

6	medium tomatoes
1	6-ounce can whole kernel corn, drained
1 ½	cups soft bread crumbs
½	small onion, chopped
1	cup sharp Cheddar cheese, grated
8	ounces warm beer
	salt and pepper

Slice tops from tomatoes. Scoop out inside of fruit, leaving a shell about ½ - inch thick. Sprinkle inside with salt and pepper to taste. Set aside.

Chop up tomato pulp. Drain off excess liquid. Add drained corn kernels, chopped onion, grated Cheddar cheese, and bread crumbs. Mix thoroughly. Spoon mixture into tomato shells.

Arrange stuffed tomatoes on greased baking pan. Spoon beer evenly over top of fruit. Bake in a 350-degree oven for 20 to 25 minutes, or until tomatoes are done and tops are lightly brown. Do not overcook.

Plan one stuffed tomato per happy diner.

Brussels Sprouts

Brussels sprouts, born of the European family of vegetables, are named after the capital of Belgium, close to where they originated. These aristocrats of the cabbage family, known since the 13th century, have a pronounced flavor that goes well with beer. Early descriptions of them were obviously made by botanists who had never seen the plant. One American scientist, writing in the early 1800's, speaks of the plant as a "thousand headed cabbage."

Cook them using this simple preparation and, if desired, enhance them with your favorite cream sauce.

10	ounces frozen Brussels sprouts, or 1 pound fresh
12	ounces warm beer
2	tablespoons butter
	salt and pepper

Boil sprouts in a combination of water and beer if they are fresh. If you're using the frozen, follow package directions, but substitute beer for water. Be careful not to overcook. When just barely tender, drain vegetables. Season with butter, salt and pepper.

For an unusual variation, add ¾ cup of seedless grapes. Cook both together. Another interesting way to serve them up is with crumbled bacon – about 6 slices should do – and 3 tablespoons of parsley as a garnish.

Finally, a cream sauce, a Bechamel, Mornay or Cheddar, makes a fine douse. Serve with your favorite meal and, if you can find it, some Belgian Jupiler lager.

Makes 4-6 servings.

Heather Ale

There is a legend among the Scots that there once existed a recipe for a brew that surpassed all praise. Robert Louis Stevenson describes it this way in his poem "Heather Ale: A Galloway Legend."

> From the bonny bells of heather,
> They brewed a drink langsyne,
> Was sweeter far than honey,
> Was stronger far than wine.

Heather ale was the secret of the Picts, who were wiped out by the Scots in the 6th century A.D. According to the story, which has more interest as a tale than historical validity, the conquering Scottish king offered the last of the Picts his life and freedom for the recipe of the famous brew. The old man chose death; so, as an 18th century writer laments, "the secret of preparing it perished with them."

Candied Sweet Potatoes

Yams or sweet potatoes were cultivated in North and South America long before Europeans arrived in their "floating houses" and "long canoes." There is some difference of opinion about exactly what happened next: One version has the Spanish carrying the tasty item back to Europe; another claims that slavers from Senegal brought it to Africa first, calling it *nyami* – their word for "eat" – which became our "yam."

Possibly both stories are true. But regardless of where and when they traveled, yams thrive in subtropical soil, so they soon became a staple in both the European and African diet, just as they had been in the New World.

In America, sweet potatoes, especially the candied kind, have become associated with holidays and festive tables.

2	pounds sweet potatoes
4	ounces brown sugar
8	ounces dark ale
2	teaspoons grated orange rind
½	teaspoon salt
½	teaspoon ground ginger

Wash sweet potatoes. Cook in boiling water until tender, but still firm. Cool, peel and cut in slices about ½-inch thick. Arrange in a shallow baking dish. Note: if you're in a rush, you can use canned sweet potatoes.

Mix brown sugar, orange rind, salt and ginger with beer.

Heat in a sauce pan over a low flame until sugar melts, stirring continuously.

Pour sauce over sweet potatoes. Bake in a 400-degree oven for 20 minutes, or until brown. Turn once.

Makes 6 to 8 servings.

From the Wood

This old term refers to the procedure of drawing beer directly from the keg, without the use of beer engines or gas pressure.

Mandarin Carrots

Variety was not a conspicuous quality in medieval European bills of fare. The foods they ate were often as not subject to the ravages of travel and storage. Spices, from abroad, were highly valued because they disguised the all too familiar and sometimes less than fresh smell of local food.

Vegetables such as carrots became staples because they were common and they kept all winter long. They were also thought to cure many common ills. It is not surprising to find that when oranges arrived from China, via India with their festive aura and complimentary coloring, they were joined with carrots to make this glazed holiday dish.

2	10-ounce packages frozen carrots
4-6	ounces brown sugar
3	ounces warm beer
2	tablespoons butter
1	12-ounce can mandarin oranges, drained

Prepare frozen carrots as directed on package, using butter and beer instead of water. When tender, stir in the sugar and at the last minute, just before serving, stir in the orange slices.

Makes 6 servings as a side dish with meat, poultry or fish.

Charlemagne the Great on Beer Policy

The Emperor Charlemagne, who began his long reign in 768 A.D., had numerous estates, run by his vassals, each with a brewery. For his vassals he set forth detailed sets of rules, Capitulare Caroli Magni de Villis, for running his estates – rules on all aspects of estate management – and he did not skimp on brewing directions. A sampling follows:

"The administrators must ensure that workers who use their hands in the preparation of beer keep themselves particularly clean." ("Employees using the rest room must wash hands thoroughly before returning to work." Sound familiar?)

When Charles the Great visited an estate, the vassal had to bring out the best: "We wish that the intendant on duty bring before Our Person samples of beer. We also wish that they bring along their brewmaster so that they can brew for Us good beer in Our presence."

"We also wish that our intendants compose an annual inventory ledger at Christmas time. We also want a list of the beers they brew so that we know which quantities of the different products are available." This is an annual report. There weren't any CPAs in the 8th century, but there could certainly be an audit!

Baked Red Onions

By about 25,000 B.C. hunters had learned to freeze or dry meat to preserve it, while gatherers had learned what was safe to consume. Early man pretty much ate what was available. When times were hard and the weather worse, onions and turnips were everyone's bulwark against starvation. Root vegetables stayed in the garden longer, protected by the soil from extremes of heat and cold, and in winter they could be stored in a cellar.

Cooking was another story. Meat was grilled on a stick, or roasted. Vegetables were just placed on flat rocks near the fire. What wouldn't our earliest ancestors have done for a grill and a bit of aluminum foil?

6	medium red onions
8	ounces warm beer
3	ounces butter
2-3	dashes garlic salt
2-3	dashes Angostura bitters
	salt and pepper

Wash and peel onions. Marinate them in beer for at least 1 hour before cooking. Turn once in a while so they have a chance to absorb the barley/hop flavor evenly.

Cut a cross in the top of each onion, about ¾ inch deep. Place 1 tablespoon of butter in the slits. Dust with garlic powder, salt and pepper to taste. Sprinkle with a few drops of bitters.

Wrap each onion separately in its own piece of aluminum foil. Place on grill over coals for 10 to 15 minutes, or in a 400-degree oven for 30 to 40 minutes. The cooking times may vary depending on the size of the onions, so check for doneness before serving. If you're having a cookout or barbecue, be sure to use heavy-duty foil.

Plan one onion per person.

A Bumper of Ale, Sir?

"Bumper" is a word associated with the English, with numerous rounds of toasts to various people's health, and with foaming mugs of nut-brown ale. Actually, the word is a corruption of a special custom observed by many Catholics in olden times, who, at the end of a meal, often rose and drank a toast to the Pope, _au bon Père_.

Breaded Eggplant

Many American cooks pass over this unusual visitor from India because they think it tastes bitter. To acquire an eggplant habit, begin with a simple recipe like this one. You will quickly discover why it's a fixture throughout Asia Minor, Turkey, Greece and the Balkans. When you're hooked, you can add to your collection of baked, fried and stewed eggplant dishes; there are even a couple of recipe books around devoted entirely to this colorful, rotund, fruitlike vegetable.

1	medium eggplant, peeled and sliced
1	egg, beaten well
½	cup warm beer
½	cup dry bread crumbs
¼	cup cooking oil
2	tablespoons grated Parmesan cheese
2	tablespoons salt (optional)
	salt and pepper

Peel eggplant and cut into ½ -inch slices. Stack the slices on a flat plate, lightly salting each layer. Next place a second plate on top of the slices with a light weight, to keep a gentle pressure on the fruit. Allow this construction to rest in the refrigerator for an hour or so. Pour off the brackish liquid that forms and dry the slices thoroughly. This salting and pressing step removes bitterness and makes the eggplant absorb less oil during cooking.

Set three plates by the stove. Pour warm beer into the first, the beaten egg into the second and the bread crumbs, mixed with the Parmesan cheese, into the third. Dip both sides of eggplant slices into beer, the egg, and, finally, the bread crumbs to coat. Drop slices – gently, so they don't splatter – into medium hot oil. Fry 5-7 minutes per side, until golden brown. Avoid overcooking. Drain off excess oil on paper towels. The eggplant should be firm, not soggy, when served. Keep hot in oven.

Dust with salt and pepper to taste. Breaded eggplant goes well with most meat and poultry, especially lamb and chicken.

Makes 4 servings.

Penalty Horns

The Edda, a 9th century collection of Northern European mythology, describes many curious German beer conventions and customs. If a warrior violated one of these, he was required to expiate the offense by emptying a special cup, reserved for such occasions.

Penalty horns, as they were called, often contained two quarts or more and had to be downed in one or two swallows for the offender to regain his status and not be marked as a weakling.

Red Cabbage

This slow-cooker recipe is a Dutch or German dish.

1	small head red cabbage, finely shredded
2	apples, peeled and sliced
¼	onion, thinly sliced
4	ounces warm beer
2	ounces vinegar
1 ½	tablespoons sugar
2	tablespoons butter
1	dash ground cloves
½	teaspoon of lemon juice

Get out the crockpot. Shred the cabbage. Pour some boiling water over the cabbage and drain it. Place the ingredients in the crockpot in this order: cabbage, apple and onion slices, beer, vinegar, sugar, butter, ground cloves, and lemon juice. (The lemon juice helps the cabbage retain most of its rich color.)

Cover with lid. Set selector for low heat and forget for 3 to 4 hours. Just before serving, stir in a little more butter. In Germany, this is served as a traditional companion to duck, pork, and goose.

Makes 4 to 6 servings.

Middle Ages Staple

Beer provided a considerable proportion of people's daily calories in medieval northern and eastern Europe. Beer was drunk daily at all meals by all social classes. Since water was often contaminated and foul, alcoholic drinks were safer because boiling was part of the brewing process. In England, Belgium, and the Netherlands, per-capita beer consumption was over sixty gallons a year by about 1500. Preparing for Lent, German monks made sure that their beer was hearty and heavy. With its complex carbohydrates and the satisfying way it sat on the stomach, beer took the place of bread during Lenten fasting.

Southern Europeans and Arabs, able to grow grapes in their more temperate climate, were comfortable with wine and mostly unacquainted with beer. Thus, the disrepute of beer among physicians, both those of ancient Greece and their successors, the Moorish doctors of the Middle Ages. One 13th-century Arab physician damned beer with this faint praise: "But from whichever it is made, whether from oats, barley or wheat, it harms the head and the stomach, it causes bad breath and ruins the teeth, it fills the stomach with bad fumes, and as a result anyone who drinks it along with wine becomes drunk quickly; but it does have the property of facilitating urination and makes one's flesh white and smooth."

CHAPTER SEVEN

THE SANDWICH CONNECTION: FROM SNACK TO BANQUET

Broiled Hamburgers

Great Hamburgers

Salisbury Steak

Smithfield Special

Coney Island Franks

Prairie Dog Sandwiches

Red Hots and Kraut

Bratwurst in Ale

Barbecue Pork Sandwiches

Barbecue Beef Sandwiches

Reuben Sandwiches

The Queen of Denver

Grilled Cheese on Rye

Saucy Steak Sandwich

Broiled Hamburgers

Ground beef, using smaller pieces of meat that might normally be considered waste, has been a staple in lower-income diets for centuries.

The name hamburger, though, is of more recent origin, originating on the New York waterfront, where German sailors asked for their meat Hamburg style. In 1904 at the St. Louis Exposition, grilled hamburgers were introduced. They proved an instant success. By the 1920's America's love affair with the beef patty bloomed as hundreds of hamburger chains sprang up across the nation.

The "double burger with everything" was a cultural icon in Southern California in the 1950's. This burger, in a scene with drive-ins, car hops, and cars, cars, cars – hot-rods and customs – became the touchstone of teenagers' existence. It's hard to imagine driving in your chopped deuce to your favorite joint on a Friday night to get a mere toasted cheese sandwich.

2	pounds ground beef
2	slices day-old rye bread
1	medium onion, minced
½	cup warm beer
½	teaspoon ground sage
½	teaspoon salt
½	teaspoon fresh ground black pepper
8	hamburger buns

Trim crusts from bread and discard. Crumble slices into mixing bowl. Cover with warm beer. Let stand until liquid is absorbed. Mix in ground beef, minced onion, sage, salt and pepper. Form into eight generous patties. Stack in the refrigerator for about an hour – this gives the flavors time to blend.

Grill to taste – rare to overdone – in oven broiler or over hot coals for a classic summer barbecue. Toast buns at the same time.

Serve hot. Offer your own special add-ons: Sliced tomatoes, sliced onion, lettuce, soft cheese, ketchup, mustard, mayo, olives or olive tapenade, sweet relish, or any other delectable sandwich addition.

Don't forget the beer.

Makes 8 generous hamburgers.

Great Hamburgers

The story of Angostura – orange bitters – began in Venezuela in 1824, when a German doctor developed a compound of native herbs and spices, including the blossom of the white gentian, for his ailing wife. Sailors, visiting the harbor of Angostura, heard about the remedy and discovered that it was also an excellent cure for seasickness.

In the course of spreading its medical fame to all the ports of the world, a few braver souls experimented with a few drops in their rum. That altered the course of bitters forever; it soon became the essential ingredient in the Manhattan cocktail. And don't be surprised if someday you hear a wise old bartender prescribing soda and bitters for a queasy stomach.

Only recently have bitters been recruited to add their unique contribution to food. Here's an easy open-faced, drippy hamburger that will add variety to summer or winter meals.

1	pound lean ground beef
¾	cup quick-cooking rolled oats
1	clove minced garlic
2	tablespoons ketchup
4	ounces warm beer or ale
1	teaspoon salt
1	teaspoon Angostura bitters
8	hamburger buns

Mix the first seven ingredients thoroughly in a bowl.

Cut buns in half. Toast briefly, cut side up, under broiler.

Distribute the meat mixture among them. Place on a cookie sheet or rack. Slide under the broiler for 8 to 10 minutes, or until done to taste.

Serve hot with a relish plate of fresh sliced vegetables, a favorite dunking dip, and some Miller High Life.

Makes 8 servings.

Salisbury Steak

When the Tartars swept out of the Russian Steppes in the 13th century, they subsisted on food that was quick to prepare, since they often ate on horseback. These energetic warriors were particularly fond of chopped meat, seasoned with onion juice and spices, that they often wolfed down raw – we call this version Tartar Steak. As the idea spread from the Balkans to greater Europe, less active folks began to fry the meat, or at least sear it on the outside.

It was the peoples of Great Britain, the English and the Irish, who began frying the meat through thoroughly, culminating in the efforts of one Dr. James H. Salisbury, who in 1888 prescribed it to his patients three times a day – preceded and followed by a glass of (what a crying shame!) hot water.

During the First World War, the name Salisbury Steak replaced the German-sounding name "hamburger" in the Allied countries. Fortunately, we've called them "hamburgers" again for a good 50 years. Fortunately too, we can pass up the hot water in favor of beer.

1 ½	pounds ground beef
½	cup chili sauce
½	cup warm beer or ale
3	tablespoons water
2	teaspoons salt
1	tablespoon butter
1	teaspoon sugar
¼	teaspoon black pepper, freshly ground
1	teaspoon Worcestershire sauce
	Tabasco sauce

Lightly mix together the ground beef, 1 teaspoon of salt, the pepper, and the water. Form into 6 to 8 patties. Heat butter in frying pan. An old, well-cured black iron skillet with a heavy bottom works well. Brown meat on both sides. Do not cook thoroughly now. Set pan aside when done.

Mix together the beer, the remaining salt, the chili, Worcestershire and Tabasco sauces, and sugar. Pour this mixture over the meat patties. Return pan to heat. Cook to your pleasure, about 5 minutes more. NOTE: Save the sauce. It makes a nice, hot on-the-table relish. Serve the burgers in buns with hot potato salad and crisp bottles of beer.

These burgers are also great without buns as a meat dish. If this is your choice, add lots of sauce, fried onions, mashed potatoes, and creamed peas. Drink some Watney's Red Barrel.

If you plan two Salisbury steaks per customer, this recipe serves from 3 to 4.

Smithfield Special

Now, this may sound like the name of a police show, but Smithfield, Virginia, has been internationally celebrated for its fine hams for centuries. And what's better than a juicy ham sandwich?

1   slice of smoked ham, sandwich-size, ¼ - ½ -inch thick
1   clove fresh garlic
8   ounces room-temperature ale

Rub the inside of a frying pan with garlic. Slide in one ham slice for each sandwich. Pour in beer. Cover with a lid. Bring to a boil, reduce heat, and simmer 15-20 minutes.

Remove ham hunks. Nestle between slices of fresh cut bread. Cover with Dusseldorf mustard. Add a crisp new pickle to munch and a bottle of Heineken to sip. This is the life!

Ale in Song and Verse

This drinking song in praise of ale came from a 17th -century play:

Submit, Bunch of Grapes,
To the strong Barley ear;
The weak wine no longer
The laurel shall wear.

Sack, and all drinks else,
Desist from the strife:
Ale's the only Aqua Vitae,
And liquor of life.

Then come my boon fellows,
Let's drink it around,
It keeps us from grave,
Though it lays us on ground.

Ale's a Physician,
No Mountebank Bragger
Can cure the chill Ague
Though it be with the Stagger.

Ale's a strong Wrestler,
Flings all it hath met;
And makes the ground slipp'ry,
Though it be not wet.

Ale is both Ceres
And good Neptune too,
Ale's froth was the sea,
From which Venus grew.

Ale is immortal
And be there no stops
In bonny lad's quaffing
Can live without hops.

Then come my boon fellows,
Let's drink it around,
It keeps us from grave,
Though it lays us on ground.

Coney Island Franks

The American hotdog is associated with many pleasures of life – summertime, pool parties, baseball, and bowl games.

Hotdogs got their name at the name at the New York Polo Grounds. The year was 1905 and Harry K. Stevens, a well-known concessionaire, was selling hot frankfurters on a bun. One cold day, he told his hawkers to yell, "Get your red hots here!" T.A. "Tad" Dorgan, the famed sports journalist, was also there that day. In his column, he whimsically characterized the "red hots" as an elongated bun containing a dachshund.

From there, sports fans caught by the fun of the allusion and the peculiarity of the word "dachshund," quickly picked up the phrase "hot dog." The name entered our slang and spread from ball parks to picnics to carnivals. Here's the way some old timers insist traditional "red hot dachshunds" must be served – Coney Island style.

1	pound frankfurters, scored
1	small onion, sliced very thin
12	ounces warm beer
1	jar pickle relish or sliced fresh pickles of your choice
1	jar mustard (basic yellow is considered the most authentic)
6-8	hot dog buns

Prepare the franks by scoring them. This is not a detail to simply make them look nice; it's important for holding the various condiments in place. Begin by cutting a continuous spiral, about ⅛ -inch deep, along the entire length of the meat with a sharp paring knife. For another variation, cut a series of tiny notches along the four sides of the wiener, with a couple of cross-cuts on the ends.

Place the scored franks in a bowl with the beer and sliced onion. Cover. Allow to marinate in the refrigerator for at least 3 hours, or even better, overnight.

Grill in the oven, on a hibachi or barbecue, or over an open fire. Slide into bun and lace with goodies. You may want to toast the bun with the franks, or, if you want to serve them New York style, use a "virgin" bun – unheated.

Serve with whatever makes a picnic memorable, but especially potato chips and a fine Big Apple beer, like Gennesee Cream Ale.

Prairie Dog Sandwiches

Among the legendary peace officers of the old west, Wyatt Earp and Bat Masterson stand tall. They were close friends but disagreed on one point, whether to give lessons on shooting a six-gun.

Earp was against helping anyone – who just might be a future foe – learn anything about their esoteric craft. Masterson, though, would teach students for $25.00 a day. His rules were simplicity itself: Shoot first, aim at the belt buckle, and don't miss.

When not taming towns, according to at least two unreliable sources, he liked to eat hot dogs prepared this way. Although everybody called them prairie dog sandwiches, they bear no resemblance to small social burrowing mammals. Maybe Masterson himself was the old prairie dog.

1	pound frankfurters
12	ounces warm beer
3-4	teaspoons ground sage
3-4	teaspoons prepared mustard
1	fresh dill pickle, sliced thin
1	ounce Worcestershire sauce
6-8	hot dog buns

Split franks almost all the way through, lengthwise. Marinate in the beer and pickle slices for three hours or so. Dry meat and fold each frank open. Rub inside of split with lots of ground sage. Broil in the oven or on the grill, about 3 inches from the flame.

Split buns down the middle. On one side spread mustard and on the other Worcestershire sauce. Line with marinated pickle slices. Slip broiled meat into place and fold shut.

For a variation, fill the franks with drained sauerkraut instead of the sage just before broiling.

Serve with tall glasses of Rocky Mountain Kool-Aid (that's Coors, to lowlanders), or Lone Star beer.

Makes 6 to 8 prairie dog sandwiches.

Red Hots and Kraut

This traditional combination, celebrated in song and story, was originally introduced in a Coney Island beer garden over a century ago. Its inventor, Charles Feltman, was a newly arrived German butcher who was an expert in the old-world arts of sausage making.

For the first few decades of its existence, the frankfurter was served on a hard roll. It didn't ally with the soft bun until the St. Louis Exposition in 1904. Renamed the hot dog, this peculiar culinary delight reached its epicurean zenith a number of years later when Eleanor Roosevelt served them at Hyde Park to King George VI and Queen Elizabeth.

1	pound frankfurters
8	ounces warm beer or ale
16	ounces water
1	1-pound can sauerkraut
6-8	hot dog buns
¼	teaspoon caraway seeds (optional)
1	small onion, chopped (optional)

Pour water and beer into a sauce pan. Add caraway seeds and franks. Cover with a lid. Heat slowly and remove with tongs. Do not boil vigorously nor pierce with a fork.

Open and drain the can of sauerkraut. Pour kraut into a sauce pan with just enough beer to cover it. Simmer slowly for about 15 minutes.

Place the meat on a hot dog bun with a heap of sauerkraut on top. Now sprinkle with chopped onion and a spoonful of hot mustard. Back it up with the most famous St. Louis beer of them all, Budweiser – it's not too late to celebrate the 1904 Exposition – or a crisp German lager.

You can improve the flavor of Knockwurst, Polish or Vienna sausage, or any similar meat, by preparing it this way in beer.

Makes 6 to 8 kraut dogs.

Bratwurst in Ale

The idea of smoking or salting meat to preserve it goes back at least to the ancient Egyptians. We know the Greek employed the process, for in 423 B.C. the comic playwright Aristophanes has one of his outrageous characters in the satire "The Clouds" offer to educate the youth in this novel manner: "Let them make sausages of me and serve me up to the students."

The Romans also enjoyed eating sausages, but it is the Germans that we must chiefly thank for serving up the many and diverse varieties we enjoy today.

1	pound bratwurst
1	medium onion, minced
12	ounces warm beer or ale
4	tablespoons butter
1	bay leaf
2	tablespoons flour
	salt and pepper

Prick skin of each bratwurst. Drop into a skillet, with enough water to cover. Simmer for 5-10 minutes. Pour off liquid. Add 3 tablespoons of butter. Brown the sausage.

Pour in beer or ale, add bay leaf, and bring to a boil. Cover skillet and reduce heat. Simmer for about 20-25 minutes. Remove lid and continue to simmer until half the liquid is gone.

In another pan melt the remaining tablespoon of butter. Add minced onion. Sauté until lightly brown. Stir in flour. Simmer over low heat for a few minutes. Pour remaining liquid from bratwurst into flour mixture, stir until smooth, and allow to thicken. Add salt and pepper to taste.

Split bratwurst. Place on bread. Pour sauce on each brat. Serve with a fine savory potato salad - and a "Cool Blonde," a name given to the traditional Dortmunder style beers like DAB.

Makes 4 servings.

High Society
At a celebration given in 1575 in honor of Queen Elizabeth I of England, 23,000 gallons of beer were consumed. Imperial gallons, to be sure!

148

Barbecue Pork Sandwiches

What do barbecue and buccaneer have in common? They were originally different words for the same thing, that open-fire meat-cooking device early explorers and privateers found Haitian natives using. The Spanish called the device a *barbacoa*, while the French used the word *boucan*, which entered English as our word "buccaneer."

12-15	slices leftover roast pork
1/2	cup finely chopped onion
1/4	cup cider vinegar
3/4	teaspoon liquid smoke
1/4	teaspoon celery seeds
1	cup tomato catsup
8	ounces warm beer
2	tablespoons brown sugar
1	teaspoon paprika
8	drops hot pepper sauce
5-6	hard rolls, cut lengthwise
5-6	tablespoons butter, softened

Mix chopped onion, vinegar, liquid smoke, celery seeds, catsup, beer, brown sugar, paprika and hot pepper sauce in a sauce pan. Simmer 15 minutes or so, until flavors blend. Do not boil! Drop slices of pork into skillet on low heat. Pour sauce over meat. Heat but don't boil.

Butter the rolls. Brown slightly in oven. Place pork slices on bread. Spoon on some sauce. Serve open- or closed-face with a relish plate of raw vegetables and siedels of cold beer.

Makes 5 to 6 sandwiches.

Bottles, Barrels, Cans, and Box-o'-Beer

Ancient imbibers kept their beer in pretty much anything concave that didn't leak faster than they could drink. Their earthenware pots, skin bags, and hollowed-out gourds didn't do much for preservation or long-term storage. Beer is fragile and tough to stabilize because ambient air is full of wild microbes that can make it go bad. Barrels made of wooden slats and hoops were an improvement because they were sturdy and could be sealed and transported. Wood barrels prevailed till the 20th century introduced metal barrels.

Bottles for beer were hand-blown flasks before manufacturers standardized size and shape and made bottles using molds. The realization that clear glass turned beer skunky led to the prevalence of brown and green bottles, and pasteurization finally tamed the problems of most wild microbes. Cans are more popular at present than glass beer bottles, but some small breweries now even sell beer in corrugated boxes lined with a fitted plastic container.

Barbecue Beef Sandwiches

If you want the reputation of a great outdoor cook who can also feed a small army, keep this one handy. It's easy and adaptable: If your dinner choice is Mexican, add a snappy salsa, or for an old-hickory touch, use catsup and a dash of liquid smoke. Variations are simple and numerous.

3-4	pounds beef brisket
1	14-ounce bottle of (your choice) barbecue sauce, Mexican salsa, or catsup
12	ounces warm beer
20-24	slices of bread, OR
10-12	French rolls (if you serve the sandwiches open-face, you need only 5-6)

Trim excess fat from meat. Cut into thick slices – 4 to 5 inches thick. Drop meat into a slow cooker or crock pot. Add beer and catsup, or other sauce. Cover. Simmer slowly for 8 to 10 hours at about 250 degrees (low) until meat is tender when pierced with a fork.

Remove beef from pot. Allow to cool a few minutes. Shred with a fork. Save the sauce. Toast bread or rolls. Spread with a generous layer of shredded meat. Top with a couple of tablespoons of warm sauce.

Serve with a tossed salad, chili beans and a cold tapper of Budweiser.

Makes 10 to 12 healthy servings.

The First Brewers' Trademark

Historically, English documents suggest that the small red triangle, the world-famous Bass Ale logo, was the first registered trademark in the world. It was officially certified as a designation for the pale ale in 1876, a full hundred years after the founding of the company by William Bass. Maybe it represented an Egyptian pyramid – ancient civilizations all around the Mediterranean built monuments and drank beer while doing so, and Bassareus was a name given to one of their beer gods – or maybe it was just a convenient shipping mark of the day.

This sturdy symbol of a fine brew was immortalized a few years later by the French impressionist Manet in his 1882 painting of a comely bartender at the Folies-Bergères.

Reuben Sandwiches

Nebraskans and New Yorkers both claim the origin of the Reuben sandwich for their state. Nebraskans say an Omaha man named Reuben Kulakofsky invented the sandwich in the 1920s for his poker buddies. Manhattanites say the sandwich first appeared in Manhattan's Reuben restaurant, which closed in the 1960s. Whatever its origin, the sandwich is delicious! Even people who dislike sauerkraut and corned beef agree that combining them with nutty-flavored cheese, rye bread, and dressing yields a dish fit for gods.

Okay, there's no beer in this recipe, but there's beer in every single other recipe in this cookbook. This is, however, the world's best sandwich to eat *with* beer.

3	cups sauerkraut
24	slices cooked corned beef
12	slices Jarlberg or Swiss cheese
1	cup Thousand Island or Russian dressing
18	slices dark rye bread
2	dozen wooden toothpicks
4-6	tablespoons butter

Spread 6 slices of bread with dressing. Place a slice of cheese, 2 slices of beef and about ¼ cup of sauerkraut on each. Spread dressing on both sides of another 6 slices of bread, and lay them on your first 6 slices. Atop these stacks build another layer of meat, cheese and kraut. Cover the edifice with the last slices of bread spread with dressing.

Secure each sandwich with long toothpicks. Spread outside with butter. Grill sandwiches in an iron skillet until heated all the way through and the cheese starts to melt. Cut diagonally in three places, leaving at least one pick in each section. (Make sure your eaters can see the picks.)

Serve with crisp Kosher dills, a little coleslaw and a bottle or three of Western Australian Swan beer.

Makes 6 large sandwiches.

Special Delivery

When the first railroad train in Germany ran from Nürnberg to Fürth in 1835, its only cargo was two kegs of beer.

Once Upon a Riddle

"What is it that walks on four legs in the morning, two legs at noon, and three legs in the evening?" the Sphinx asked unwary Theban travelers. When they couldn't answer the riddle correctly, she killed them. One day, of course, she met the wise young Oedipus, who promptly answered "man." And, even while he was explaining the ages of man (four legs as a crawling child, two as an adult, and three in old age, when walking with the aid of a stick), the contrite monster, the terrorizer of cities, politely did herself in — some say because of a long-standing pact with the gods, and others because of Oedipus' long-windedness.

Now, try this one. "What is not alive, but stands on one foot?" This is another old riddle based on the potter's name for the bottom of a bowl or jug, a "foot." So if you answered "my beer mug or glass," you're safe. Not to worry about a Sphinx getting you.

Does anything stand on "no feet?" Be careful! If you say "nothing" you might end up in a metaphysical argument about the nature of reality. A safer response would be the same as above, "my beer mug." In the 16th and 17th centuries most land travelers went via coaches, which rocked and creaked over poor roads and through inclement weather, stopping periodically at inns and taverns to change horses and allow the battered passengers a few moments' respite. To keep the occupants from dawdling when the coach horn sounded, they were served their beer and ale in specially designed "coach glasses" that had no foot. Thus drinkers were not tempted to put the pint down and rest between draughts. It was drink and be gone or — as was known to happen — be left behind.

Another special glass on these occasions was the "yard of ale," an extremely long-necked vessel that was handed up to the coachman in the box. It too was without a foot.

What about today? Are you safe from these ploys? By and large, yes, but, human nature being what it is, be on guard. When on the road, traveler, be wary. If you're ever offered a choice between a coach glass full of flat beer and a yard of ale, there is no riddle. Take the ale.

After all, no one can stand the first, while the second always has three feet.

The Queen of Denver

Sometimes called a Western Sandwich, this many-versioned favorite isn't just something to slap between two slices of bread. Think of it rather as a symphony of culinary imagination. The exact origin of the treat is disputed, but it was most likely the product of a Chinese cook, hired to feed hungry miners, gandy dancers and timber jacks during the explosive expansion period of the American West. It was called a "Denver" probably because that was where Easterners, traveling by train, got their first taste of the West.

This is a good recipe to experiment with, so try adding some of your favorites – bacon, a bit of sausage, mushrooms, slices of franks, tomatoes, cheese, avocados, cheese, ripe olives or whatever you find loose.

¼	cup chopped green pepper
¼	cup chopped onion
2-3	eggs, beaten
¼	cup ham chunks
2	tablespoons cold beer
2	tablespoons butter
4	slices bread
	hot pepper sauce
	salt and pepper

Melt the butter in any large frying pan or skillet. Sauté onions with green peppers until soft. Add ham and heat thoroughly.

Beat eggs with cold beer. Pour over warm onions, peppers and ham. Do not stir. Allow to brown on one side. Turn once. Season to taste with pepper sauce, salt and pepper.

When done, divide and place between slices of bread. Or, if the sun has just come up, serve as an omelet with buttered slices of toast on the side. When in its sandwich manifestation, serve with cold cans of Coors.

Makes 2 sandwiches or 1 omelet.

Grilled Cheese on Rye

Full-flavored pumpernickel bread forms the base for this tasty sandwich.

Ever wonder how that bread got such a peculiar name? There are at least three theories. (1) A French horseman was offered the bread and disdainfully said it was good food for his horse, Nicol: *pain pour Nicol*. Probably not true. (2) *Pumpern* was an old German word for breaking wind, and Old Nick was the devil. So – pumpernickel was the devil's fart. Probably equally untrue. (3) *Pumpernickel* was a common German insult meaning a lout, a booby, or a jerk. But why attach the name to a delicious dark sourdough?

The Oxford English Dictionary doesn't vote with either of the first two theories. It nods briefly at the third, but concludes "origin uncertain."

1	pound sharp Cheddar cheese, grated
½	teaspoon garlic powder
4	ounces warm beer
½	teaspoon dry mustard
6-8	slices pumpernickel
6-8	slices bacon (optional)
1	sliced tomato (optional)
	paprika
	salt and pepper

Combine grated cheese, garlic powder and dry mustard with beer to form a thick paste. Add salt and pepper to taste. Spread mixture heavily on slices of bread. Dust top with paprika.

Broil in oven until cheese melts and turns bubbly. Watch carefully.

Add slices of crisp bacon and/or tomato if desired. Serve with a reliable English brew, like John Courage.

Makes a snappy snack or lunch for 4.

Beere in Shakespeare's Time

By far the most popular drinks in the 16th and 17th century England, on all levels of society, were beer and ale, which "beare the greatest brunt of drinking." According to William Harrison in 1587, "There is such headie ale and beere in most [markets and fairs], as for the mightinesse thereof among such as seeke it out is commonlie called huffecap, the mad dog, father whoresonne, angels food, dragons milke, go by the wall, stride wide, lift leg, &c. . . ."

Saucy Steak Sandwich

The sandwich was developed by John Montagu, Fourth Earl of Sandwich, an inveterate gambler. One evening in the late 18th century, at the height of a particularly interesting game, he was annoyed at the thought of having to stop to eat, so he called for a slice of beef, which he ate between two slices of bread.

The beef sandwich offered here does require a knife and fork. Even though it does not leave any hands free to hold cards, it is not a gamble in good taste.

4	beef eye-of-round steaks, ½ inch thick
4	slices light rye bread
1	cup grated Cheddar cheese
1	cup warm beer or ale
2	tablespoons butter
2	tablespoons flour
1	teaspoon sugar
¼	teaspoon dry mustard
⅛	teaspoon thyme
8	slices tomato
	salt and pepper to taste

Melt butter in a sauce pan. Stir in flour, mustard, thyme, sugar, salt and pepper, and beer. Heat, stirring continuously, until mixture thickens. Reduce heat and add cheese. Continue stirring until cheese melts and sauce is smooth. Set aside in a warm place.

Grill, broil or pan-fry steak. Dust with salt and pepper. Turn once and cook until done to taste. Butter bread and toast on grill or under broiler.

Serve steaks on toast. Top with sliced tomatoes and cheese sauce. Serve with a pint of good English ale or bitter such as Ben Truman – or Bass, perhaps.

Makes 4 servings.

CHAPTER EIGHT

DISHES WITH CHEESE AND EGGS

Spanish Omelet

Egg Foo Young

Huevos Rancheros

Eggs Parmesan

Gascony Fried Eggs

Creole Soufflé

Eggs Provençal

Baked Eggs Español

Welsh Rabbit

Heathen Welsh Hare

Alpine Fondue

Spanish Omelet

First, there is nothing Spanish about a Spanish omelet. It was developed in the Old West, somewhere in the area bounded by Texas, Colorado and California, from a panful of available whatevers by a grizzled cook, often referred to as a bean-master or biscuit-shooter. This particular version contains tomatoes and sour cream, ingredients rarely found in chuck wagons – but you wouldn't want to be so foolishly authentic as to leave them out. If you want to try a Mexican omelet, add chopped chilis – the amount and type of chili used will determine the basic fire quotient.

The word "omelet" in English, or *omelette*, in French, originated with the Latin *lamella*, meaning a small plate. Would I lie to you?

1	medium onion, sliced thin
¼	cup chopped green pepper
5	tablespoons butter
¼	cup sour cream
1	chopped tomato with seeds removed
½	teaspoon dill weed
	salt and pepper
6	eggs, beaten
2	tablespoons cold beer
4-6	sprigs parsley
10-12	black olives (optional)

Peel onion. Slice very thin. Separate into rings. Sauté briefly in butter with green pepper until onions are tender but still slightly crisp. Add sour cream, tomatoes, dill weed, and ¼ teaspoon of salt and pepper. Stir together thoroughly. Set aside in a warm place. Wash skillet to remove any salt residue.

Melt remaining butter in skillet. Beat eggs with cold beer. Pour quickly into bubbling pan. Cook on medium heat until eggs begin to set on bottom. Now, using the tines of a fork, raise the edges of the omelet and allow the uncooked portion to run underneath.

Spoon onion mixture onto half the omelet when almost done. Fold the remaining side over the top. Check doneness by piercing with a sharp knife. The blade should come out clean. Or, press lightly with a finger tip; a finished omelet will spring back. Don't overcook!

Slide the omelet onto a warm plate. Garnish with parsley and black olives. At breakfast time, serve immediately with toast and butter or hot croissants. For the Mexican version, serve with salsa.

Omelets also make great snacks and fine-to-behold sandwiches. Serve them on fresh-cut slices of French bread or croissants with a tall glass of Kronenbourg beer.

Makes 2 to 3 servings, depending on how much you improvise and add.

Being at Loggerheads

During the Revolutionary period, one of the most renowned public houses in the New York area was France's Tavern. It was known for its patrons, such as General George Washington, its witty conversation, and its hot drinks for a cold climate. There, of an evening, one could enjoy a Stonewall, which was half rum and half hard cider, or a Flip, made from strong beer, molasses, dried pumpkin, and a gill of rum.

Gentlemen customarily kept their drinks warm by plunging a special red-hot poker, called a flip dog, hottle, or loggerhead — because of a round ball at the business end — into their drinks. Not surprisingly, after a few Flips, when debates became truly spirited, some patrons found themselves shaking their miniature pokers at one another, obviously unable to convince their opponent and thus "at loggerheads" in their argument.

The Little Mermaid, Gift of Beer

She sits quietly atop a large rock, at the edge of the harbor of Copenhagen, wistfully watching the sea to which she can never return. This famous statue, commemorating perhaps the most famous of the tales of Hans Christian Anderson, was sculpted and cast in bronze by Edward Erikson in 1913. It was commissioned and donated to the city by Carl Jacobson, owner of Carlsberg Brewery, as a gift to all lovers of that bittersweet story.

This example of the brewer's philanthropy is not the only objet d'art given by Jacobson. Other activities of the Carlsberg Foundation include the restoration of Frederiksburg Castle, the establishment of a National History Museum, funds for the Danish Royal Ballet and Symphony Orchestra, a planetarium, and numerous individual art masterpieces, all for the public's enjoyment.

Egg Foo Young

The story of this dish is convoluted; it is in fact a joining of two legends from two different places. It begins with the great Emperor, Chiang Lung, who during the Ching Dynasty stopped at a humble food stand. He asked to be fed the best. The peasant in charge was both very poor and very afraid, fearing that his cuisine would offend such a noble taste. To solve his dilemma, he prepared a normal meal but renamed it "Red Beaked Parrot with Gold-Trimmed Jade Cake."

A few days later, at the palace, the Emperor decided he wanted more. He ordered his chefs to duplicate the meal. When they were failed, they were executed. Finally running out of patience (and chefs), the ruler summoned the poor man to his presence. Under the combined weight of threats and a treasure of real gold and jade, the man admitted he had served his royal guest spinach, crimson beet root, and fried bean curd.

In a later century, labor recruiters enticed many Chinese coolies to this country with the story of an entire mountain of jade. In America the Chinese toiled, building the Southern Pacific Railroad and digging in the gold fields, bringing along much of their culture.

Egg Foo Young is one of those authentic America-out-of-China dishes. American because it was developed in California during the 19th century; Chinese because the cook who devised it knew the story of mixing humble ingredients together under an exotic name. He never found his jade mountain (for if it does exist, it probably lies under the surface of the Pacific Ocean), but we all gained a fine dish, so simple to prepare that if you can make scrambled eggs, you'll find Egg Foo Young a snap.

¼	cup chopped pork, or chicken, shrimp, or mushrooms
2	tablespoons butter
2	tablespoons chopped onion
¼	cup chopped green onions
3	eggs, beaten
2	tablespoons cold beer
3	tablespoons chopped water chestnuts
½	cup bean sprouts
2	tablespoons cooking oil

Trim fat from pork. Brown meat in cooking oil. Remove from pan. Set aside in a warm place. Wash pan. Melt butter. Sauté onions and green onions lightly. Do not overcook; they should be a little crunchy.

Beat eggs with cold beer. Add water chestnuts, bean sprouts, meat and onions.

Heat cooking oil until moderately hot, about 275-300 degrees. Drop egg mixture into pan a spoonful at a time. Allow to brown on one side. Turn once. When done, keep warm in the oven. Serve while still hot on warm plates. Top with sauce made with the directions here.

Sauce for Egg Foo Young

2	tablespoons cornstarch
1-2	tablespoons warm beer
¼	cup soy sauce
1-1 ½	tablespoons beef or chicken soup base
1	cup water
	dash of coriander

Dissolve cornstarch in beer and soy sauce. Heat stock in saucepan with water. Add cornstarch paste. Heat until mixture thickens and sauce becomes transparent. Add a pinch of coriander or fresh parsley.

Makes 1 ½ cups of Egg Foo Young sauce.

This dish makes a fine accompaniment plate for an appropriate meat recipe, such as pork or chicken, and bowls of rice. Another nice factor is that Chinese food likes beer. Why not try some Chinese Tsing Tao or, if you like something a little stronger, some Thai Singha ale.

Makes 2 to 3 servings.

Wager Cups

The Dutch once designed a drinking cup that looked much like an old-fashioned school bell, having a bowl and stem but no foot to set it down on. The idea was obvious, for once it was full, the drinker was bound to finish it off in one draught.

Some of the more ornate models had small windmills built into the handles. When using these, the owner would bet that he could blow the tiny windmill sail, set it spinning, and then drink his beer down before it stopped.

Strangers were wise, as strangers still are, not to wager against someone who makes a ridiculous claim in a tavern — and is willing to back it up with hard cash.

As one spokesman for the cautious explained, "If a stranger comes up to you in a bar and bets you ten dollars that the Jack of Spades will step out of a sealed deck of playing cards, climb up your arm and piss in your left ear, and you agree, be prepared to lose the ten and go home with a wet ear."

Huevos Rancheros

Herb doctors, *brujos*, and other practitioners of folk medicine and magic in the Mexican culture often use eggs in curative rituals for their cleansing, restorative, and protective powers. Most often, an egg is rubbed over wherever the pain is coming from, and a chant or prayer is said. The egg draws out and captures the evil spirit causing the illness. Sometimes, to strengthen the cure, the sufferer is told to throw the egg away in running water or along the road, or even, in serious cases, to bury it in holy ground.

As food, eggs offer excellent nutrition in addition to wonderful flavor. Eggs form the basis of countless dishes, and special sauces are also a tradition. No pain or suffering – just pleasure – is associated with *huevos rancheros*.

2	corn tortillas
2	tablespoons cooking oil
4	tablespoons minced onion
1	clove minced garlic
¼	teaspoon dried red pepper
4	ounces fresh or canned salsa
4	tablespoons cold beer
	salt and pepper
4	eggs
2	tablespoons butter

Fry tortillas in oil until golden brown but still limp. Do not brown or crisp. Place in oven to keep warm.

Sauté onions lightly with dried pepper and garlic in the same oil. Pour off liquid from salsa. Add beer. Mix and pour into pan. Season with salt and pepper to taste. Be careful here because Mexican salsas tend to be salty.

Melt butter in another pan. Fry eggs sunny-side-up. Place two eggs on each tortilla. Spoon lots of sauce over them.

Serve with toast, hot tortillas, or *pan dulces* and fresh fruit. In Mexico, this macho breakfast is often accompanied with a couple of bottles of beer. The selection of excellent imported beer is broad. Superior and Dos Equis lager are special favorites.

Makes enough for 2.

Eggs Parmesan

A Massachusetts tale tells about the Yankee peddler who found himself somehow burdened with a load of coconuts he couldn't get rid of, no matter how much he discounted them. He finally hit on the idea of selling them to unwitting housewives as gollywhopper eggs. He explained that inside each shell was a splendid, unhatched gollywhopper, a rare and handsome bird, cheap to feed, that would protect poultry from marauding hawks, weasels and foxes.

Business was brisk until one woman became skeptical, sawed one open, and found only water and white lining. She invited the peddler to her house and sat him down to a huge breakfast of eggs, cheese and bacon. While he ate, she quietly gathered a number of her friends and told them her findings. When the peddler finished his meal, there, surrounding his cart, were seven of the meanest-eyed women he'd ever encountered, each armed with a pitchfork. Sheepishly he returned all their money and left the area knowing that, at least in that village, somebody knew a coconut from a gollywhopper egg.

Originally, this breakfast was made with wine, but the substitution of beer did no disservice to this gollywhopper treat.

2	tablespoons butter
2	tablespoons warm beer
4	eggs
1	dash *each* hot pepper sauce, salt, and pepper
2	tablespoons grated Parmesan cheese
2	English muffins, cut in half
4	slices Canadian bacon

Fry Canadian bacon and keep warm in oven. Melt butter in a medium-size skillet – one with a heat-resistant handle. Increase heat and stir the beer into the butter. Crack and add eggs when mixture is bubbling. Poach in simmering liquid until egg whites are just barely done. Splash a couple of drops of hot pepper sauce on each egg yolk. Salt and pepper to taste. Finally, sprinkle cheese on top of everything.

Turn on broiler in oven. Place English muffins, cut side up, in oven about six inches from heat. Slip entire egg dish under broiler, too. When cheese begins to brown but egg yolks are still soft, remove from oven.

Serve on buttered muffins with a slice of fried Canadian bacon.

Makes 4 to 6 servings.

Gascony Fried Eggs

The French of Gascony do magnificent things with eggplant – as they also do with truffles, Armagnac, chestnuts, and other food elements cherished in this Midi-Pyrénées region. Here's an egg and eggplant recipe that even musketeer D'Artagnan, the most famous fictional Gascon, would have relished.

4	slices eggplant
¼	cup warm beer
¼	cup flour
3	tablespoons olive oil
4	eggs
½	cup tomato sauce
4	thin slices ham
1	sprig parsley
	salt and fresh pepper

Cut eggplant into ¼ -inch slices. Dip each into beer and then into flour.

Heat fresh olive oil in an iron skillet. Fry eggplant slices for about three minutes a side or until nicely brown

Turn eggplant slices. Break an egg on top of each. Cover with a lid. Cook over low heat until egg whites are firm.

Place on a warm serving dish when done. Top with thin-sliced ham and heated tomato sauce. Garnish with a parsley sprig.

Serve hot with a dish of extra sauce on the side. If you lean more toward spicy food, use a hot Mexican salsa in place of the tomato sauce.

Makes 4 delicious breakfast servings.

Flip-Top Coup

The "tab top" or flip-top can, introduced in 1962, was a blockbuster in modern packaging. The move, by Alcoa Aluminum and Pittsburgh Brewing Company, was made only after a very careful market study, far from home. If you were living in Richmond, Virginia, that year, and drank Iron City Beer, you probably helped pull the whole thing off.

Creole Soufflé

Fluffy omelets and subtle soufflés are popular in areas that follow the custom of abstaining from meat during Lent. Mardi Gras, or "Fat Tuesday" is the last hurrah before the forty days of Lenten penitence. In the Christian holy calendar, *carne vale*, literally meaning "farewell to meat," was marked by a spate of masked revels which hark back to Roman times.

The date of the first such celebration in this country is unknown, but the custom was probably carried here by French trappers in the 18th century. Mardi Gras was already a well established fête in New Orleans prior to the Louisiana Purchase in 1803.

Here's a delicious onion dish that has gotten many cooks through a meatless meal without having to hide behind a carnival mask.

12	ounces warm beer
⅓	cup minced dried onion
⅓	cup sliced green onion
¼	teaspoon salt
6	eggs, separated
6	tablespoons flour
½	teaspoon cornstarch
¼	teaspoon sugar
	dash of cayenne pepper
6	tablespoons butter, softened

Mix warm beer, dried onions and green onions, and salt in a heavy sauce pan. Bring to a boil. Lower heat. Simmer about 5 minutes or until onions are tender. Remove from heat. Let cool.

Beat egg yolks in a bowl until creamy. Blend in flour, cornstarch, sugar, and cayenne and mix together thoroughly. Add butter. Continue to blend until mixture becomes a thick, smooth paste. Add about half the cool beer from the sauce pan. Stir again until smooth.

Pour egg mixture into sauce pan with remaining beer. Return to heat. Bring almost to a boil. Keep stirring. The final product should have the consistency of a thick custard.

Beat egg whites in a separate bowl until stiff, but not dry. Fold them slowly into the soufflé, turning gently until blended. Do not beat!

Spread butter on the bottom and sides of a 1 ½ - quart oven dish. Dust lightly with flour. Pour soufflé gently into the dish until it comes to about an inch from the top.

Bake in moderate, 375-degree oven for 45 to 50 minutes, or until the soufflé is firm.

166

Soufflés are a little tricky to prepare. Try one or two before you invite company over. Plan to serve them immediately; as they cool, they tend to deflate. (They still taste great.)

Accompany your soufflé with a green or fruit salad and a light lager beer from down south. Dixie beer, brewed independently in New Orleans since 1903, rarely ends up on connoisseurs' lists of world class beers, but it's been able to retain its local devotees in spite of numerous attempts by national breweries to invade the Crescent City market.

Makes 4 to 6 servings.

What Prohibition?

Beer drinkers all over the U.S. cried into their near beer all during Prohibition, 1919-1933. But the beer drinkers of Kansas really had something to mourn: The state of Kansas went dry in 1880 when a state Constitutional amendment prohibited the production and sale of any drink containing more than one half of one percent alcohol. This was thirty years before the Volstead Act (1919, ruled unconstitutional in 1933) killed a decade and a half of joy. Kansas remained dry until 1948, longer than any other state. Carrie Nation, poster girl of Prohibition, came from Kansas.

Whereas prohibition laws shut most breweries down or made them change production to soft drinks or near beer, in Atchison, Kansas, the Ziebold-Haegelin Brewery continued producing the good stuff through Kansas' early Prohibition years with very little static from the law.

Kansas Governor John A. Martin lived in Atchison, and Joseph Haegelin and Herman Ziebold were his buddies. The way he saw it, their brewery was way up in northeast Kansas, so close to Missouri that it was in effect in a Missouri border town.

Anytime citizens objected too strongly, he had the sheriff go and arrest one of the owners. The arrestee, either Mr. Ziebold or Mr. Haegelin, would play cards at the jail with the sheriff for a while and then go back home. Whichever partner was not arrested would maintain business as usual at the plant..

Mencken on Sobriety

H. L. Mencken, noted American author and journalist, delivered this observation about temperance: "All the great villainies of history have been perpetrated by sober men, and chiefly by teetotalers. All the charming and beautiful things, from the Song of Songs to terrapin à la Maryland, and from the nine Beethoven Symphonies to the Martini cocktail, have been given to humanity by men who, when the hour came, turned from well water to something with color to it. . . ."

Eggs Provençal

In the former Duchy of Lorraine, where the elements of this dish were originally combined, cooks and housewives carefully crushed the egg shells they used after breaking them. This was because many people believed that witches could use the empty shells as a means of transportation. In the trial of Anne Baites, in 1673, witnesses swear they saw her riding in an egg shell, both in her kitchen and over surrounding fields.

Fortunately, there's nothing supernatural about this classic egg dish, but it still might be a good idea to keep the shells out of temptation's way.

¼	pound butter
2	cups chopped onion
1	clove minced garlic
3	green bell peppers, chopped
12	eggs
½	cup Cheddar grated cheese
½	cup dry bread crumbs
12	ounces warm beer
	salt and pepper

Melt the butter in a skillet, except for 2 tablespoons. Sauté onions, peppers and garlic for about 10 minutes. Spoon mixture equally into 6 ramekins or other small baking dishes.

Carefully break two eggs into each dish – keep the yolks intact.

Mix the cheese with the bread crumbs. Sprinkle evenly over the top of the eggs. Pour about 2 ounces of beer into each cup. Dot finally with a dab of butter.

Bake ramekins in a 375-degree oven for 10 minutes or until eggs set to your liking. Serve with hot croissants and butter.

Make 6 servings.

Baked Eggs Español

"Columbus's egg" refers to a deed that, once someone has done it for the first time, anyone can do. Girolamo Benzoni wrote, in his 1565 *Story of the New World*, that Columbus " . . . was dining with many nobles when one of them said: 'Sir Christopher, even if your lordship had not discovered the Indies, there would have been, here in Spain which is a country abundant with great men knowledgeable in cosmography and literature, one who would have started a similar adventure with the same result.'

"Columbus did not respond to these words but asked for a whole egg to be brought to him. He placed it on the table and said: 'My lords, I will lay a wager with any of you that you are unable to make this egg stand on its end like I will do without any kind of help or aid.' They all tried without success and when the egg returned to Columbus, he tapped it gently on the table breaking it slightly and, with this, the egg stood on its end. All those present were confounded and understood what he meant: That once the feat has been done, anyone knows how to do it."

Got eggs? Make this delicious breakfast for family or friends.

1	medium Spanish onion, minced
1	clove garlic, minced
½	pound bulk chorizo (Spanish sausage)
2	tablespoons olive oil
1	10 ½-ounce can tomato or tomato bisque soup
4	ounces warm beer
¼	teaspoon Tabasco sauce
	salt and pepper
6-8	eggs
½	cup grated Parmesan cheese
½	cup grated Swiss cheese

Sauté minced onion and garlic lightly in olive oil. Add the chorizo and cook till it's golden. Add the tomato soup, warm beer, Tabasco sauce, and salt and pepper to taste. Warm it over moderate heat.

Pour about half of the sauce from the pan into a shallow 2-quart baking dish. Break eggs into dish carefully, keeping the yolks whole. Sprinkle about half of each cheese on top of eggs. Now cover with remaining tomato sauce and the rest of the cheese.

Bake in a 350-degree oven about 15 minutes, or until eggs are done the way you like them.

Serve to 3 or 4 folks along with hot crescent rolls or crusty bread and lots of fresh butter.

Welsh Rabbit

It seems there's a "new" version of this classic cheese dish around every corner. Connoisseurs' opinions differ widely on which ingredients are best, how much of what goes into it, and the various techniques of preparation. Even the name is a hot point of debate. "Rabbit" and "rarebit" are both in the unabridged Webster dictionary. The folklore behind the dish speaks of a Welsh chieftain, who, discovering to his chagrin that there was no game in the larder to serve some unexpected guests, instructed his cook, on pain of unspeakable consequences, to come up with something good – and fast.

The poor man raced about the kitchen, but all he cold find was some old cheese, a few eggs, and a few spices, hardly a suitable meal. He was just taking a sip of ale to prepare for his impending demise when he had an inspiration. Why not mix the cheese and eggs and flavor them with mustard and ale? He did. And just for good measure, to misdirect the diners' curiosity, he called the dish a rabbit. Welsh, of course.

This pleasant tale speaks to the ingenuity of an ancient cook, the gullibility of his masters, and, if you're inclined to believe the story, the snobbery of later cookbook authors who insisted on substituting the more genteel "rarebit" for the all too common bunny.

2	egg yolks
½	cup warm ale or dark beer
2	tablespoon butter
1	pound sharp grated Cheddar cheese
1	teaspoon Worcestershire sauce
½	teaspoon salt
¼	teaspoon dry mustard
1-2	dashes cayenne pepper
4	slices crisp, buttered toast or 4 English muffins, split, open-face paprika

Beat egg yolks into ale until smooth. Set bowl aside.

Melt butter in a double boiler over steaming water. Add grated cheese and stir. (Purists become livid if anything other than a wooden spoon is used or the mixture is stirred in more than one direction. Personally, we do not sweat this sort of thing.) Mix in Worcestershire sauce, salt, dry mustard, and cayenne pepper. NOTE: Heartier souls may wish to substitute a more fiery curry powder for the cayenne pepper. As ingredients blend, slowly pour in beer and egg mixture until everything is smooth and bubbly. Don't ever boil your rabbit!

Serve on hot buttered toast or English muffins. Dust with a fine cloud of paprika. Welsh rabbit makes an excellent late evening snack, or, accompanied with a little green salad, a tasty lunch or light dinner. Naturally, it goes well with beer. In this case, offer a fuller bodied brew, a brown ale such as Double Maxim, or an old ale such as Old Peculier. This recipe also works nicely in a chafing dish or fondue pot, but watch the heat and keep stirring.

For variety, consider a California or Latin variation of the basic theme. Sprinkle in some chopped green onion or some diced green and red bell peppers for color. Or, for *calor* (heat), a few minced Jalapeno peppers.

This particular rabbit serves 2 to 4.

And Speaking of Ale

Originally Burton Ale referred to a distinguished ale, brewed as early as the 12th century by monks of the Burton-on-Trent abbey. In <u>Ivanhoe</u>, Sir Walter Scott refers to the brew as one that preceded the reign of Richard the Lionhearted. The water in this area is quite hard – generally good for ale making – and lends a distinctive bitterness to Burton ale. Today the name is used to identify any fairly heavy, dark, hoppy ale, such as Britain's popular Double Diamond. There is still a winter ale made in Burton called "old ale" which is usually drunk half-and-half with a lighter brew.

There is a fragment of an old song that praises the ale of Burton, though not the generosity of its abbot.

> The abbot of Burton brewed good ale
> On Fridays when they fasted.
> But the Abbot of Burton never tasted his own
> As long as his neighbor's lasted.

Hob Nobbing

This early American slang comes to us from the popular custom of sitting around a warm stove while engaged in pleasant conversation on a chilly day, often as not smoothed by a mug or two of beer. Old standing stoves were equipped with a convenient projection called a "hob," just where an eloquent speaker could rest his foot during the discourse.

Not everyone, of course, found such pursuits laudatory; hence there was a sting embedded in the phrase that emerged. "Nob" is an old English term for someone of high status; thus a "hob nobber" was one who spent more time chatting up his betters than working.

Heathen Welsh Hare

The more popular a dish, the more variety in stories of its origin. This account is offered in George Leonard Herter's wonderful *Bull Cook and Authentic Historical Recipes and Practices*. According to his research the dish was invented in the 7th century by Mary Cameron, who resided in Wales near Glamorgan. One day, when she saw her husband, Arthur, returning empty-handed from a hare hunt, she quickly picked up some cheese, cut it into small pieces and mixed it in a pot with bacon drippings and a pint of ale. She served the mélange on stale bread.

The fame of Mary's recipe spread throughout the British Isles, where there must have been a great deal of old cheese and stale bread – because, over 1300 years later, we still know the name of this famous alewife of Wales.

This recipe version does not use Worcestershire sauce, eggs, cayenne pepper or curry powder, which, according to Mr. Herter, ruin most attempts at making a good old-time Welsh rabbit.

1	pound sharp Cheddar cheese, grated
½	teaspoon garlic powder
½	teaspoon dry mustard
½	cup warm beer or ale
4-5	slices pumpernickel, toasted
	salt, pepper and paprika

Mix grated cheese, garlic powder and dry mustard with liquid to form a thick, smooth paste. Shake on salt and pepper to taste. Spread mixture on toasted bread slices. Dust with a tad of paprika. Broil in oven until cheese melts and turns bubbly brown.

For a little variety, slip a slice of Canadian bacon or fresh tomato onto the bread before grilling. Many English enjoy a dish called Buck Rabbit that's made by adding a poached egg on top of the toasted cheese.

This grilled rabbit makes an easy breakfast, lunch or midnight snack for 4. Depending on the time of day, accompany it with a spot of Earl Grey tea or a fine Pale Ale from Bass.

A variation of this recipe doubles as an appetizer. Use basic white bread. Remove the crusts and spread thickly with cheese spread. You might mix in a bit of chopped ham, olives or mushrooms for fun. Roll the bread fairly tightly like an old-fashioned jelly roll. Secure with toothpicks and bake in a 425-degree oven on a cookie sheet for 5-7 minutes. Turn once or twice to brown. When done, cool and slice into canapé wheels.

Alpine Fondue

This festive dish, which originated in Switzerland, can be doubly enjoyed with friends, a few ground rules, and some pleasant penalties. First, the recipe:

If you use a fondue pot, it's a good idea to prepare your fondue on the stove. Those little burners are only good to keep the finished cheese stew hot.

5	tablespoons butter
	salt to taste
1	tablespoon sweet hot mustard
1	teaspoon Worcestershire sauce
¼	cup all purpose flour
1 ½	cups warm beer or ale
8	ounces shredded Swiss cheese
8	ounces shredded Cheddar cheese
1	loaf French, Italian or pumpernickel bread, cut in 1-inch cubes

Melt butter in fondue pot or double boiler. Add salt, mustard and Worcestershire sauce. Stir thoroughly. Mix flour and beer together. Add to the pot a little at a time, stirring continuously. Use a medium flame until the mixture begins to thicken and bubble.

Reduce heat. Add cheeses a handful or so at a time. Continue to stir until all the cheese is in the pot and the fondue is smooth.

Place the finished fondue in the center of the table in a fondue pot holder with a small flame beneath to keep it warm. If you serve your fondue this way, stir it once in a while to keep it smooth and to avoid burning or sticking.

Accompany it with a tossed green salad or a relish plate of bite-size-cut vegetables and fruits, such as broccoli, cauliflower, seedless grapes, apple cubes, and such.

Arm each guest with a goodly supply of bread cubes and other dippables and a fondue fork – the long-tined European ones are best. Now, each person, in turn, dips, swirls and tries to bring the skewered morsel to his or her mouth without losing it in the pot or dropping it en route. If a person is successful, it's the next one's turn; if not, there's a penalty due. For the gentlemen, it's his turn to buy more beer or the next bottle of wine. For the ladies, a kiss is due each man at the table – payable immediately.

You know, some folks just never get good at eating fondue. And you can believe that!

For a beer? Danish Tuborg, the "golden beer of kings," a Swiss Löwenbräu or a comparable German lager would be appropriate.

CHAPTER NINE

THE BAKERY – BREADS AND SWEET STUFF

Radio Beer Bread

Cheese Bread

Soft Rye Bread

Raisin Cheese Nut Bread

Beer, Olive, and Sun-Dried Tomato Bread

Sesame Beer Bread Sticks

Superlight Beer Pancakes

Quick Beer-Batter Crêpes

Hot Spice Cake

Chocolate Cake

Universal Chocolate Frosting

Date Cake from the Desert

Alice's Unbirthday Fruit Cake

Brit Lemon Cake

Cherry Cake

Old English Plum Pudding

Butterscotch Tarts

New York Cheesecake

Radio Beer Bread

Brewing and baking are natural companions because they both rely on the same chemical interaction of grain and yeast. During the Medieval Period in Europe, the baker was often the town brewmaster, too. Even earlier, according to Pliny the Elder, the ancient Gauls and Iberians skimmed beer while it was fermenting and used the foam as a leavening to improve their breads.

This recipe is so uncomplicated and widely used that many people have memorized it – dozens of folks have quoted it to me verbatim. This loaf is sometimes called Radio Beer Bread because it was broadcast so often, on programs like the "Magic Chef," during the Golden Age of Radio between 1930 and 1950.

3	cups self-rising flour***
½	cup melted butter
2	tablespoons sugar
12	ounces warm beer, ale or stout
1	tablespoon cornmeal

Use a wooden spoon to mix flour, butter, sugar, and beer. (Purists call for mixing in a clockwise direction only.) Let dough stand for about half an hour or so.

Some warnings are in order here. Measure ingredients carefully: Too much beer can spoil the loaf. Don't use light beers; this reaction requires beer containing at least 6% alcohol.

Generously grease a 9 x 5-inch bread pan. Dust it with cornmeal. Mold bread into a loaf shape. Place in pan and drizzle melted butter over top. Bake in 350-degree oven 1 hour, or until a wooden toothpick comes out clean when slid into the very center of the loaf. Remove bread from pan and cool on an open rack.

This is a fun recipe to experiment with because the type of beer or ale used will affect the flavor of the bread. For more interesting variety, add additional ingredients to the dough. A cup of grated, sharp Cheddar cheese makes a fine cheese bread, or 1 cup of finely chopped onion for onion bread. What else? Try a spoonful of fresh garlic, sage, caraway seed, a handful of chopped pitted kalamata olives, or whatever tickles you.

Makes 1 tasty loaf.

*** Don't have self-rising flour? Just combine these according to the following proportions, sift together, and you have self-rising flour. Measure out your 3 cups and you're good to go.

1	cup all-purpose flour
½	teaspoon salt
1 ½	teaspoons baking powder

Cheese Bread

The rise of civilization and bread making are virtually the same. Indeed, people were baking bread long before recorded history. Here are a few taboos from our past that clearly show the interweaving of bread and fate.

- swearing while holding bread is bad luck
- so is toasting bread on a knife
- throwing bread to the ground is very unlucky
- selling or giving away a loaf of bread without first tearing off a small piece tempts the fates
- placing bread on the table face down is a bad omen
- stolen bread gives the thief hiccups
- giving away the first slice of bread cut is giving away luck
- sticking a knife into a loaf of bread and leaving it there will lead to a dire event

Here's a way to serve up French bread that needs no luck to be a success. You wouldn't want to take any chances, though – no swearing, no foodfights – you know the drill.

1	pound natural Swiss or Jarlsberg cheese, grated fine
2	loaves fresh French bread
1	teaspoon dry mustard
2	tablespoons tomato paste
4	ounces warm beer
1-2	dashes hot pepper sauce
¼	teaspoon garlic powder

Mix grated cheese, dry mustard, garlic powder, tomato paste and pepper sauce with enough warm beer to make an easily spreadable paste.

Cut bread, crosswise, into 1-inch slices. To hold the loaf together, do not cut all the way through the bottom crust. Separate the slices and spread generous amounts of cheese mixture evenly between them.

Wrap bread in aluminum foil. Bake in a 400-degree oven for 15 or 20 minutes.

Serve piping hot. This is also a good one to make in advance, freeze and then take along on the next camping trip.

Makes enough spread for 2 good-sized loaves of bread.

Soft Rye Bread

Some food, like champagne and caviar, are associated with high social status, while others connote a common but healthy life style. Rye bread aligns itself with the latter group because it grows well in poor soils, places unsuited for wheat. Today we reach for this chewy, uniquely flavored favorite and pair it with heaps of thinly sliced ham or corned beef.

This recipe is for soft bread, called *limpa* by the Swedish. But with a couple of changes (see below), it can double for traditional harder rye bread.

2 ¼	cups rye flour
3 ½	cups all-purpose white flour
1	package active dry yeast
1	cup warm beer or ale
¼	cup brown sugar, packed
1	tablespoon light molasses
¼	cup shortening or bacon fat
1	cup warm water
2	tablespoons grated orange peel
1	tablespoons salt
1	tablespoons caraway seeds (optional)

Heat beer gently until it bubbles, to drive off alcohol. Add shortening or bacon fat, brown sugar, molasses, salt, and grated orange peel to liquid. Stir. Cool liquid to lukewarm.

Dissolve yeast in warm water. Mix thoroughly. Add to beer mixture. Beat in rye flour and enough white flour to make a soft dough. Turn out onto a floured breadboard. Knead until it is evenly smooth and elastic. Place dough in a greased bowl – turn over once or twice so that the entire outside of the dough is greased. Cover and put in a warm place. Have a beer or two while you allow the dough to rise to double its previous size.

Throw the dough back on the floured breadboard and think of something you don't like. Punch and knead again, until the dough is smooth or you just feel better. Keep board floured. Roll the dough into a 12 x 15-inch rectangle. Then, starting on one side, roll it tightly into a loaf. Place on greased baking sheet. With a sharp knife, cut diagonal slashes into the top at 2 ½ -inch intervals. Cover with a cloth and let rise again.

If you'd like to make regular rye bread, add caraway seeds to the dough ingredients and use ¾ cup instead of a whole cup of the two liquids. After the dough has risen, skip the fancy rolling. Shape it into a round or oblong loaf. Slash the top decoratively with a sharp knife.

Bake in a 350-degree oven for 45 to 50 minutes, or till loaf sounds hollow when thumped.

Makes 1 handsome loaf of bread.

Raisin Cheese Nut Bread

The Greeks, though great wine drinkers, understood that grapes did not grow everywhere in the ancient world. According to ancient historian Diodorus, these lesser climes were given the consolation prize of beer by Dionysus, the Greek god of wine and revelry. Other stories say Dionysus was so partial to his grape that he fled Mesopotamia when he discovered that all the people there drank beer.

As for consolation, even if your grape crop shrivels in the heat of less fortunate climes, at least you have raisins to put in your bread.

2	cups beer
1	15-ounce package raisins
5	cups sifted flour
1 ¼	cup sugar
1	tablespoon baking soda
½	teaspoon salt
1 ½	teaspoons nutmeg
3	eggs, well beaten
2 ½	cups American cheese, grated
2	cups chopped walnuts

Put beer and raisins in saucepan and heat just to boiling. Let stand until cool and raisins plump up and absorb liquid. Mix flour, sugar, soda, salt and nutmeg. Add beer and raisins, eggs, grated cheese, and walnuts. Mix well.

Spoon batter into 2 greased loaf pans. Bake at 350 degrees for 45 minutes or until toothpick inserted in center comes out clean.

Serve warm or cold. Offer with butter or cream cheese.

When Taxes Were Really Sticky

When beer was first taxed in England, in 1660, the year of the Restoration of the monarchy in the person of Charles II, rates were based on the potency of the brews. According to Frederick Hackwood's Inns, Ales and Drinking Customs of Old England (1911), the tax arbitrators, called ale conners, literally judged this by the seat of their pants.

They wore special leather trousers and sat, for a few moments, in a puddle of ale. The extent to which they "stuck" decided whether the brew was "strong" or "light," and thus how much tax was due. The numerous easier ways to judge ale's strength might cast a bit of doubt on this narrative. But when you get a story like this one, it would be a pity to reject it outright.

Beer, Olive, and Sun-Dried Tomato Bread

Ceres, known as Demeter to the Romans, was one of the twelve Olympians of classical Greek mythology. She was the goddess of agriculture generally and of grain specifically. Her name was lent to the Gallo-Latin word for beer, *cerevisiae*, and our modern word cereal, meaning "of grain." Today, though the ancient Greeks and their gods are gone, Ceres' heritage is found in the scientific designation for brewer's yeast, *saccharomyces cerevisiae*, and in words for beer, which is *cervoise* in medieval French, *cerveza* in Spanish, and *cerveja* in Portuguese.

Ceres has doubly blessed this marriage of bread and brew.

½	cup sun-dried tomatoes in oil
3 ½	cup all-purpose flour
½	teaspoon. salt
½	teaspoon baking soda
1	teaspoon double-acting baking powder
1	egg
1	12-ounce bottle lager beer
⅓	cup coarsely chopped pitted kalamata olives

Preheat oven to 350 degrees. Grease and flour a loaf pan.

Drain the tomatoes, but keep 1 teaspoon of their oil. Chop the tomatoes coarsely. Mix together flour, salt, baking soda and baking powder in a large bowl. Beat the egg lightly in a separate bowl.

Add egg and beer to flour mixture, mixing until just combined. Fold in the tomatoes, tomato oil and olives. (Feel free to substitute green olives for the kalamata olives if desired.)

Pour batter into pan and bake on middle rack for 40 minutes or until a toothpick inserted in bread comes out clean. Turn bread out onto a rack and let it cool.

Travelers Take Care!

The city fathers of Frankfurt were concerned about the quality of their beer in a curiously paternalistic way. The mayor in 1466 declared that "The beer brewers shall sell no beer to the citizens unless it be three weeks old; to the foreigners they may knowingly sell younger beer."

Sesame Beer Breadsticks

People have eaten sesame seed for thousands of years. It was used in Babylon to flavor cakes and wine, and its oil was used in cooking. Sesame seeds were found in Egyptian King Tut's tomb. In the story "Ali Baba and the Forty Thieves," Ali used "open sesame" as the magic word to open the cave, maybe because ripe sesame seed pods pop open when touched lightly.

Make these sesame-laced breadsticks and pop open a great cold beer.

1	package instant yeast
4	cups all-purpose flour or whole-wheat flour
¾	cup warm water
¾	cup vegetable oil
¾	cup room-temperature beer
¼	cup melted butter
½	cup sesame seeds
	coarse salt

Make sure you have instant yeast so that you don't have to dissolve the yeast in water before adding it to the remaining ingredients.

Combine yeast and flour in a large bowl. Add the remaining ingredients and mix well. Cover and let rise in a warm place about 1 ½ to 2 hours or until double in volume. Lightly grease two baking sheets. Preheat oven to 350 degrees.

Punch down the dough. Pinch off pieces about the size of a ping-pong ball and roll each into a stick about 8 inches long. Place on prepared baking pans. Brush sticks with melted butter. Sprinkle with sesame seeds and coarse salt. Bake 20-30 minutes till lightly brown.

Makes 3 to 4 dozen breadsticks.

Not Toasting With Beer

For years some people wouldn't use beer for drinking a toast. The reason is something like this: In 1848-49 Hungarians tried to throw off the Austrian yoke. They were successful at first, but the Austrians, under the leadership of General Haynau, clamped down. When the victorious Austrians toasted their victory over the Hungarian revolutionaries with beer, the defeated but outraged patriots declared a 150-year ban on ever toasting with beer. As of 1998, however, everybody got to toast with beer again. Some of today's Hungarians speak their toast, then bang the beer glass on the table and say "F*** you, Haynau!"

Superlight Beer Pancakes

The clown in Shakespeare's "All's Well that Ends Well" praises a thing as being "as fit as a pancake for Shrove Tuesday." That day, the day before Ash Wednesday, was people's last chance for even a minor celebration before the season of penitence began. Lent in some cultures required giving up not only meat, but also other rich and pleasurable foods like eggs and most fat. So on Shrove Tuesday people traditionally ate pancakes to use up these ingredients.

1	cup sifted all-purpose flour
¼	cup white sugar
¾	teaspoon baking powder
½	teaspoon salt
1	egg, beaten
1	cup beer

In a large bowl, stir together the flour, sugar, baking powder and salt. Pour in the egg, beer and melted butter; whisk together just until blended – do not overbeat.

To a skillet or griddle over medium heat, add a thin layer of vegetable oil or cooking spray. For each pancake, pour about ¼ cup of batter onto the hot surface. When the tops of the pancakes bubble and the edges start to look dry, turn the pancakes and cook them until the other side is brown.

Serve with butter and assorted other toppings - maple syrup, chopped pecans, fruit, jam, even sliced bananas and brown sugar.

For Whom the Beer Bell Tolls

Brewing beer, even for one's own consumption, was a highly formalized activity in medieval Germany. The city of Erfurt in 1351 issued this directive to those householders who had paid their brewing tax and thus would be allowed the privilege of replenishing their stores. "No citizen shall brew more than twice a year; for each time he shall use three chests of malt, filled to the brim, no more and no less. On Wednesday evening before St. Michael, when the beer-bell is tolled, and no sooner, the fire shall be lit and the brewing commensed."

The remainder of the ordinance addresses quality, price, and punishments for infractions. The latter were stiff – either a fine of ten gold groshen for a first offender, all the way up to banishment from the city.

Other cities were equally stern toward bad brewers: City of Danzig, 11th Century: "Whoever makes a poor beer is transferred to the dunghill." City of Augsburg, 13th Century: "The selling of bad beer is a crime against Christian love."

Quick Beer-Batter Crêpes

February 2, Candlemas Day, in France is called *la Chandeleur, Fête de la Lumière*, or crêpe day. Crêpes are served, along with a fortune-telling game. The player holds a gold coin in his or her dominant hand and a crêpe pan in the other hand. The challenge is to flip the fragile crêpe into the air and catch it in the pan without tearing it or landing it on floor or ceiling. Catching the crêpe neatly in the pan means the person will be rich for the rest of the year. It was also held that eating crêpes on Candlemas Day led to a good harvest the following fall.

Make your crêpes with beer and they'll be so light they'll almost float.

3	eggs, lightly beaten
1 ¼	cup milk (or ½ cup heavy cream and ¾ cup milk)
1	cup beer
1 ¾	cups all-purpose flour
1	pinch salt
2	tablespoons vegetable oil
2	tablespoons butter

Whisk together the eggs, milk (and cream if you use it) and beer. Gradually whisk in flour. Add salt and oil, then beat the batter vigorously 3 - 5 minutes. Let stand for 1 hour.

Heat a 10-inch non-stick skillet or crêpe pan over medium heat. Brush it with butter, and when it's hot but not smoking, pour ⅓ cup of batter into the center of the skillet, and immediately tip the pan so the batter thinly covers the whole bottom of the pan. Cook the crepe 1-2 minutes until it is just golden on the bottom. Turn it and cook until it is golden on the other side, about 30 seconds. Transfer to a plate, and keep it warm by covering with foil. Brush pan with butter again and continue until all of the batter is used.

These can be served with either sweet or salty fillings/toppings. Serves 10-12 people.

For dessert crêpes, use fruit sauces, whipped cream, caramel or chocolate pudding, fresh sliced strawberries or peaches, or ice cream – or offer all of them and let guests choose.

For brunch or other main-dish crêpes, fill with creamed chicken, beef in mushroom sauce, or cheese sauce with crumbled bacon.

Hot Spice Cake

The state of California owes a debt to Armenian immigrants who came to the great San Joaquin valley in the middle of the last century. They immediately recognized the area as ideal for growing grapes, and from this sprang the multi-billion dollar grape, wine, and raisin industries. The lowly raisin did not initially enjoy the success its growers hoped for. In fact, when marketed as "dried grapes," the response was not enthusiastic. Then an enterprising advertising person hit on the idea of a new name, the raisin, and the slogan, "Have you had your iron today?" After that, raisins became not only a popular snack but a major ingredient in many recipes, such as this fine spice cake.

1	cup light molasses
⅓	cup cooking oil
2	eggs
2 ½	cups all-purpose flour
1 ½	teaspoon baking soda
½	teaspoon ground ginger
¼	teaspoon *each* ground cinnamon, cloves, and nutmeg
½	cup warm beer
½	cup chopped walnuts
½	cup dark raisins

Combine molasses and cooking oil in a bowl. Add eggs. Beat well. In a larger bowl stir flour together with baking soda and spices. Add molasses-oil-egg mixture, a little at a time, with beer, and beat well. Fold in chopped nuts and raisins.

Pour cake mixture into a greased and floured 13 x 9 x 2-inch baking pan. Bake in a 350-degree oven for 25 to 30 minutes. It's done when the center of the cake springs back after being lightly touched with a finger. Remove cake from oven and allow it to cool a little while preparing this sterling hot sauce to accompany it.

¼	cup brown sugar
4	tablespoons flour
½	cup warm beer or ale
½	cup water
2	tablespoons butter
¼	teaspoon vanilla

Mix brown sugar and flour in a saucepan. Gradually stir in beer and water to form a smooth mixture. Heat slowly until sauce thickens and begins to bubble. Add butter and vanilla. Heat a few minutes longer. You'll have about 1 ½ cups of sauce.

Cut warm spice cake into twelve 3-inch squares. Pour hot sauce on top of each. Serve immediately.

Chocolate Cake

The discovery of the New World had many consequences, some, with the sharp clash of cultures, highly damaging to native populations. Of the more favorable results of the opening of the new continents, changes in the European diet were probably the most beneficial. Among the new foodstuffs were corn, tomatoes, potatoes, chilis and cocoa.

In pre-Colombian Mexico cocoa beans were used as money. They made a common medium of exchange among various peoples from the northern deserts to the Central American jungles. Montezuma himself received an annual tithe of over six million beans from one city in his empire. Only the richest could afford to grind up their wealth and drink it in the form of chocolate. Fortunately, today there are enough of these beautiful black spheroids available to flavor many of our foods, such as this international favorite.

¾	cup shortening
1 ½	cups sugar
4	eggs
2 ½	cups all-purpose flour
1	teaspoon baking soda
1	teaspoon salt
1	cup warm beer
3	squares unsweetened chocolate

Melt chocolate slowly in a greased pan. Set aside to cool.

Mix shortening and sugar until smooth and creamy. Add eggs, one at a time, beating after each. Sift flour, baking soda and salt together in a bowl. Add dry ingredients to shortening-sugar-egg mixture alternately with beer. Beat until smooth. Stir in chocolate and beat thoroughly. Turn batter into greased and floured cake pans. If you have 8-inch pans, use three; if yours are 9-inch pans, use two.

Bake in a 350-degree oven. Test for doneness after 30 minutes. (Center of layer should spring back when touched lightly with a finger, and layer edges should pull away from sides of pan.)

Remove from oven. Allow to stand 5 minutes. Remove from pans and let cool on a rack.

Fill and frost cake with whipped cream or a chocolate-butter frosting (described on next page).

Makes 8 servings.

Universal Chocolate Frosting

It has been said by connoisseurs that a fine icing justifies any cake. Here is one that does exactly that and beats anything that comes from a can.

    2   cups confectioner's sugar
    3   tablespoons butter
    1   square unsweetened chocolate
    2-3   tablespoons warm beer

Sift confectioner's sugar. Soften butter in microwave for a few seconds at half power. Slowly mix butter with sugar in a medium sized bowl.

Melt chocolate over very low flame in a greased pan. Remove from heat and gradually add to the butter/sugar mixture. Blend well.

Stir in beer, a little at a time, until the frosting is of spreading consistency. Continue beating until smooth.

Spread frosting generously over cakes, doughnuts, cupcakes or whatever needs a chocolate lift.

Makes about 1 cup of frosting.

What's More Serious Than a Double Cross?

At one time or another we've all seen lithographs of tall sailing ships on the verge of leaving port. The docks are usually depicted as a pandemonium of people, cargo, and paraphernalia of those distant times. Somewhere among the scurrying sailors, stevedores, and local loungers, amid the boxes, bales, and crates, there is bound to be a stack of wooden barrels bearing X, XX, and XXX markings.

These are beer barrels awaiting shipment. The Xs designated the strength of the brew, not its quality. The first was "small beere," sometimes called "single beer." It was the cheapest and most often consumed drink in the American colonies. The second classification, referred to as "middling beer," "sailors' beere," or "table beere," was stronger, kept better, and demanded a higher price than small beer. The last, "strong" or "double" beer, was the heartiest, cost the most, and was likely destined for some rich man's table or cellar.

Date Cake from the Desert

A high proportion of the dates in this country come to us from California. Each year, at the Indio Date Festival, southeast of Palm Springs, this small fruit is honored with marching bands, celebrants and camels. Yes, camels.

Just before the Civil War, Lincoln's Secretary of War, Jefferson Davis, organized the Dromedary Service, to haul goods across the great deserts between Albuquerque and the outskirts of Los Angeles – prior to the completion of the railroads, of course. The idea, one of those marvelous failures in history, led to numerous stories, including the legend that a ghost camel and its dead rider still haunt the desert near Yuma, Arizona.

Dates became a popular treat during the last half of the 19th century. California dates were sometimes stuffed with walnuts and rolled in sugar. It's not surprising to discover that some cooks simply added some flour, a few eggs, and spices to create this specialty cake.

1	cup butter or shortening
2	cups firmly packed brown sugar
2	beaten eggs
3	cups all-purpose flour
½	teaspoon salt
2	teaspoons baking soda
1	teaspoon ground cinnamon
½	teaspoon *each* ground allspice and ground cloves
2	cups warm beer
2	cups chopped dates
1	cup chopped walnuts

In a large bowl, cream the butter and sugar until mixture is light. Beat eggs separately and add to bowl. Beat. Sift dry ingredients together – flour, salt, baking soda and spices – in a different bowl. Set aside 2 tablespoons of dry mixture.

Add remaining dry mixture in parts, alternating with the beer, into the bowl with the shortening and eggs. Beat batter earnestly. Coat dates and nuts with reserve dry-ingredient mix. Fold into bowl. Pour batter into a generously greased and floured 10-inch tube pan. Baked in a preheated, 350-degree oven for 1 ¼ hours. Remove cake from oven. Let cool for about 5 minutes before inverting the pan onto a serving dish. Cover the dish and refrigerate for a couple of hours – overnight is even better.

To serve the cake, dust it with confectioner's sugar, or frost it with whipped cream or caramel frosting, or make a quick Lemon Glaze by beating together 3-4 tablespoons of fresh lemon juice and 1 ½ cups powdered sugar to spread atop the cake.

Makes 12 to 14 servings.

Alice's Unbirthday Fruit Cake

Cakes have traditionally been associated with festivities and special events. In Europe and especially England, many centuries ago, "Twelve Cakes" were served on the Eve of the Epiphany (also called Twelfth Night) in a curious admixture of Christian and pagan ceremonies. The elaborately decorated cake contained a silver coin or a bean. The guest who found it became the King or Queen of the party and was expected to bless the rafters of the house against the work of devils and evil spirits. As time passed, parties became more secular. The coins were left out; the good luck was symbolized by the cake itself; and the cakes were not limited to Twelfth Night but might be presented on one's saint's day.

This recipe was reportedly found among the effects of Mr. Charles Lutwidge Dodgson (*nom de plume* Lewis Carroll, author of *Alice in Wonderland*) many years after his death. It was not noted earlier because he'd included it in his lesser notes on photography, writing in the dark, and improving the game of backgammon.

¾	cups butter, softened in microwave on low power
3	cups all-purpose flour
2	teaspoon baking powder
1	teaspoon salt
½	teaspoon ground allspice
2	teaspoon ground cinnamon
½	teaspoon *each* of ground cloves and ground nutmeg
2 ½	cups candied mixed fruit
1 ¼	cups *each* of candied cherries and candied pineapple
½	cup candied citron
1	pound raisins
2	cups chopped nuts
4	eggs
1 ¾	cups packed brown sugar
1	cup warm dark beer
¼	cup molasses

Soften butter and set aside to cool. Sift flour, baking powder, salt, allspice, cinnamon, cloves and nutmeg together in a large mixing bowl. Add all candied fruit, raisins, and nuts. Mix together until all fruit is coated thoroughly with dry ingredients. Set bowl aside.

In another bowl, beat eggs until they foam. Gradually add brown sugar. Continue beating until mixture is smooth. Blend in warm beer, molasses and melted butter. Add to flour and fruit mixture. Stir thoroughly until all ingredients are combined evenly.

Grease two 13 x 9 x 2-inch baking pans. Line with waxed paper. Fill each about ¾ full of batter. Bake slowly in a preheated 275-degree oven for 2 ½ to 3 hours. Remove cakes from oven. Allow to cool thoroughly before attempting to remove from pans.

Wrap fruit cakes in aluminum foil for storage. Since fruit cakes improve with age, store them in something airtight. Periodically, you may tend your charges by basting them with a little rum, brandy, or bourbon – just to keep them moist, of course.

All you have to do now is wait for any of Alice's un-birthdays to celebrate. (Keep in mind that she had only one birthday, so you have a lot of days open to you.) Fruit cakes, called *napfkuchen* in German, also make wonderful gifts, especially around Christmas time.

This recipe makes two tasty 9 x 13-inch *napfkuchen*.

Toby Mugs

Although the Toby Mug is quintessentially British, the word "mug" is Scandinavian in origin. The old Norwegian word for an earthen vessel was _mugga_; the Swedish was _mugg_. The word probably came to the British Isles during the invasions of the Vikings in the 9th century.

The word was in wide usage many years later when potters began fashioning beer mugs in the shape of human and not-so-human faces. This idea might also have a Viking origin, in the legendary promise of eternal bliss in Valhalla, where warriors passed the days drinking ale from cups fashioned from the skulls of their enemies. Echoes of this are heard still in the sanguine toast _Skoal!_ which literally means "skull."

Later, industrious English potters turned their talents to fashioning more festive drinking mugs in various shapes and sizes. The most familiar of these depict romantic characters from literature and folklore. Colorful figures such as Mr. Pickwick, Dick Turpin, Robin Hood, a jolly coachman, and an anonymous red-cheeked squire in a three-cornered hat holding his own brimming Toby Mug grace many a mantel and shelf, their real life sources and counterparts lost behind their eternal glaze of nostalgia and good cheer.

The Toby is a direct descendent of the Bellarmine mug, an ugly political caricature of the 17th century Cardinal Robert Bellarmine. This earlier version, with its leering, satanic face, was designed and produced by Protestant potters in Holland to express their adverse opinion of the intolerant Catholic cleric. Toby Mugs, with their dramatic characterizations in clay of either good or evil, are still popular and highly collectible.

Brit Lemon Cake

Halloween, short for All Hallows Even, is observed on October 31, the day before All Saint's Day or All Hallows. In Great Britain, also, the celebration of All Hallows on November 1 begins the evening before, on what they call Cake Night. The cakes were sometimes called soulcakes. These were given to beggars who were then obliged to pray for the departed souls. In Yorkshire, carolers would sing from house to house:

Soul! Soul! For a soul-cake I pray, Good mistress, a soul-cake,
An apple or pear, a plum or cherry, Any good thing to make us merry,
One for Peter, two for Paul, Three for Him who made us all.

Surely a lemon cake would qualify.

1	16- or 18-ounce package yellow cake mix
1	4-ounce package instant lemon pudding mix
1	cup warm beer
¼	cup cooking oil
4	eggs

Combine packages of cake mix and lemon pudding mix in a large mixing bowl. Stir until thoroughly mixed together. Add beer and oil. Continue stirring mixture.

Beat eggs in a separate bowl. Combine with other ingredients. Mix with an electric mixer, set on high speed, until batter is smooth and creamy – about 2 minutes.

Pour cake mixture into a greased and floured two-piece tube pan with legs. Bake in a 350-degree oven for 55 minutes. Remove cake from oven. Invert over serving dish and let cool.

The cooled cake can be iced or not. Lemon Glaze (see Date Cake recipe, p. 188), would give this cake some soul.

Beer Money

For many decades the English Army supplied its noncommissioned officers and regular soldiers with a daily ration of beer or spirits. The custom was discontinued in 1800, but so as not to undermine morale, each man was given an extra penny a day subsidy. Beer money, as it was called, was abolished entirely in 1873 at the height of the British Empire. During this period, too, servants working in large households also received a penny a day for their libations.

Cherry Cake

When Frederick the Great of Prussia discovered that Germans were increasingly becoming coffee drinkers, he issued this declaration on September 13, 1770: "It is disgusting to notice the increase in the quantity of coffee used by my subjects and the amount of money that goes out of the country in consequence. . . . My people must drink beer. His Majesty was brought up on beer and so were his ancestors and his officers. Many battles have been fought and won by soldiers nourished on beer, and the King does not believe that coffee-drinking soldiers can be depended on to endure the hardship or to beat his enemies in case of the occurrence of another war." Beer resumed its ascendency in Germany and coffee became a luxury.

If you can overcome the weight of His Majesty's indignation long enough to pour a cup of java, this easy cake will be a great accompaniment. And the beer in it is bound to strengthen your soldierly endurance.

1	cup maraschino cherries
2	cups all-purpose flour
2	teaspoons baking powder
¼	teaspoon salt
4	eggs, at room temperature
2	cups sugar
2	teaspoons vanilla
2	tablespoons melted butter
1	cup cherry wheat beer
½	cup chopped pecans (optional)
1	cup powdered sugar
2	more tablespoons cherry wheat beer

Drain cherries. Save syrup. Chop them coarsely and dry them with paper towels. Preheat oven to 375 degrees. Generously grease and flour a tube pan, or use baking-pan spray liberally. Sift together flour, baking powder, and salt. Beat eggs 3-5 minutes. Add vanilla. Beat in sugar, ⅓ at a time. Fold flour mixture into egg and sugar mixture.

Heat 1 cup of the beer just until bubbles begin to rise around the edge of the pan. Add warm beer along with melted butter to the batter, stirring gently to combine. Batter will seem thin. Pour half of it into the prepared pan. Sprinkle the chopped cherries over the top of the batter. Pour in the other half of the batter. Add the remaining chopped cherries and the nuts (if desired). If cherries and nuts sink, don't worry – it looks pretty that way.

Bake 35 minutes. Test for doneness. When toothpick inserted in cake comes out clean, remove from oven. Invert and let cool. Loosen cake around the inner and outer edges of the pan with a knife. Turn out onto cakeplate. Loosen and remove tube pan bottom. Poke holes in top of cake and spoon the cherry syrup into the holes. Mix powdered sugar and 2 tablespoons of the beer to form icing. Drizzle the icing over the cake.

Makes 8 to 10 servings

Pilsner Urquell

Pilsner is, for most beer lovers, the hallmark of brewing excellence. It has been produced in the Pilsen region of what is now the Czech Republic since 1292 when King Wenceslaus granted the people of the area the right to brew beer. Outside of its homeland it's usually spelled pilsener or abbreviated to just pils.

Pilsner Urquell, the brand most familiar internationally, is really not a separate variety of beer but rather a superbly brewed light lager. In fact, the name means the "original, the source of all Pilsners." Since it uses Bohemian hops, a glass of classic pilsner has a characteristic well-hopped flavor. Serve it cold but not in Pilsner glasses; their shape allows the collar to dissipate too rapidly.

The greatest testimonial to the fame of Pilsner Urquell is the fact that it is Germany's biggest imported beer. Talk about bringing coals to Newcastle! But the Czech brewers' devotion to quality is found in the words of one of their executives, during a 1972 Playboy Magazine interview, when he commented: "We spend two years studying each new brewing technique as it comes along — before rejecting it."

On September 18, 1961, Czechoslovakia became the first nation to commemorate its brewing industry on a postage stamp. On that day a 60 haleru stamp was issued, picturing a hop vine, the Pilsner medallion and a foaming glass of beer.

The Holy Hour

In Dublin, until the year 1988 the taverns and pubs closed down between the hours of 2:30 and 3:30 each afternoon. Some residents explained the so-called "holy hour" as a gesture to temperance and calm demeanor. Other wags accounted for it as the time the parish priest could drink his beer in peace.

Old English Plum Pudding

This famous delight is a "pudding" in the English sense of a rich dessert cake, similar to fruit cake. In Henry VIII's time the puddings were made by the dozens at Christmas time. Good luck certainly would follow if one ate a pudding each night of the twelve days between Christmas and Epiphany, "making a wish on the first mouthful each day." Conversely – and this was probably dreamed up by a beleaguered cook – anyone who nibbled a pudding before the proper time risked twelve months of dire fortune.

The most famous flouter of this custom was a young man named John Horner. He was detailed by the king to accompany a large, specially prepared pudding to London. On the way, temptation mastered him and he broke the crust with his thumb. Expecting to extricate a plum treat, he was astounded to find no fruit inside, but instead the deeds to twelve manor houses! The tale of his luck spread quickly through England. One witty scribbler wrote a satirical rhyme to accompany the story and these words, memorized by generations of children, immortalized Little Jack Horner's well timed audacity.

¾	cup *each* of dark seedless raisins and golden raisins (sultanas)
¼	cup *each* chopped candied citron, candied fruits, and candied orange peel
1 ½	cups beer
4	eggs
1 ½	cups firmly packed brown sugar
1	cup chopped nuts
½	cup fine dry bread crumbs
1	cup lard or minced suet
1	cup sifted all-purpose flour
1	teaspoon salt
1 ½	teaspoons baking powder
¾	teaspoon baking soda
1	teaspoon ground cinnamon
⅛	teaspoon *each* ground cloves and allspice

Combine fruits and peel in bowl; add beer and let stand for at least an hour. Beat eggs with brown sugar and add fruit-beer mixture. Stir in nuts, crumbs, and suet. Sift dry ingredients and spices; stir into fruit mixture. Stir into two well-greased 2-quart pudding molds or other 2-quart pans, filling three quarters full. Cover tightly. Put on rack in deep kettle; pour in boiling water to half the depth of the molds. Cover; steam for 2 ½ hours, adding more water if necessary. Remove from steamer; immediately remove the top. Cool completely. Store, covered, in refrigerator. Warm before serving, by steaming again for about 35 minutes.

To make a quick hard sauce for this cake, cream together ¾ cup butter, 3 cups of sifted confectioners' sugar, 2 tablespoons cream, dash of salt, and 2 teaspoons rum extract. Spoon over warm slices of cake.

Butterscotch Tarts

Tarts are forever linked with the Queen of Hearts, one of the high ranking members of the royal family of cards. Playing cards themselves were probably invented in Egypt during the 17th century for a French prince's amusement. They were designed to correspond to the astronomical signs and calculations of the Egyptians; the colors, red and black, for instance, stand for the equinoxes. The suits represent the four seasons: the Heart is a cup for winter, the Spade, an acorn for autumn, the Club, a trefoil (or clover) for spring, and the Diamond, a rose for summer.

The twelve count cards – Kings, Queens, and Jacks – represent the months of the year. The pack, fifty-two cards in all, stands for the weeks. The suits, composed of thirteen cards each, correspond to the weeks in a lunar quarter. The total number of pips, or spots on the cards, are equal to three hundred and sixty-five, if one counts using numerical equivalents for the face cards, such as eleven for Jacks or Knaves, twelve for Queens, and so on.

All of this information and much more can be found in *The Unerring Fortune-Teller* (1866), about Madame le Normand, the Emperor Napoleon's counselor and seer.

And now to the tarts:

1	3 ⅝-ounce package butterscotch pudding and pie filling mix
1 ½	cups milk
½	cup warm beer
1	cup whipped topping
1	tablespoon pumpkin pie spice
1	teaspoon instant coffee powder
6	baked tart shells

Empty packaged ingredients into a mixing bowl. Prepare pudding as directed on package using beer and milk as the liquid. When pudding begins to thicken, stir in pumpkin pie spice and instant coffee. Before cooling, to keep the surface from forming a thick skin, cover the pudding with plastic wrap, placing it right on top of the pudding. Cool in refrigerator.

Arrange tart shells on serving dish. Beat pudding with a wire whisk to make it fluffy.

Spoon mixture evenly into shells. Again cover each dessert with plastic wrap. Chill finished tarts until icy cold.

Serve tarts with a dollop of whipped topping and a flourish of pumpkin pie spice at the next social gathering.

New York Cheesecake

Cheesecake was not invented at Lindy's in New York, though Lindy's made it famous. Cheesecakes aren't even a modern idea. In a letter written to a friend in 310 B.C., a Greek traveler named Hippolochus described a wedding he'd recently attended in Macedonia. After the entertainment and dining, the guests were served sweetmeats and "cheesecakes of every kind known."

As the centuries wore on, the secret of the delicacy spread to many lands. This version, though, is definitely New York City.

1 ½	cups graham cracker crumbs
¼	cup butter
¼	cup heavy cream
¼	cup warm beer
½	cup grated Cheddar cheese
1	teaspoon vanilla
4	eggs
2	egg yolks
4	8-ounce packages cream cheese
1 ½	cups sugar
½	cup chopped walnuts

Mix graham cracker crumbs with melted butter in a large bowl. Press firmly into a 9-inch spring-form pan. Make sure the sides and bottom are covered evenly.

Beat cream cheese in another bowl until it's soft. Continue to beat mixture as you add Cheddar cheese and sugar. When thoroughly mixed, add vanilla. Beat eggs and extra egg yolks into the batter one at a time. Mix smoothly. Finally, fold in heavy cream and beer.

Pour cheese batter into pie shell. Bake in a preheated 300-degree oven for 1 ½ hours, or until the filling sets. When done, turn off heat. Allow cheese cake to remain in oven, with the door ajar, for half an hour.

Cool on a rack and chill in refrigerator before serving.

Note: If you like fruit cheesecake, you can spread a can of prepared apple pie filling or other fruit filling in the pie shell just before you pour in the cheese filling. Or top the finished cheese cake with a fruit topping.

Makes 8 servings.

INDEX TO BEER RECIPES

A

Alice's Unbirthday Fruit Cake, 189
Alpine Fondue, 173
Amsterdam Fried Cheese, 3
Apples
    Bratwurst and Sauerkraut, 53
    Pork and Apple Ragout, 91
Asparagus and Shrimp, 113

B

Baja Bean Dip, 5
Baked Curried Chicken, 102
Baked Eggs Español, 169
Baked Ham, 61
Baked Onion Soup, 28
Baked Polish Sausage, 52
Baked Red Onions, 136
Bananas
    Latin Pochero, 62
Barbecue Beef Sandwiches, 150
Barbecue Pork Sandwiches, 149
Barbecued Chicken, 95
Bartender's Chili, 81
Bavarian Pickled Eggs, 9
Beans
    Baja Bean Dip, 4
    Bartender's Chili, 81
    British Banger Soup, 22
    California Salad, 35
    Chili Azteca, 83
    Four-Bean Salad, 36
    Frijoles Borrachos, 125
    Latin Pochero, 62,
    New England Baked Beans, 88
Beef
    Barbecue Beef Sandwiches, 150
    Bartender's Chili, 81
    Beef and Cheese Nosh, 12
    Beef Canton, 90
    Beef Rolls de Paris, 54
    Beef Stroganoff, 56
    Beer-Braised Pot Roast of Beef, 39
    Broiled Hamburgers, 141
    Chili Azteca, 83
    Corned Beef Brisket, 45
    Danish Meat Balls, 59
    Doughboy Stew, 69
    Flemish Carbonnes, 65
    German Meat Balls, 58
    Great Hamburgers, 142
    Hearty Steak and Guinness Pie, 73
    Humbles and Onions, 47
    Hungarian Goulash, 67
    International Meat Loaf, 60
    Latin Pochero, 62
    Mushroom Steak, 43
    Old Time Beef Jerky, 15
    Reuben Sandwiches, 151
    Salisbury Steak, 143
    Saucy Steak Sandwich, 155
    Seaman's Beef, 40
    Shish Kebabs, 46
    Spaghetti with Meat Sauce, 84
    Steak and Kidney Pie, 71
    Steak Iberia, 44
    Stuffed Green Peppers, 86
    Texas Flank Steak, 41
    Uncle Sam's Barley Stew, 68
    Vampire Steak, 42
Beef and Cheese Nosh, 12
Beef Canton, 90
Beef Rolls de Paris, 54
Beef Stroganoff, 56
Beer, Olive, and Sun-Dried Tomato Bread, 181
Beer-Braised Pot Roast of Beef, 39
Bowery Cheese Crock, 4
Braised Cabbage, 122
Bratwurst and Sauerkraut, 53
Bratwurst in Ale, 148
Bread
    Beer, Olive, and Sun-Dried Tomato Bread, 181
    Cheese Bread, 178
    Radio Beer Bread, 177
    Raisin Cheese Nut Bread, 180
    Sesame Beer Bread Sticks, 182
    Soft Rye Bread, 179
Breaded Eggplant, 137
Brit Lemon Cake, 191
British Banger Soup, 22
Broiled Hamburgers, 141
Brussels Sprouts, 133
Butterscotch Tarts, 195

C

Cabbage
    Braised Cabbage, 122
    Bratwurst and Sauerkraut, 53
    Cabbage and Noodles, 121
    Chops and Kraut, 48
    Gypsy Steak, 50
    Latin Pochero, 62
    Pennsylvania Slaw, 34
    Polish Delight, 75
    Red Cabbage Salad, 29
    Red Cabbage, 138
    Red Hots and Kraut, 147
    Reuben Sandwiches, 151
    Spanish Paella, 105
Cabbage and Noodles, 121
Caesar Salad, 33
Cakes
    Alice's Unbirthday Fruit Cake, 189
    Brit Lemon Cake, 191
    Cherry Cake, 192
    Chocolate Cake, 186
    Date Cake from the Desert, 188
    Hot Spice Cake, 185
    Old English Plum Pudding, 194
California Salad, 35
Canadian Salmon Steaks, 108
Candied Sweet Potatoes, 134
Carnitas Jalisco, 49
Carrots
    Mandarin Carrots, 135
Cheddar Bisque, 23
Cheese
    Alpine Fondue, 173
    Amsterdam Fried Cheese, 3
    Beef and Cheese Nosh, 12
    Bowery Cheese Crock, 4
    Cheddar Bisque, 23
    Cheese Bread, 178
    Grilled Cheese on Rye, 154
    Heathen Welsh Hare, 172
    Raisin Cheese Nut Bread, 180
    Reuben Sandwiches, 151
    Saucy Steak Sandwich, 155
    Welsh Rabbit, 170
    Yankee Tavern Soup, 21
Cheese Bread, 178
Cheesecake
    New York Cheesecake, 196
Cherry Cake, 192
Chicken
    Baked Curried Chicken, 102
    Barbecued Chicken, 95
    Chicken Ecuador, 100
    Chicken Stuffed with Rice, 104

Flemish Chicken, 97
Gold Rush Chicken Livers, 10
Irish Chicken Cretloe, 96
Chicken Ecuador, 100
Chicken Stuffed with Rice, 104
Chili Azteca, 83
Chocolate Cake, 186
Chops and Kraut, 48
Clams
Spanish Paella, 105
Colorado Mushrooms, 14
Coney Island Franks, 145
Corn on the Cob, 124
Corned Beef Brisket, 45
Cornish Hens
Hoosier Game Hens, 99
Creole Soufflé, 166

D

Danish Beer Soup, 26
Danish Meat Balls, 59
Date Cake from the Desert, 188
Dixie Fish Turbans, 110
Doughboy Stew, 69
Dressing
Sesame Seed Dressing, 30

E

Eggplant
Breaded Eggplant, 137
Gascony Fried Eggs, 165
Eggs
Baked Eggs Español, 169
Bavarian Pickled Eggs, 9
Creole Soufflé, 166
Egg Foo Young, 161
Eggs Parmesan, 164
Eggs Provençal, 168
Gascony Fried Eggs, 165
Huevos Diablos, 8
Huevos Rancheros, 163
Spanish Omelet, 159
The Queen of Denver, 153
Toad in the Hole, 18
Egg Foo Young, 161
Eggs Parmesan, 164
Eggs Provençal, 168

F

Fish
Canadian Salmon Steaks, 108
Dixie Fish Turbans, 110
Fish and Chips, 106
Rolled Sole with Peanuts, 109
Fish and Chips, 106
Flemish Carbonnes, 65
Flemish Chicken, 97
Four-Bean Salad, 36

French Fried Onion Rings, 118
Fried Green Tomatoes, 123
Frijoles Borrachos, 125
Frosting, Universal Chocolate, 187

G

Gascony Fried Eggs, 165
German Meat Balls, 58
Gold Rush Chicken Livers, 10
Great Hamburgers, 142
Grilled Cheese on Rye, 154
Gypsy Steak, 50

H

Hearty Steak and Guinness Pie, 73
Heathen Welsh Hare, 172
Hoosier Game Hens, 99
Hot German Potato Salad, 32
Hot Spice Cake, 185
Huevos Diablos, 8
Huevos Rancheros, 163
Humbles and Onions, 47
Hungarian Goulash, 67

I

International Meat Loaf, 60
Irish Chicken Cretloe, 96

L

Lamb
Mexican Lamb Stew, 76
Smuggler's Ribs, 51
Steak and Kidney Pie, 71
Latin Pochero, 62
Lettuce
Caesar Salad, 33
California Salad, 35
Liverwurst Pâté, 13
Lobster
Spanish Paella, 105

M

Mandarin Carrots, 135
Mexican Lamb Stew, 76
Mushrooms
Colorado Mushrooms, 14
Mushroom Steak, 43
Mushroom Steak, 43

N

New England Baked Beans, 88
New York Cheesecake, 196

O

Old English Plum Pudding, 194
Old World Potato Salad, 31
Old-Time Beef Jerky, 15
Onions
Baked Onion Soup, 28

Baked Red Onions, 136
French Fried Onion Rings, 118
Humbles and Onions, 47
Oriental Fried Rice, 130

P

Pancakes and Crêpes
Quick Beer-Batter Crêpes, 184
Superlight Beer Pancakes, 183
Peanuts
Rolled Sole with Peanuts, 109
Peas
Stone Soup, 24
Pecos Chili, 80
Pennsylvania Slaw, 34
Peppers
Stuffed Green Peppers, 86
Pie
Butterscotch Tarts, 195
Polish Delight, 75
Pork
Baked Ham, 61
Barbecue Pork Sandwiches, 149
Carnitas Jalisco, 49
Chops and Kraut, 48
Danish Meat Balls, 59
Eggs Parmesan, 164
Gascony Fried Eggs, 165
Gypsy Steak, 50
Irish Chicken Cretloe, 96
New England Baked Beans, 88
Pecos Chili, 80
Pork and Apple Ragout, 91
Pork Chili Verde, 78
Smithfield Special, 144
Stone Soup, 24
The Queen of Denver, 153
Pork and Apple Ragout, 91
Pork Chili Verde, 78
Potatoes
Hot German Potato Salad, 32
Old World Potato Salad, 31
Potato Casserole, 127
Saratoga Chips, 17
Spuds Au Gratin, 129
Potato Casserole, 127
Prairie Dog Sandwiches, 146

Q

Quick Beer-Batter Crêpes, 184

R

Radio Beer Bread, 177
Raisin Cheese Nut Bread, 180

200

Red Cabbage Salad, 29
Red Cabbage, 138
Red Hots and Kraut, 147
Reuben Sandwiches, 151
Rice
  Chicken Stuffed with Rice,
    104
  Dixie Fish Turbans, 110
  Oriental Fried Rice, 130
  Spanish Paella, 105
  Spanish Rice, 117

Rolled Sole with Peanuts, 109

S
Salad
  Caesar Salad, 33
  California Salad, 35
  Four-Bean Salad, 36
  Hot German Potato Salad, 32
  Old World Potato Salad, 31
  Pennsylvania Slaw, 34
  Red Cabbage Salad, 29
Salisbury Steak, 143
Saratoga Chips, 17
Saucy Steak Sandwich, 155
Sausage
  Baked Eggs Español, 169
  Baked Polish Sausage, 52
  Bratwurst and Sauerkraut, 53
  Bratwurst in Ale, 148
  British Banger Soup, 22
  Coney Island Franks, 145
  Latin Pochero, 62,
  Liverwurst Pâté, 13

Polish Delight, 75
Prairie Dog Sandwiches, 146
Red Hots and Kraut, 147
Stone Soup, 24
Toad in the Hole, 18
Seaman's Beef, 40
Sesame Beer Bread Sticks, 182
Sesame Seed Dressing, 30
Shish Kebabs, 46
Shrimp
  Asparagus and Shrimp, 113,
  Shrimps Daphne, 7
  Spanish Paella, 105
  Texas Gulf Shrimp, 112
Shrimps Daphne, 7
Smithfield Special, 144
Smuggler's Ribs, 51
Soft Rye Bread, 179
Soup
  Baked Onion Soup, 28
  British Banger Soup, 22
  Cheddar Bisque, 23
  Danish Beer Soup, 26
  Stone Soup, 24
  Yankee Tavern Soup, 21
Spaghetti with Meat Sauce, 84
Spanish Omelet, 159
Spanish Paella, 105
Spanish Rice, 117
Spreads
  Bowery Cheese Crock, 4
Spuds Au Gratin, 129
Steak and Kidney Pie, 71
Steak Iberia, 44

Stone Soup, 24
Stuffed Green Peppers, 86
Stuffed Tomatoes, 132
Succotash, 120
Superlight Beer Pancakes, 183
Sweet Potatoes
  Candied Sweet Potatoes, 134
T
Texas Flank Steak, 41
Texas Gulf Shrimp, 112
The Queen of Denver, 153
Toad in the Hole, 18
Tomatoes
  Bartender's Chile, 81
  Fried Green Tomatoes, 123
  Pecos Chile, 80
  Pork Chile Verde, 78
  Spaghetti with Meat Sauce,
    84
  Stuffed Tomatoes, 132
U
Uncle Sam's Barley Stew, 68
Universal Chocolate Frosting,
  187
V
Vampire Steak, 42
W
Welsh Rabbit, 170
Y
Yankee Tavern Soup, 21

INDEX TO BEER TRIVIA

A
Abbey Beers, 65
**Agony of Prohibition, From a
  Cockroach's Point of View,
  The, 87**
Ale Conners, 180
Ale in Song and Verse, 144
Algeria, 23
Ali Baba, 182
Alice in Wonderland, 189
Allsopp, Hugh de, 98
Allsopp, Samuel, 98
American Can Company, 53
American Language, The, 99
Amyloglucosidase, 27
And Speaking of Ale, 171
And Speaking of Heat, 82
Anderson, Hans Christian, 160
Angostura, 142

Anthony, Susan B., 83
Aphrodite, 132
Apollo, 7
Archy the Cockroach, 87
Aristophanes, 148
Armenian Grape Growers, 185
Augustus, 30
Australia, 106
Australia, First Beer in, 3
Aztec, 6, 78, 79, 83, 101
B
Bacall, Lauren, 8
Baites, Anne, 168
Ballot, 22,
Ballotas, 22
Bananas, 62
Barbarossa, Frederick I, 35,
Barley Wine, 66
Bartender 'Bot, 79

Bass Beer Trademark, 150
Bass, William, 150
Bassareus, 150
Bean Eaters, 22
Bean-master, 159
Beer Cans, 100
Beer CEOs, 18
Beer Comes to Japan, 102
Beer Diets, 27
Beer Dreams Foretell Future, 119
Beer Flood, 124
Beer Gardens, 32
Beer in Politics, 57
Beer Law and Policy, 40, 135, 183
Beer Lovers Party, 57
Beer Money, 191
Beer Production Champs, 30
Beer Street, 74
Beer Turns Up Down Under, 3
Beer Witches, 82

Beere in Shakespeare's Time, 154

Being at Loggerheads, 160

Bell, Book, Candle, 111

Bellarmine, Cardinal Robert, 190

Belly-Robber, 41

Benedictine, 35

Benzoni, Girolamo, 169

Betting and Beer, 162

Biggest Cabbage Plant, 122

Biscuit-shooter, 159

Bittering, 66

Black and Tan, 107

Blackball, 22,

Blue Hen State, 104

Blue Ribbon Tweak, 83

Boat We All Miss, A, 12

Bock, 57

Bohemia, King of, 44

Bon Père, 136

Bonner, Bishop, 126

Boston, John, 3

Boswell, James, 71

Bottles, Barrels, Cans, and Box-o'-Beer, 149

Bottom Fermenting, 66

Bowery, 4

Bradford, Governor, 52

Brian Boru, 97

Bridger, Jim, 15

Brody, Steve, 4

Buccaneer, 149

Buck Rabbit, 172

Bull Cook and Authentic Historical Recipes, 172

Bumper of Ale, Sir?, 136

Burns, Robert, 119

Burton Ale, 171

But Mr. Tax Man, It's Almost the Same as Bread, 40

C

Cabbage Thief Moon, 121

Caesar's Restaurant, 33

Cake Night, 191

Caldwell, Captain, 104

California Gold Rush, 10, 69

California Steam Beer, 11

California, 11

Camels in U.S. Service, 188

Cameron, Mary, 172

Candlemas Day, 184

Cannibal, 3

Carlsberg Brewery, 160

Carne Vale, 166

Carroll, Lewis, 189

Carrots Medicinal, 135

Cartier, Jacques, 121

Carver, George Washington, 109

Catherine the Great, 56

Cazuela, 76

Celts, 131

Ceres, 181

Cervantes, Miguel de, 44

Charlemagne the Great on Beer Policy, 135

Charlemagne, 135

Charles II, 180

Charles V of Spain, 101

Chiang Lung, Emperor, 161

Chickens, 102

China, Chinese, 84, 90

Ching Dynasty, 161

Chips, Saratoga, 17

Church Key, 53

Civil War, 41, 109

Clinking Glasses, 111

Coach Glasses, 152

Coach Horn, 21

Cock Fights, 104

Cocoa Beans as Money, 186

Cocoa, Origin of, 186

Columbus, Christopher, 169

Columbus's Egg, 169

Cone Mouth Beer Cans, 100

Coney Island, 145, 147

Confucius, 101

Conquistadores, 78, 83

Containers for Beer, 149

Conversion of Hathor, The, 29

Cook, Captain, 55

Copeland, William, 101

Copenhagen, 160

Cortez, Hernan, 78

Crum, George, 17

Cuauhtemoc, 79

Curb Your Enthusiasm and Hitch Your Pony, 12

D

D'Artagnan, 165

Dalrymple, Sir John, 55

Daphne, 7

Davis, Jefferson, 188

Demeter, 181

Denver Sandwich, 153

Devil's Table, 111

Dextrins, 27

Díaz, Porfirio, 49

Diodorus, 180

Dionysus, 180

Diuretic, 27

Dixies, 110

Domitian, 131

Don Quixote, 44

Doppelbock, 57, 66

Dorgan, T.A. "Tad", 145

Doughboys, 69

Dracula, 42

Drawing Straws, 108

Dreams of Beer, 119

Drink Responsibly, 9

Dromedary Service, 188

Drunken Beans, 125

E

Earp, Wyatt, 146

Earth Apple, 127

Edda, 137

Eggs, 8, 163

Egypt, Egyptians, 33, 40, 42, 118, 119, 122, 148, 195

Election-Fixing, 22,

Elizabeth I, 17, 148

Emmett, Daniel D., 109

En Chen Tsai, 101

Eric the Red and Green Ale, 61

Eric the Red, 61

Erikson, Edward, 160

Evil Eye, 42

F

Feltman, Charles, 147

First Bottle of Beer, The, 126

First Brewers' Trademark, The, 150

First Brewery in New World, 101

First Brewery in U.S., 101

First Railroad Cargo, 151

First Registered Trademark, 150

Flanders, 97

Flip-Top Coup, 165

Floating Brewery, 12

Floating Kingdom, 101

Flowery Death, 6

Folk Beliefs,

    Bread and Luck, 178

    Caraway Protective, 50

    Carrots Medicinal, 135

    Crêpes, Gold, and Luck, 184

    Eggs Magical, 8, 163

    Garlic Protective, 42

    Mushrooms and Black Magic, 14

    Mushrooms and Lightning, 14

    Onion Symbol of Eternity, 118

    Onion Proof Against Witches, Snakes, and Disease, 118

    Paprika Medicinal and Protective, 50

    Pork and Sauerkraut on New Year's Day, 50

    Pudding and Luck, 194

    Tomatoes Aphrodisiac, 132

    Tomatoes Poison, 132

    Witches, 82, 168

For Whom the Beer Bell Tolls, 183

France's Tavern, 160

Franklin, Benjamin, 129

Frederick the Great, 192

Frederiksburg Castle, 160

Free Lunch, 128

Friend Indeed, A, 34

From the Wood, 134
Frothingslosh, Olde, 13

G

Gambrinus, 111
Garden of Eden, Hindu, 62
Garlic, 42
Gaul, 131
Genghis Khan, 48
George VI, 147
Gerard, John, 122
Gin Lane, 74
Gladiators, 111
Go to Bed, Tom, Drunk or Sober, 89
Gods, 6
Gods
 Aphrodite, 132
 Apollo, 7
 Bacchus, 111
 Bassareus, 150
 Ceres, 181
 Demeter, 181
 Dionysus, 180
 Hathor, 29
 Huitzilpochtli, 6
 Odin, 59
 Ra, 29
 Shiva, 130
 Tlaloc, 6
 Tontiu, 6
Gollywhopper Eggs, 164
Good Queen Bess, 17
Goodhead, Job, 98
Grafenburg, 111
Great American Beer Festival, 35
Great Britain Beer Festival, 18
Greece, Greeks, 95, 180
Greenland, 61
Gretz Brothers, 39
Growler, Rushing the, 103
Guinness at the Pole, 89
Gullible Stew, 24

H

H.M.S. Menestheus, 12
H.M.S.Surprise, 3
Haakon the Good, 12
Hackwood, Frederick, 180
Haegelin, Joseph, 167
Hail to the Queen!, 17
Half and Half, 107
Hamburg, 45, 141
Hangovers, 122
Happy Birthday, Granddad, 41
Hardy, Thomas, 77
Harrison, William, 154
Hate to Pick a Favorite Beer, But . . ., 18
Hathor, 29
Haynau, General, 182

Heather Ale, 133
Hebrides, 131
Henry VIII, 17
Herball, 122
Herrera, Alfonso de, 101
Herter, George Leonard, 172
Hetzmek Ceremony, 8
High Society, 148
Hildegarde von Bingen, 35
Hippolochus, 196
Hob Nobbing, 171
Hogarth, William, 74
Holy Experiment, 34
Holy Hour, The, 193
Homer, 52
Hoosier, 99
Hops, 35
Horner, Little Jack, 194
Horseback, 12
Hot Beer, 45
Huitzilpochtli, 6
Hungarians, 182
Hunter, Governor, 3
Hutchinson, Col., 89

I

I Think He Liked the Beer, 77
In Vassar Halls, 72
Indestructible Guinness, 91
India Pale Ale, 98
Indio Date Festival, 188
Indoor Beer Gardens, 32
Industrial Revolution, 127
Inns, Ales and Drinking Customs of Old England, 180
International Potato Center, 127

J

Jacobson, Carl, 160
Jefferson, Thomas, 132
Jennings, Gary, 6
Jerky, 15
Johnson, Samuel, 71

K

K'ung Fu-Tzu, 101
Kaiser Bill, 60
King Gambrinus, 111
King of Bohemia, 44
Kirin, 101
Krausening, 11
Kulakofsky, Reuben, 151

L

Lawrie, Sir Robert, 119
Lehman, George, 122
Lent, 138, 166, 183
Lenten Fasting, 138
Lett, George Killian, 97
Liberty Cabbage, 29
Lindy's, 196

Little Mermaid, Gift of Beer, The, 160
Loggerheads, 160
London Beer Flood – Free Beer by Force of Nature, 124
Longevity, 66
Louis XIV, 14
Love Apple, 132
Love Apple, 3
Low-Calorie Beer, 27

M

Magic, 14
Malverde, Jesus, 49
Manet, Edouard, 150
March Beer, 58
Marines, 40
Marquis, Don, 87
Martin, John A., 167
Martyns, Peter, 86
Masterson, Bat, 146
Maya, 8
Mencken on Sobriety, 167
Mencken, H. L., 99, 167
Mendoza, Antonio de, 101
Menestheus, H.M.S., 12
Mesopotamia, 108, 180
Metamorphoses, 7
Middle Ages Staple, 138
Middle Ages, 45
Mighty Aztec Brew, The, 6
Mind Your P's and Q's, 48
Minuit, Gov. Peter, 85
Miss Old Frothingslosh, 13
Molson Oldest Operating Brewer in North America, 41
Monks, Cistercian, 65
Montague, John, Earl of Sandwich, 155
Montezuma, 6, 78, 186
Moon's Lake House, 17
Mouthful of Beer Proverbs, A, 128
Muggling, 16
Mughouse, 16
Mugs and Muggling, 16
Munich, 58
Mushrooms, 14

N

Napoleon, 195
Nation, Carrie, 167
Naval Secrets Revealed, 55
Navy Beer Stories, 80
Near Beer, 95
New Heights for Beer, 80
New Nation's First Brewery, A, 52
New York Polo Grounds, 145

Nikita, Galina, 57
Noble Compliment, A, 44
Noggin of Old Rattle Skull, A, 70
Normand, Madame le, 195
Not Toasting With Beer, 182
Nowell, Alexander, 126

O

Odin, 59
Odysseus, 52
Oedipus, 152
Oktoberfest, 58
Old Ben's Elbow, 129
Old German Proverbs, 55
Old World Connection, 101
Olde Frothingslosh, 13
Øllebrod, 26
Once Upon a Riddle, 152
Onion, 118
Only the Yeast Knows, 66
Ovid, 7

P

P's and Q's, 48
Pabst, Capt. Frederick, 83
Peanuts, 109
Pecos Bill, 80
Penalty Horns, 137
Penn, William, 34
Pennsylvania Dutch, 24
Penny Subsidy for Beer, 191
Peru, 127
Peru, 31
Pharaoh, 48
Picts, 133
Pilsner Urquell, 193
Pint and a Gill, A, 125
Plains Indians, 15
Playing Cards, 195
Pliny the Elder, 177
Pochero, 62
Poems and Verses
    Ale in Song and Verse, 144
    Drink and Longevity, 66
    Heather Ale, 133
    I Sing of a Whistle, 119
    Soul-Cake, 191
    Tavernkeeper's Verse, 79
    The Abbot's Ale, 171
    The Agony of Prohibition,
        From a Cockroach's Point
        of View, 87
Polo, Marco, 84
Pope, 136
Population Explosion, 127
Porter: A Strong Man's Drink, 107
Potato Famine, 129
Potato, 127, 129
Potter, Harry, 16

Present Remedies Against the Plague, 118
Primus, Jan, 111
Pringle, Sir John, 55
Probus, 131
Prohibition, 83, 87, 95, 103, 167
Proverbs on Beer, 128
Public Bakers, 71
Pudding and Luck, 194
Pudding, 194
Pulque, 101
Pulque, 6
Pumpernickel, 154
Puritans, 52
Puritans, 88

Q

Quaker, 34

R

Ra, 29
Rabbit, 170
Raleigh, Sir Walter, 129
Rally Round the Flagon, 126
Rarebit, 170
Rattle Skull, 70
**Record of Hops' Value Comes
    from Dark Ages Abbess, 35**
Red Hots, , 145
Restoration, 180
Rice, 117, 130
Richard the Lion-Hearted , 98, 171
Robot Bartender, 79
Roosevelt, Eleanor, 147
Root Vegetables, 136
Roughing It, 69
Rumford, Count, 71
Rushing the Growler, 103
Russians Take Beer Seriously, 57

S

Saarland, University of, 79
Sabbath, 88
Salisbury, James H., 143
Sam, Uncle, 68
Sancho Panza, 44
**Scholars' Theory Gauls
    Germans, 131**
Scott, Sir Walter, 171
Sedgewick, Capt., 52
Sesame, 182
Shakespeare, 154, 183
Shiva, 130
Shu-Bad, Queen, 108
Sign of Prohibition, 95
Silver Whistle, 119
Skinny on Low-Cal Beer, The, 27
Smithfield Ham, 61

Smuggling, 51
**So Can Beer Help Me Lose
    Weight?, 27,**
Spanish Main, 126
Special Delivery, 151
Sphinx, 152
Spring Cleaning Myth, 57
St. Boniface, 23,
St. Gallen, Switzerland, 82
St. Louis Exposition, 141
St. Louis Exposition, 147
Standish, Miles, 52
Steak Tartare, 60
Steam Beer, 11
Stevens, Harry K., 145
Stevenson, Robert L., 133
Stone Street, 85
Story of the New World, 169
Strange Names for Bad Drinks, 70
Strengths of Beer, 187
Stroganoff, Count George, 56
Sub Rosa, 30
Sumerians, 108
Surprise, H.M.S., 3

T

Tab Top Can, 165
Take It to the Judge, 23
Tall, Tall Cornstalk, 124
Tankard, Whistle, 8
Tartar Steak, 143
Tartars, 143
Tatoo, 89
Tavernkeeper's Verse, 79
Taverns, 6, 21, 36, 48
Tegnersee Monastery, 58
Tenochtitlan, 6, 78
Tepache, 75
**Three Cheers for Uncle Sam! And
    Some of His Beery Relatives, 30**
Three Companions, 5
Three Sheates to the Wind, 131
Three Shreads, 107
Tip a Black and Tan, 107
Tipping a Yard, 25
Tlaloc, 6
Toby Mugs, 190
Tomato, 132
Tonga, 3
Tooner Schooners, 39
Top Fermenting, 66
Travelers Take Care!, 181
Tricking the Trickster, 6
Trickster, 6
Troubles, The, 107
Trumpet Major, The, 77
Tutankhamen, 182
Twain, Mark, 69
Twelfth Night, 189
Twelve Cakes, 189

204

U

Ubiquitous Church Key, The, 53

Umbles, 47
Uncle Sam, 30, 68
Unerring Fortune-Teller, The, 195
Ur, 108

V

Valhalla, 190
Valkyries, 59
Vassar, Matthew, 72
Victoria, Queen, 61
Volstead Act, 167

W

Wager Cups, 162
Wenceslaus, King, 193
Wet Your Whistle, 119

What Prohibition?, 167
What's Behind the Clink?, 111
What's More Serious Than a Double Cross?, 187
When Taxes Were Really Sticky, 180
When There WAS a Free Lunch, 128
Whistle for It!, 8
Whistle-Belly Vengeance, 36
Why We Drink – It's the Longevity, 66
Wilhelm, Kaiser, 60
William of Orange, 74
Wilson, Samuel, 68
Winter Garden, 32
Witches, 82, 168

World Championship Chili Cookoff, 81

X

XXX, 187

Y

Yams, Origin, 134
Yankee Peddler, 21, 164
Yankee Trader, 6
Yard of Ale, 25, 152
Yeast, 66
Yechburg, Fatima, 13
Yuengling Oldest Operating Brewer in U.S., 41

Z

Ziebold-Haegelin Brewery, 167
Ziebold, Herman, 167

www.ingramcontent.com/pod-product-compliance
Lightning Source LLC
Chambersburg PA
CBHW031251090426
42742CB00007B/404